# CATULLUS AND ROM

In the past century, scholars have observed a veritable full cast of characters from Roman comedy in the poetry of Catullus. Despite this growing recognition of comedy's allusive presence in Catullus' work, there has never been an extended analysis of how he engaged with this foundational Roman genre. This book sketches a more coherent picture of Catullus' use of Roman comedy and shows that individual points of contact with the theater in his corpus are part of a larger, more sustained poetic program than has been recognized. Roman comedy, it argues, offered Catullus a common cultural vocabulary, drawn from the public stage and shared with his audience, with which to explore and convey private ideas about love, friendship, and social rivalry. It also demonstrates that Roman comedy continued to present writers after the second century BCE with a meaningful source of social, cultural, and artistic value.

CHRISTOPHER B. POLT is an Assistant Professor of Classical Studies at Boston College. He has published extensively on Latin poetry of the Republic and early Empire. He was the recipient of the Linda Dykstra Distinguished Dissertation Award in the Humanities and Fine Arts at UNC-Chapel Hill.

# CATULLUS AND ROMAN COMEDY

*Theatricality and Personal Drama in the Late Republic*

CHRISTOPHER B. POLT

*Boston College*

## CAMBRIDGE
### UNIVERSITY PRESS

University Printing House, Cambridge CB2 8BS, United Kingdom

One Liberty Plaza, 20th Floor, New York, NY 10006, USA

477 Williamstown Road, Port Melbourne, VIC 3207, Australia

314-321, 3rd Floor, Plot 3, Splendor Forum, Jasola District Centre, New Delhi - 110025, India

103 Penang Road, #05-06/07, Visioncrest Commercial, Singapore 238467

Cambridge University Press is part of the University of Cambridge.

It furthers the University's mission by disseminating knowledge in the pursuit of
education, learning and research at the highest international levels of excellence.

www.cambridge.org
Information on this title: www.cambridge.org/9781108813747
DOI: 10.1017/9781108885195

© Christopher B. Polt 2021

First published 2021
First paperback edition 2022

*A catalogue record for this publication is available from the British Library*

ISBN 978-1-108-83981-5 Hardback
ISBN 978-1-108-81374-7 Paperback

To Ann Holt, for starting me on this path,
and
David Runkle, for supporting me through everything

# Contents

| | | |
|---|---|---|
| *Acknowledgments* | | *page* ix |
| *Note on the Text* | | xii |

Introduction     1
    *Romanus Palliatus*: Comedy's Catullan Allure     8
    Nugatory Sensibilities (Poems 1, 16, 12, and 25)     8
    Domestic, Urban, and Local Perspectives (Poems 10, 31, and 51)     24
    Greco-Roman Hybridity and Translation (Poems 70 and 68)     36

1   Through the Comic Looking Glass     45
    Theatricality and Metatheater in the Late Republic     46
    Masks of the Self: Persona, Performance, and Exemplarity     62

2   The Best Medicine: Comic Cures for Love in the First
    Century BCE     70
    Erotocatharsis, Comic *Adulescentes*, and Terence's *Eunuchus*     73
    The *Adulescens Amator* as Antidote: Cicero's *Eunuchus* (*Tusc.* 4.65–76)     79
    The *Adulescens Amator* as Gateway Drug: Lucretius' *Eunuchus* (*DRN* 4)     91
    The *Adulescens Amator* as Restorative Therapy: Catullus' *Eunuchus*
       (Poems 5, 7, 6, 8, 51, 85, 75, 72, and 109)     107

3   Heroic Badness and Catullus' Plautine Plots     126
    Entrapping Aurelius (Poems 15 and 21)     132
    Boy for Sale (Poems 48, 99, 24, 81, 23, and 106)     136
    Patrons and Parasites (Poem 49)     143

4   Naughty Girls: Comic Figures and Gendered Control
    in Catullus     148
    Lessons from the Ladies at Pompey's Theater (Poems 55 and 58B)     154
    Watching It Burn (Poems 37 and 36)     167

*Contents*

Epilogue: The Show Goes On: From Roman Comedy to Latin
Love Elegy                                                                                          174
    Catullus' Comic Economics and Elegy's "Greedy Girl" (Poem 110)        183

*Bibliography*                                                                                  189
*Subject Index*                                                                              209
*Index Locorum*                                                                            212

# *Acknowledgments*

While a graduate student at the University of North Carolina–Chapel Hill, I had the good fortune in spring 2006 to take seminars on Catullus with James O'Hara and Roman comedy with Sharon James. This project grew out of that serendipitous mash-up and countless conversations with Jim and Sharon, whom I owe an immense debt for their guidance and friendship over many years. My thanks go first to them, as well as to my dissertation readers, Robert Babcock, Mario Erasmo, and Werner Riess. Dan Curley, Timothy Moore, and Christopher Nappa generously read and discussed the entire manuscript, and their sage advice was instrumental in bringing this book to publication. Parts of the Introduction, Chapters 3 and 4, and the Epilogue benefited from feedback by audiences at the Classical Association of the Middle West and South (2010, 2015), the Society for Classical Studies (2011), Wake Forest University (2013), Texas Tech University (2014), the University of Wisconsin–Madison (2014), Boston College (2015), the Classical Association of Massachusetts (2016), and Wellesley College (2017). Special thanks to all the participants at the MACTe Junior Faculty Forum, especially Sophie Klein and Meredith Safran, whose suggestions and encouragement were invaluable.

Thanks to Michael Sharp, Hal Churchman, Rebecca Grainger, Mary Bongiovi, Ishwarya Mathavan, Stephanie Sakson, and the Syndics of Cambridge University Press for their invaluable help in bringing this book to publication. I am deeply grateful to the anonymous readers, whose constructive critiques were transformative. If I have learned anything from studying Catullus and Roman comedy, it is that "hackneyed" is not the same as "false" or "meaningless," and in that spirit: all deficiencies that remain in this book despite the best efforts of everyone named above are entirely my own.

I am grateful for support from the USF Humanities Institute, which let me devote summer 2014 to revisions. The Office of the Provost at Boston College provided a Manuscript Mini-Conference Award, without which this book would not exist, and I thank Shaylonda Barton and Gail Rider for facilitating this grant (and for the immeasurable help they have given me every term at BC). At Boston College, Fr. Gregory Kalscheur, Dean of the Morrissey College of Arts and Sciences, and David Quigley, Provost and Dean of Faculties, supported a Faculty Fellowship and pre-tenure leave in fall 2017, for which I am deeply grateful. Anjali Prabhu, Director of the Suzy Newhouse Center for the Humanities at Wellesley College, offered me space during that term to work free of distractions and engage with a cohort whose enthusiasm was invigorating. Thanks to Sandy Alexandre, Gurminder Bhogal, Saikat Majumdar, Corey McMullen, Tanalís Padilla, Banu Subramaniam, Carol Dougherty, Mary Lefkowitz, and Raymond Starr. The Graduate School at UNC supported my initial work on this project through a Dissertation Completion Research Fellowship, and the Departments of Classics at UNC and Carleton College provided travel funding to present some of these ideas at conferences.

This book came about through many years and through many changes, and in the process both it and I have accrued many more debts than I can recount here. For all their support, thanks to my friends and colleagues at UNC (Emily Baragwanath, Sarah Bond, T. H. M. Gellar-Goad, Elizabeth Greene, John Henkel, George Houston, Rachel Jorgenson, Derek Keyser, Amanda Mathis, Kim Miles, Sheri Pak, Arum Park, William Race, Joy Reeber, James Rives, Liz Robinson, Peter Smith, Philip Stadter, Nicola Terrenato, David Wiltshire, Serena Witzke, Cecil Wooten, Erika Zimmerman Damer), UNC's Writing Center (Sara Agre, Vicki Behrens, Heather Branstetter, Chris Cameron, Rania Chelala, Arseniy Gutnik, Matthew Harper, Lisa Mangiamele, Chris Newsome, Julia Osman, Margaret Swezey, Gigi Taylor), Carleton College (Jackson Bryce, Clara Hardy, Maureen Jackson, Victoria Morse, Bill North, Jean Sherwin, Kathryn Steed, Nancy Wilkie, Cathy Yandell, Chico Zimmerman), Boston College (Mary Crane, Hanne Eisenfeld, Kendra Eshleman, Gail Hoffman, Mark Hogan, Elizabeth Sutherland, Mark Thatcher), and elsewhere (Corby Kelly, Dániel Kiss, Stephanie Nelson, Amy Oh, Patricia Rosenmeyer, James Uden, Elizabeth Young). I am also grateful to my mother, father, brother, and aunt Barb for a lifetime of caring. To any and all whom I have failed to name, I apologize and express my deepest gratitude.

Above all, I am forever grateful to my husband, David Runkle, for his constant love and support, and to Toby, Cleo, and Reggie for their unfailing companionship and affection.

# *Note on the Text*

Except where noted, I follow these editions for Latin texts: for Catullus, Thomson (1998); for Plautus, De Melo (2011–13); for Terence, Barsby (2001); for Lucretius, Bailey (1947); for Cicero, Clark (1905), Powell (2006), Pohlenz (1914), and Pease (1955–1958); and for Ovid, McKeown (1987). All translations are my own unless otherwise indicated.

# *Introduction*

The curtain comes down, the audience departs, the actors and stagehands and musicians finish up before heading out for the night. The play is done, and there is nothing left but to move on to the next thing – or so we often presume. When it comes to drama, we tend to focus only on the play itself and forget all the thinking about and playing with the play that we keep doing once we leave the theater. But the theater leaves with us and lingers on in our thoughts, just as the poet Lucretius observes it did with Romans in the first century BCE (4.973–83):

> et quicumque dies multos ex ordine ludis
> assiduas dederunt operas, plerumque videmus,
> cum iam destiterunt ea sensibus usurpare,                    975
> relicuas tamen esse vias in mente patentis,
> qua possint eadem rerum simulacra venire.
> per multos itaque illa dies eadem obversantur
> ante oculos, etiam vigilantes ut videantur
> cernere saltantis et mollia membra moventis               980
> et citharae liquidum carmen chordasque loquentis
> auribus accipere et consessum cernere eundem
> scaenaique simul varios splendere decores.

> And anyone who has been glued to the festivals
> for days on end without a break, we very often see,
> once they have stopped taking them in with their senses,
> there are still paths that remain open in their minds
> through which the images of these same things can enter.
> And so for many days these same things appear
> before their eyes, even while they are awake, so they seem
> to perceive dancers as they move their supple limbs
> and to hear in their ears the pure song and expressive strings
> of the cithara and to perceive that the same crowd and the
> assorted embellishments of the stage glimmer as well.

By the time Lucretius' hypothetical audience member departs, the sights and sounds of the stage have so fully infiltrated his mind that they become a sort of waking dream, playing out again and again alongside whatever new sensations and thoughts his "real" life offers. And even Lucretius himself seems to undergo a similar impulsive recall of the dramatic world, conjuring up elements from the stage throughout the fourth book of *De rerum natura*: notions about atomic properties of color bring to his mind performances beneath the vibrant awnings of crowded venues (72–86); he envisions a theatrical mask while illustrating the complex optics of mirrors (292–301); and in the ridiculous behavior of lovers he finds echoes of countless young men from Roman comedies who squander their fortunes, dignity, and well-being for the sake of their beloveds (1121–91). As he goes about his work, such reminiscences from the theater repeatedly intervene. But these are not moments of psychotic possession that hinder his ability to engage with the everyday world. In fact, quite the opposite: his theatrical visions give him tools to understand the obscure nature of things and to share those strange insights with other Romans through the familiar vocabulary of the stage.[1] Lucretius thus shows how drama embeds itself deep in the psyches of its audience, offering them a new, theatrically augmented reality with which they can more fully comprehend the world and connect with their fellow theatergoers.

This notion serves as the foundation of this book, which explores the cultural memory of theater in Rome and what happens to Roman drama, and to comedy in particular, after its *floruit* in the third and second centuries BCE. As a broader goal, I am interested in trying to identify what the Roman audience does with comedy after the show seems to be over: How does the experience of this genre change and continue, where and how does it enter the vernacular of people outside the theater and join the language of literary allusion, and in what ways does it find fresh life for new ends in unfamiliar venues? My attention rests especially in the last years of the Roman Republic and in the work of one of Lucretius' contemporaries, the poet Catullus, whose engagement with Roman comedy has long and often been noted, albeit in scattershot fashion. More than a century ago, E. P. Morris first pointed out that Catullus' poem 8 (*miser Catulle, desinas ineptire*) recalls the plaintive soliloquy of the *adulescens amator*, or "young lover" stock type from Roman comedy, though his

---

[1] On Lucretius' engagement with the theater in *DRN* 4, see L. R. Taylor (1952), Rosivach (1980), Brown (1987 ad locc.), Goldberg (2005, 98), Hanses (2015, 91–107), B. Taylor (2016), and Chapter 2.

argument took decades to gain any foothold in Catullan scholarship. Indeed, despite the refinement of Morris' observations by Marilyn Skinner and others, there remains skepticism that Roman comedy ought to be seen as a meaningful element of the poem, an issue that Sander Goldberg captures succinctly:[2]

> Whether [the speaker of Catullus' poem 8] will be any more successful in his resolve than comedy's Phaedria or Calidorus may well be an open question. It is not, however, the kind of question that Catullan scholarship likes to entertain. Though the language, form, and thought of this poem may have comic analogues, scholars are reluctant to accept its comic roots.... At heart, this resistance is less to the influence of comedy in general than to that of Roman comedy in particular.... This Greek focus is the legacy of Friedrich Leo, who was a great lover of Plautus but nevertheless thought only a "falsche Methode" would attribute the affinities of comedy and later love poetry to anything more than similarities of subject and a common grounding in Greek precedents.

James Uden voices a similar sentiment in his study of Catullus' allusions to the "young lover" of Roman comedy in his epigrams, where he remarks that "despite these apparent correspondences, the degree to which Catullus' passionate persona is indebted to the comic *adulescens* has been a matter of rather scattered debate."[3] He and others have observed numerous moments throughout the corpus when Catullus appropriates Roman comedy's erotic discourses while reflecting on the literary, personal, and public experience of love.[4] It is difficult, however, for readers to square up an author who seems so genuine, unfiltered, and intimate with a genre that revels in its ostensible superficiality and staginess. Elizabeth Manwell notes that "most of his readers persist in a belief that Catullus offers us a window into his life, a sincere emotional outpouring of love or disgust. The source of anxiety for many lies in an attempt to reconcile (or more frequently, to ignore) those aspects of the Catullan poetic identity that do not accord

---

[2] Morris (1909). Wheeler (1934, 227–30) was an early proponent of his interpretation, but it was rejected or ignored by scholars (e.g., Elder [1951, 104]) until the 1960s, when Commager (1965, 91–92) and others began endorsing it. Especially useful developments of Morris' ideas are found in Skinner (1971), McCormick (1981), Thomas (1984), Selden (1992, 500–505), Gaisser (2009, 56–57). Quotation is from Goldberg (2005, 102); Leo remarks (1912, 143), "Es ist aber Zweifel, dass Tibull Properz Ovid jede andere Lektüre eher als die der plautinischen Komödien getrieben haben."

[3] Uden (2006, 19).

[4] Besides Uden (2006), see, e.g., Konstan (1986), Minarini (1987, 59–79), Agnesini (2004), O'Bryhim (2007), and Hanses (2015, 107–36).

with the persona of the sincere lover."[5] How could such a paragon of
sincerity find anything meaningful in the clichés of comic theater?

But Roman comedy's clichés abound in Catullus, and if we work the
question backward from that fact, we find a partial answer: Catullus is not
"sincere," at least as the Romantics would use the term, spontaneously
pouring out emotion and unfiltered experience. Rather, he voices his work
through a carefully constructed persona. The idea of the literary persona is
now sufficiently established in scholarship that we need not rehash it here,
except to observe that the gap between comic *adulescentes* like Plautus'
Calidorus or Terence's Phaedria and "Catullus," the speaker in the poems
of the first-century BCE poet Gaius Valerius Catullus, is illusory, since
each of these is a fictional young man whose role is scripted by a Roman
poet.[6] However curious or provocative it might be to find the Catullan
speaker impersonating stock types from Roman comedy (and one of my
aims in this book is to show that this choice *is* curious and provocative),
the basic notion that one literary figure can be made to act like another one
should not surprise.

But another part of the answer can be found in an observation by Uden,
namely that even living, breathing, "real" Romans found utility and
convenience in conforming their characters to cultural and literary stereotypes and, what is more, that "the new comic *adulescens* had acquired its
own cultural force as the popular archetype of the irresponsible young man
in love."[7] On the one hand, comedy's "young lover" was an appealing
target for allusion and emulation precisely because he is familiar and seems,
in his own ridiculous way, to endure the tribulations common to actual
young people in love. This is certainly how Lucretius employs the *adulescens* at 4.1121–91, where he serves as the textbook case of terminal
lovesickness and exhibits all of the symptoms from which his reader might
diagnose erotic mania.[8] Feelings need not be novel and unique to an
individual for them to be meaningful, and anyway no emotion under
the sun is new, as Terence implies in the famous prologue to his *Eunuchus*

---

[5] Manwell (2007, 121).

[6] Persona theory first came to prominence in English studies with Kernan (1959) and found its way
into Classical scholarship through Anderson (1964 and 1982), Winkler (1983), and Braund (1988).
For good overviews of the persona in Catullan scholarship, see Nappa (2001, 15–35) and Wray
(2001, 1–35, 161–67, 203–6), with fuller survey in Polt (2018). I use the name "Catullus"
throughout this book to refer to both the poet and his speaker, but when context does not make
clear which I mean, I try to clarify.

[7] Uden (2006, 23)

[8] Rosivach (1980) and Brown (1987, 248–307). For similar psychological readings of Catull. 8's comic
elements, see Skinner (1971) and Gaisser (2009, 55–60), alongside remarks by Uden (2006, 20).

(35–41), a prime model, we will see, for Catullan erotics: "But if our poet can't use the same characters as others do, how on earth can he write of . . . love, hatred, and suspicion? After all, there's nothing said now that hasn't been said before."[9] If everything that we experience is always already hackneyed and generic, what could be more useful for understanding and expressing those experiences than the most hackneyed and generic characters?

On the other hand, although personal poetry is ostensibly an inward-looking genre, it also represents a public expression of character and values. This idea, Uden points out, is the basis of conflict in Catullus' poem 16 (*pedicabo ego vos et irrumabo*), in which the speaker aggressively rebukes Furius and Aurelius for reading the character of the poet's work onto the character of the poet himself. However we interpret the complexities of the poem, it clearly implies that Catullus' contemporary readers understood poetry as one of the myriad ways by which Romans in the late Republic could engage in self-fashioning and self-positioning within the hierarchy of elite social discourse.[10] An allusion to the *adulescens amator* stock type was not merely a game of literary navel-gazing, but rather acted as shorthand for a whole set of ethical suppositions that the writer could convey quickly to readers in the theatrical know. And the particular values (or rather, antivalues) that the comic "young lover" embodies – indifference or hostility to *negotium* and *pietas*, prioritization of personal pleasure over public responsibility, rejection of emotional restraint and stability, and so on – gave Catullus and other Romans who were disillusioned with the *mos maiorum* an alternative model and a recognizable stance from which to critique aristocratic social norms.[11] To align oneself with the comic "young lover" was to embrace "a cultural paradigm that violates the protocols of expected behaviour for elite males," not unlike American men channeling James Dean's rebel without a cause, Jim Stark, or Matthew Broderick's Ferris Bueller.[12]

Although the stock character of the young lover has, unsurprisingly, received the bulk of attention in scholarship on Catullus' engagement with Roman comedy, the *adulescens amator* is not the only comic figure that has

---

[9] Ter. *Eun.* 35–41: *quod si personis isdem huic uti non licet, / qui mage licet . . . scribere . . . / amare, odisse, suspicari? denique / nullumst iam dictum quod non dictum sit prius.*

[10] For poetry as expression of character, see Clay (1998), Mayer (2003), and Iddeng (2005).

[11] See Duckworth (1952, 237–42) on the generic attributes of the comic *adulescens*, explored more fully in Chapters 2 and 3. Janan (1994) and Wray (2001) trace some of the ways in which Catullus challenges elite citizen male norms.

[12] Uden (2006, 21).

been sighted in his poetry. Skinner and Christopher Nappa, for example, show that Catullus employs the comic parasite as an invective marker in several poems about social competition, while David Wray, Rüdiger Bernek, and Julia Gaisser likewise discern the presence of the *miles gloriosus*, or "braggart soldier," in similar contexts.[13] Indeed, an almost full cast of comic characters has been spotted in the Catullan corpus: besides the stock types that I name above, scholars have also glimpsed the *meretrix*, or sex laborer; the *senex durus*, or "harsh old man"; the pimp; and so forth.[14] It is no coincidence, I think, that many of these scholars have also played critical roles in introducing and normalizing persona theory in work on Catullus: the idea that the Catullan speaker is a fictive "mask" (the basic meaning of the Latin word *persona*) that the poet crafts and speaks through has set the stage for readers to observe him impersonating other theatrical roles as well, and the past decade and a half of scholarship has gradually revealed that Catullus repeatedly turns to the Roman comic tradition for inspiration.[15]

Despite this growing recognition of comedy's presence in Catullus' poetry, though, there has never been a large-scale, systematic account of how this foundational Roman genre operates in the Catullan corpus. Indeed, although separate allusions have been readily acknowledged, the notion that Roman comedy as a whole presented writers after the second century BCE a meaningful source of cultural and artistic value (in the same way that, say, the genre of epic or Callimachean aesthetics are seen clearly to have done) still is not fully appreciated.[16] What is missing, and what this book aims to provide – if only in part – is this larger contextualization and answers to related questions, such as: What do these allusions to Roman comedy that appear throughout his poetry do for Catullus, his speaker, and his audience? How are Romans of Catullus' day experiencing comedy and how does that experience, either of plays themselves or of allusions to them outside the theater, relate to their contemporary values,

[13] Skinner (1979), Nappa (2001, 85–105 and 112–14), Wray (2001, 80–87), Bernek (2004), Gaisser (2009, 51–55).
[14] On the *senex durus*, see Nappa (2001, 54–55); on the *meretrix*, Skinner (1989) and Selden (1992); on the *leno*, Goldberg (2005, 105–14). Note that I use "sex laborer" throughout this book to translate the word *meretrix* for the reasons articulated by Witzke (2015) except when trying to convey the value judgments that particular ancient individuals bring to the term.
[15] *OLD* s.v. *persona* 1; see Chapter 1 for discussion of the significance of this meaning and related etymologies for the Roman conception of the self.
[16] Newman (1990, 3–24) draws attention to the emphasis on Alexandrian aesthetics in Catullus' work to the exclusion of influences from Roman comedy, tracing some ways in which Plautus is a more likely source for ideas and terms that have been traditionally associated with Callimachus (e.g., *nugae*, *lepus*).

interests, and anxieties? What mechanisms stand behind allusions to drama in non-dramatic poetry and how does their integration into personal poetry shape the trajectory of literature in Rome? Besides contributing to the catalog of Catullus' comic allusions further examples that have gone unnoticed or inadequately treated, I aim to sketch a more coherent picture of Catullus' engagement with Roman comedy and to show that individual points of contact with this genre in his work are part of a larger, more sustained poetic program than has been recognized.

Roman comedy, I argue, offers Catullus a common cultural vocabulary, drawn from the public stage and shared with his audience, with which to explore and convey private ideas about love, friendship, and social rivalry. Further, Catullus' use of Roman comedy is not isolated, but represents part of a larger communicative phenomenon among Romans of his era. The gods and heroes of tragedy remained eloquent symbols for ancient writers, but comedy – long considered *infra dignitatem* for "respectable" authors of the first century BCE – also offered them a powerful tool for navigating their complex social relations.[17] Roman comedy developed hand-in-hand with Rome itself in the third and second centuries BCE, working together and in tension with one another in establishing political, social, and cultural values, as well as a sense of unity and stability for their population.[18] But as these began to break down in the twilight of the Republic, comedy served as both a touchstone of Romans' cultural patrimony and contested space for ethical discourse that the elite used to define their communal and personal identities in the face of a century of civil unrest and the consequent disruptions of traditional values. For some, such as Cicero, Roman comedy came to represent an instrument to recall, promote, and reinforce the *mos maiorum*, how things had been at the height of Rome's self-confidence as the ascendant power in the Mediterranean, when the genre first materialized and flourished on the public stage. For others, such as Catullus, the genre's everyday anti-values would offer a means to reflect on and critique those very same

---

[17] Sharrock (2009, ix–x) discusses this attitude among scholars, which Fontaine (2014, 180) summarizes: "Roman comedy frequently embarrasses Latinists . . . it is usually seen as an outlier, a misfit that does not really belong with the rest of Latin literature." Even Wheeler (1934), who first drew Morris (1909) to wider attention, attributed the poem's comic elements to Catullus' "knowledge of Greek literature" (228); see also Wheeler (1910), who remarks that "the Augustan elegists did not read Plautus and Terence" (442), and Griffin (1985, 199), who asserts that the absence of Plautus' and Terence's names from Augustan poetry "proves only that they were not creditable, not in fashion, not that they had made no contribution."

[18] For relationships between the genre's development and that of Roman society itself, see Leigh (2004) and Richlin (2014).

mores, as well as to contemplate the paradoxes involved in revolting against a system in which they nevertheless yearned to participate. And for everyone in Rome, traditionalist and iconoclast alike, comedy presented a convenient set of ethical touchstones with which to identify and to site themselves and those around them within the shifting flows of Roman moral, social, and political relations.

## *Romanus Palliatus*: Comedy's Catullan Allure

We can safely posit, then, that Catullus uses Roman comedy extensively in his work. But *why comedy*? What about this genre caught Catullus' attention in the first place? I have already nodded toward some of the value I think he and other Romans found in thinking with the theater generally, and Plautus and Terence specifically, and subsequent chapters of this book examine the effects of Catullus' and his contemporaries' invocations of individual comic characters and schticks. But here seems an appropriate place to say something about the broader reasons why Catullus would find Roman comedy an appealing target of allusion and reflection. Three aspects of the genre are especially pertinent: (1) a nugatory sensibility; (2) a domestic, urban, and local perspective; and (3) an interest in Greco-Roman hybridity and translation. Throughout this book, I return to these overarching themes, as they can be seen to undergird Catullus' engagement with Roman comedy. In this introduction, though, I want to sketch their essential features by using a few examples in the Catullan corpus that highlight the poet's theatrical outlook but whose comic substructure has gone overlooked or underappreciated.

## Nugatory Sensibilities (Poems 1, 16, 12, and 25)

In his programmatic opening poem, Catullus calls his work "a charming new booklet" (*lepidum novum libellum*, 1.1) and "trifles" (*nugas*, 1.4); he makes an equally evocative literary claim in poem 16, where he defends his verses on the grounds that "they have wit and charm" (*habent salem ac leporem*, 16.4), even if they are "a bit naughty" (*parum pudicum*, 16.4). These have been read as two of the most revolutionary and distinctive statements of Catullus' poetics, as well as defining qualities of his neoteric contemporaries.[19] Their work, they assert, pulls away from the traditional,

---

[19] On the programmatic function of poem 1, see Copley (1951) and Batstone (1998, 2007). On the metapoetic significance of poem 16, see, e.g., Sandy (1971), Buchheit (1976), and Fitzgerald (1995, 34–58).

focusing on little things and social niceties their predecessors ignored, those objects and events that are peripheral to Roman thought but central to their lived experiences: an affectionate moment with a pet, a meal shared with a friend, a looming mortgage payment, erotic strife, and all the other bits and bobs that fill out most of our days but about which we spare little thought – that is, until a poet like Catullus comes along to help us sense the weight of this social, emotional, and material unconscious. Part of what makes Catullus' work successful is that he "writes what his culture defines as 'trifles,' but by virtue of the care he lavishes on them proves himself a dedicated and serious Alexandrian poet."[20]

But while the elevation of the small, graceful, and witty over the bloated and thunderous was indeed the calling card of an Alexandrian, and specifically Callimachean, poet, there is more to Catullus' elaborate polishing of the quotidian than an attempt to copy Hellenistic aesthetics.[21] The catchwords Catullus deploys so expressively in these metapoetic statements – *lepos/lepidus, nugae, sal* – came loaded with social, cultural, and literary significance in Latin literature long before the arrival of Alexandrian literature on Italian shores. J. K. Newman shows that Plautus deploys these terms as metapoetic shorthand for comic playfulness and trickery and suggests these valences should also be considered in understanding Catullus' poetic program.[22] I take his observation a step further and argue that Catullus expressly draws inspiration for his poetics, in part, from Roman comedy – and indeed, that the traditional understanding of what makes his work "nugatory" misses the mark by ignoring these words' comic connotation. *Nugae, lepos,* and *sal* are not simply about elevating the typically trivial through extreme polish; they are the characteristics of a person who can imbue people and things with alternate meaning, of the playwright who turns actors into characters, clothing into costumes, and everyday objects into stage properties that signify more than they normally could. The point of Catullus' nugatory poetics lies not merely in highlighting the quotidian, but in his ability to transform the quotidian and extraordinary alike into something else altogether.

---

[20] Fitzgerald (1995, 44), said tongue-in-cheek to critique the uncritical opposition of surface and depth in interpretations of Catullus' metapoetic statements.

[21] For primarily Callimachean readings of Catullus' programmatic poetry, see Elder (1967) and Cairns (1969). Although quotidian objects and the materiality of poetry appear in Callimachus, they do not play nearly as large a role as in Catullus; for examples, see Cameron (1995, 443) and Phillips (2013).

[22] Alexandrian poetry and poetics probably arrived in Rome at the end of the second century BCE; see Fantuzzi and Hunter (2004, 462–67) and bibliography cited there for a good overview of the chronological issues, especially as relates to Callimachus and Hellenistic epigram.

Significantly, all three of Catullus' poetic terms appear side by side in one particularly metatheatrical scene from Roman comedy. In the middle of Plautus' *Curculio*, the *choragus* (a stage professional in charge of costumes for the acting troupe) comes onstage to break the fourth wall and laud the play's eponymous parasite (462–64):[23]

> edepol **nugatorem lepidum lepide** hunc nanctust Phaedromus.
> **halophantam** an sycophantam magis ess' dicam nescio.
> ornamenta quae locavi metuo ut possim recipere.

> By Pollux, this guy that Phaedromus has gotten is a charmingly charming trifler. Whether I should say that he's a sharp fellow or a swindler, I just don't know. I'm afraid I'm not going to be able to get back the costumes that I hired out to him.

Curculio is described as *lepidus, nugator,* and *halophanta,* that is, "salt-shower" (ἅλς + φαινεῖν). I think it is not a coincidence that these are three of Catullus' most prominent poetic buzzwords (*lepidum,* 1.1; *nugas,* 1.4; *salem ac leporem,* 16.4). The context of the *choragus'* accolades suggests Plautus' comic parasite was a meaningful *exemplum* for our poet. Immediately after these lines, the *choragus* gives the audience a tour not of Epidaurus, where the play is set, but of Rome itself, where the play is being produced, pointing out places and people they would see as they turned their attention away from the *scaena* and back to their regular lives once the show was over. Timothy Moore argues persuasively that this would present a disturbing moment for the spectators. *Curculio* centers on deception and false identity, and "Plautus paints a picture of an Epidaurus with a greater share of deceit than an average comedy requires." By erasing the boundaries between the imaginary and the "real" worlds, the *choragus* implies the characters have broken out of their Epidaurian fiction and are free in Rome itself. While watching the play so far, the audience learned that the parasite has the power to trick other characters with ease and devastating consequences. Now we see Curculio is on the loose and can come for us, too – and incognito to boot, since he has raided the stage shop. The divide between literary and real breaks down, and our appreciation for the power of costumes and props goes up.[24] Indeed, Curculio is

---

[23] Newman cites this passage for understanding Catullus' terminology, but he does not develop the idea that it may be programmatic. Copley (1951, 201–2) also attributes *lepidus* to "the sphere of everyday, ordinary life and behavior" and says Catullus chose it to show poetic affiliation "not only of the amusing, agreeable, amiable, and charming, but of these qualities *in their popular guise,*" though he does not connect it to Roman comedy. Moore (1991, 343) calls this "perhaps the strangest passage in all of Plautus."

[24] Moore (1991, 360–61).

an exemplary model for understanding how far this ability to manipulate the meanings of the physical world can extend. As Ketterer and Sharrock observe, in addition to the usual things we consider "props" in Roman comedy – costume, a signet ring, a letter – Curculio even turns body parts and people into props.[25] When he dresses up as the freedman of the *miles gloriosus* to trick Lyco the banker into handing over the *puella* Planesium, he sports a patch over one eye. His other eye in turn becomes a prop that "raises the bearer to both monstrous and divine status," which banker and parasite contest, the former trying to align him with the Cyclopes and the latter merging his identity with that of Antigonus Monophthalmus and other Hellenistic kings.[26] Throughout the play Curculio regularly turns Planesium, as Ketterer demonstrates, into a living prop for whom the ring, the letter, and the money that the parasite wrests control over become onstage stand-ins for the objectified *puella*.[27] With a few words and bits of cloth, the parasite shows that he can (re)define reality itself, forcing the audience to mistrust their own senses. To Catullus, who consistently challenges the terms of the Roman social contract, the comic *parasitus* offered a role model to subvert his readers' norms and expectations.

All the terms the *choragus* employs to praise Curculio are ultimately about seeming one way and being another, using words and things to control perceptions. On *nugator* and *nugae*, Newman cites a scene from Plautus' *Trinummus* that makes this clear. The play's *sycophanta* explains, "I've hired myself out for the trifling arts" (*locavi ad artis* **nugatorias**, 844), to trick the play's *adulescens* by play-acting as a messenger from his father, describing the instructions he was given (854–60):

quae voluit mihi dixit, docuit et praemonstravit prius
quo modo quidque agerem; nunc adeo si quid ego addidero amplius,
eo conductor melius de me **nugas** conciliaverit.
ut ille me exornavit, ita sum ornatus; argentum hoc facit.
ipse ornamenta a chorago haec sumpsit suo periculo.
nunc ego si potero ornamentis hominem circumducere,
dabo operam ut me esse ipsum plane sycophantam sentiat.

The guy told me what he wanted, taught me and trained me up,
as to how to act and what to do. So now if I go above and beyond,
my contractor will have gotten all the more **trifles** out of me.

[25] Ketterer (1986a, 1986b, 1986c) and Sharrock (2008); see also Richlin (2014, 407).
[26] Sharrock (2008, 26); see also Elderkin (1934) and Slater (2000, 177) on associations between Curculio, Alexander, Antigonus, and Demetrius Poliorcetes, whose siege of Sicyon in 303 BCE may be alluded to at Pl. *Curc.* 394–95.
[27] Ketterer (1986a, 201); see also Richlin (2014, 407–8).

I'm outfitted just as he fitted me out. The money has paid for it.
He got this costume from the *choragus* and paid the deposit himself.
Now if I can use this get-up to run circles around this guy,
I'll work hard to make sure he realizes I'm quite the swindler myself.

All actors are deceivers, but *Curculio's parasitus* and *Trinummus' sycophanta* are a cut above, and their *nugae* center on dressing up in layers of deceptive coverings. For Plautus, "*nugae* describes a reality opposed to that of the soldier and businessman; the deceptive reality of the slave, the lover, the parasite, the comic playwright, irritatingly provocative because its inventors are fully conscious of its illusory or 'masked' . . . nature."[28] Costumes and props are key to this manipulation: *nugae* depend on the capacity of physical objects to bear meaning, and more importantly, playwrights' power to imbue objects with meanings they never bore before.

This nugatory sensibility undergirds Catullus' work, and the interpretation that the *nugae* of poem 1 denote merely "trivial" or "quotidian" tells an incomplete tale, as William Fitzgerald observes. The point of poem 1 is not the *libellus* that it dedicates, nor even the type of poetry it heralds; its focus is the tense little drama it produces between the speaker and the addressee, as well as between poet and audience, as he shows how easily he can use objects to (re)define the terms of our engagement with him. The booklet is a tiny thing, nonsense, not worth your time – but it deserves to endure for all time, so take it (*habe tibi quidquid hoc libelli, / qualecumque quod . . . maneat perenne*, 8–10). Catullus' fixation on his work's materiality suggests anxiety about its ability to last, but he also revels in his words' ability to transcend and become something more permanent than papyrus could ever be. The physical work belongs to Nepos; the poetry belongs to the ages. If you're going to judge Catullus' book by its cover, you'll be surprised – big things, small packages, and so forth. But appearances matter and the surprise is the point, so don't ruin it by trying not to be surprised; look at the cover, polished fine with pumice (*pumice expolitum*, 1.2), and judge it accordingly. Fitzgerald notes that "the gesture of poem 1 teases us with the notion that the *nugae are* something, without allowing us a clear separation between what is nugatory and what is something . . . The nugatory is not a matter of a particular kind of content or even style; it is a form of game with the audience," in which the poet makes what we all thought was simple and secure into something slippery.[29] It is, in other words, the same performance the comic parasite plays: both use words,

---

[28] Newman (1990, 18).     [29] Fitzgerald (1992, 427); see also Fitzgerald (1995, 38–42).

performance, and props (*ornamenta, libellus*) to force the audience to question what is before their eyes. Is the actor who he says he is? Is the poetry what it looks like? Catullus' *nugae* are slight things he uses to perform sleights of hand.

Catullus' metapoetic terms *lepidus/lepos* and *sal* carry similar implications of clever manipulation and mischievous deception, which he likewise extracts from the vocabulary of Roman comedy. As Brian Krostenko notes, *lep(idus)* in the late Republic primarily marked proper social performance that entailed verbal dexterity, and Plautus often uses it to praise comic cleverness and deception: the *choragus* of *Curculio* uses it in this way to praise the play's role-shifting eponymous parasite, and when Saturio's daughter in *Persa* expertly misleads the *leno* Dordalus, the *servus* Toxilus proudly describes her in terms typically used of the *servus callidus*, or "clever slave," saying that "she's so sharp and clever to have a discriminating heart that says what needs to be said!" (*ita cata est et callida, / ut sapiens habet cor, quam dicit quod opust!*, 622–23) and declaring that "she's played him charmingly" (***lepide** lusit*, 635).[30] Notably, in this scene she is disguised, using props and a costume that Toxilus earlier tells her father to acquire: "Bring out that daughter of yours costumed charmingly in the outfit of a foreigner ... get the costume from the *choragus*; he should give it – the aediles hired him to lend it" (*et tu gnatam tuam / ornatam adduce **lepide** in peregrinum modum / ... ornamenta aps chorago sumito; / dare debet: praebenda aediles locaverunt*, 157–60).[31] This combination of *lepidus* and *ludus* also appears in the opening to *Asinaria*, where the prologue speaker promises that "there's charm and play in this comedy" (*inest **lepos** ludusque in hac comoedia*, 13). To act *lepide* requires that you know how to play along with the humorous deceptions, to give yourself over to the idea – essential for comic playwrights and Catullus alike – that what matters is not what you see, but what you can make believe and make others believe.

A similar network of associations obtains for *sal*, which "describes a particular kind of humor, one that has an ironic, dissimulating, or deadpan quality ... that is, humor which assesses, then controverts expectations."[32]

---

[30] Krostenko (2001a, 70); see also 142–43, where he notes, "Ennius uses *lepide* for the self-congratulatory cleverness of a trickster, recalling the forte of the *servus callidus*" at *Sat.* 59–62. For the clever deceptions by Saturio's daughter, see Lowe (1989, 392–96).

[31] On costuming and metatheatrical deception in this scene, see Muecke (1986), Lowe (1989), and Hardy (2005).

[32] Krostenko (2001a, 281 n. 116; see also 220 n. 59); see Nielsen (1987) on *sal*'s deceptive and ironic nature in Catullus.

Indeed, *sal* is a prerequisite for the playfulness and deception inherent in performing *lepide*, "the spark that kindles the display of *venustas* and the exercise of *lepos*; its absence blunts perception and wit and coarsens taste and behavior."[33] The opening *canticum* of Lysidamus, the *senex amator*, or "old man in love," of Plautus' *Casina*, explores the relationship between altered appearances, *sal*, and *lepos* (217–23):

omnibus rebus credo ego amorem et nitoribus nitidis antevenire
nec potis quicquam commemorari quod **plus salis plusque leporis** [hodie]
habeat; coquos equidem nimis demiror, qui utuntur condimentis,
eos eo condimento uno non utier, omnibus quod praestat.
nam<que> ubi amor condimentum inerit, quoivis placituram <escam> credo;
nec **salsum** nec suave esse potest quicquam, ubi amor non ammiscetur:
fel quod amarum est, id mel faciet, hominem ex tristi **lepidum** et lenem.

Love, I believe, excels all things, including the bright brightnesses,
and not a thing can be mentioned that has more salt and charm.
Why, I'm really amazed that cooks, who use flavorings,
don't use this one flavoring, which surpasses all others.
When love's a flavoring in a dish, I believe everyone will enjoy it.
Nothing is salty or sweet, when it doesn't get combined with love.
Why, it turns bitter gall into honey, a stern man into a charming and mild one.

The *sal* and *lepos* of love rest in its ability to change things into something unexpected, including having a *senex durus* perform as if he were the stereotypical *adulescens amator*. In the next few lines, Lysidamus admits that his transformation relies on a particular prop, namely, a "charming perfume" (**lepidum** *unguentum*, 226) that he uses to convince the *puella* Casina that he is an apt suitor, such as the "young man in love," rather than the "harsh old man" that he is in reality. But he soon runs into his wife Cleostrata, who rebukes him for trying to use this scented prop to shift his stock type: "You're walking the streets, perfumed at your old age, you lazy fool?" (*senectan aetate unguentatus per vias, ignave, incedis?*, 240).[34]

Lysidamus is chastised for trying to manipulate appearances but failing spectacularly. Props alone are not enough to achieve this kind of transformation, and the *senex* of Roman comedy is simply not sharp enough to fool others into thinking that he is more than his stock type. Catullus, by contrast, is censured for the opposite reason in poem 16, where his poetic *sal ac lepos* (4) are so successful that Furius and Aurelius misread his

---

[33] Seager (1974, 894).
[34] Connors (1997) discusses the perfume's significance for Lysidamus' attempt to reject the norms of the *senex*. We might compare the transformative power of the *unguentum* Catullus promises will make Fabullus pray to become *totum nasum* in poem 13.

character. Selden observes that "the salt here is seasoned with paradox," since poem 16 paints a picture of Catullus that is at odds with his reality: soft verses make the poet look as if he is an effeminate who claims to be *pius* and *castus* (5), but they flow from the pen of a man who promises to penetrate his readers sexually and in the process commit *stuprum*, the opposite of *pietas* or *castitudo*.[35] Catullus uses his *versiculi* like the *nugae* of poem 1 to play games with his audience. His poems are "soft and a bit naughty" (*molliculi ac parum pudici*, 8), but if you take them at face value, you'll take it in the face. Poem 16 announces that Catullus' work is made to manipulate, like the *parasitus* of Roman comedy, and correctly playing his poetic game entails thinking outside the box and recognizing that all objects that mediate the relationship between poet and audience are props that can distract and deceive. Cornelius Nepos gets the dedication because he sees there is something to Catullus' nothings (*namque tu solebas / meas esse aliquid putare nugas*, 1.3–4). Meanwhile, Furius and Aurelius get the shaft because they don't get that Catullus says one thing to mean another (*vos, quod milia multa basiorum / legistis, male me marem putatis*, 16.12–13).[36] Salt, charm, and trifles, for both Roman comedy and Catullus, demand an appreciation of the ironies of illusion, understanding what it means to interact with people and objects beyond the quotidian surface, and recognizing there is always more to that relationship than meets the eye.

The physical *libellus* and *versiculi* are merely a couple of many objects whose meaning Catullus playfully manipulates, but his prop-mastery extends well beyond metapoetic concerns. Take an example that illustrates the comic element behind Catullus' broader nugatory approach: in poem 12, Catullus attacks Asinius Marrucinus for committing what seems on its face a trivial offense:

> Marrucine Asini, manu sinistra
> non belle uteris: in ioco atque vino
> tollis lintea neglegentiorum.
> hoc salsum esse putas? fugit te, inepte;
> quamvis sordida res et invenusta est.                    5
> non credis mihi? crede Pollioni
> fratri, qui tua furta vel talento
> mutari velit: est enim leporum

---

[35] Selden (1992, 478).
[36] My reading of poem 16 is deeply indebted to Selden (1992), Batstone (1993), and Fitzgerald (1995, 49–52), who trace the poem's paradoxes and playful manipulations.

differtus puer ac facetiarum.
10    quare aut hendecasyllabos trecentos
exspecta, aut mihi linteum remitte,
quod me non movet aestimatione,
verum est mnemosynum mei sodalis.
nam sudaria Saetaba ex Hiberis
15    miserunt mihi muneri Fabullus
et Veranius; haec amem necesse est
ut Veraniolum meum et Fabullum.

Asinius Marrucinus, you put your left hand
to use not suavely: you steal the napkins of
those who are carelessly drinking and joking.
You think this is sharp? You're out of it, tactless man.
This business is grubby and uncharming.
Don't believe me? Believe your cousin
Pollio; he'd be willing to undo your thefts,
even if it cost a talent. You see, he's a boy
chock-full of cleverness and charm.
So either look forward to three hundred
hendecasyllabic verses or give me back my napkin.
It doesn't move me because of its monetary value,
but because it's a souvenir of my buddy.
For Fabullus and Veranius sent me Saetaban
handkerchiefs from Spain as a gift.
I have to cherish them just as I cherish
my little Veranius and Fabullus.

Marrucinus' actions constitute theft, but his real crime in Catullus' eyes is his lack of grace and social propriety. He uses his hands "not suavely" (*non belle*, 2) and thinks his misappropriation of Catullus' *lintea* will be a "sharp" (**salsum**, 4) joke, but really he is just "tactless" (*inepte*, 4). These terms are all markers of social performance, of knowing how to fit in with Catullus' in-group, and Marrucinus has failed at each step.[37] His cousin Pollio would know better, and that is why he is a "boy chock-full of cleverness and charm" (**leporum** / *differtus puer ac facetiarum*, 8–9). In fact, Catullus says Pollio understands how priceless conforming to proper etiquette is: "he would be willing to undo your thefts, even if it cost a talent" (*tua furta vel talento* / *mutari velit*, 7–8). Pollio and Catullus think

---

[37] On the vocabulary of social performance here, see Krostenko (2001a, 241–46), as well as Fitzgerald (1995, 93–98), Nappa (2001, 107–20), Stroup (2010, 72–78), and Young (2015, 55–63), to whom my reading is indebted.

alike. Money pales in comparison to the value of keeping up your end of the social contract, and "the linen doesn't move me out of concern for its cost, but because it's a memento of my buddy" (*me non movet aestimatione, / verum est mnemosynum mei sodalis*, 12–13). Marrucinus, by contrast, has failed to grasp what the smart crowd knows well: objects can mean more than they seem to on their surface. Only an oaf would think the napkins' worth lay in how much they cost or who possesses them. Their real value depends on the relationship forged and signified by the gift-exchange (*muneri*, 15) between friends and their connotative function as a stand-in for Catullus' Veranius and Fabullus, whose travels take them far from him.[38] By stealing these napkins, Marrucinus effectively reenacts that separation, removing a physical link connecting Catullus to his absent *sodales* and weakening the group's social bonds.

Moreover, Marrucinus has failed to show that he understands that nothing is as it seems among the cultured elite and that belonging to this group requires one to approach life as a performance. Marrucinus' sin is being straightforward, obvious, and therefore dull. His "joke" is merely a game of peek-a-boo: the napkins were here, but now they're over here, and he's the one who moved them – surprise! None of this requires any subterfuge or subtlety; in fact, it relies on his audience seeing every step of the process. Being a thief, and being recognized for your theft, takes no *sal* or *lepos*. By contrast, Catullus and his peers are social magicians, transforming their belongings so that only those in on the act can understand what they actually mean and thereby declaring their fitness for this special in-group. The point of loading so much personal and social significance in them is to show an aesthetic that not only announces triviality but requires people to know how to read the importance of the trivial. Nothing about napkins declares, "We matter," unless you know the silent backstory with which Catullus, Veranius, and Fabullus have imbued them, that is, their "material unconscious."[39] Indeed, Catullus' explicit mention of the napkins' *aestimatio* represents a complete rejection of any

---

[38] See Uden (2011, 129) on the napkins' power to memorialize friendship, as well as Stroup (2010, 75–77) and Krostenko (2001a, 245), who notes they are "meant to suggest the private world of sentimental value." Skinner (1981, 105) observes, "In the ironic jargon of Catullus' circle, poems may be *nugae* and the craft of letters a *ludus*, but, beneath the surface frivolity, the discipline of art inculcates abiding principles of good taste which can be developed into a general code of behavior." I would add that their code of behavior does not contrast with *ludus* and *nugae*, but depends precisely on appreciating the irony they promote.

[39] Skinner (1981, 96) comments on the "deep mutual sympathy" among Catullus' circle that the hidden meanings of the napkins disclose. For "material unconscious," see Brown (1996) as well as

form of valuation that outsiders might bring to the situation. What would seem no more than something you could pawn for some quick cash or a way to announce the size of your estate to most people means far more to members of this in-group who have a different, secret, shared valuation. The napkins function as a kind of *mysterion*, which only initiates of Catullus' clique understand.

They thus also function analogously to the props of Roman comedy, which require the audience's belief that things can mean more than they should: a lamp in broad daylight can set the play at night, a sword or cape can turn a slave actor into a triumphant general or road-weary traveler, unguents can reveal that someone is in love, and a signet can change a sex laborer into a citizen daughter.[40] To someone in a Roman theater who does not know the rules of the space, the ironies inherent in props can be confounding. Take the story of the guard who saw Nero, playing the role of *Hercules insanus*, bound in chains on the stage: the soldier breaks the fourth wall and rushes up to help the emperor, failing to grasp that the props were not real and Nero was never in any danger.[41] Even within the dramatic world, the significance of props can vary, and Marshall observes that the "discrepant understanding of an object's value by characters creates dramatic tension … particularly when relatively valueless objects provide the means of identification of a character as freeborn. A stage property's symbolic value therefore exists only in relationship to something or someone else."[42] The drama of poem 12 derives from this basic truth, and indeed much of the humor, cleverness, and even plots both of Catullus' poems and of Roman comedy depends on ironies that arise when different people evaluate objects differently.

One Plautine scene parallels poem 12's attitude, if not its situation. In *Rudens*, Gripus, a slave of the *senex* Daemones, is out fishing and hauls up a trunk he daydreams is full of treasure that will let him buy his freedom and become a real rags to *reges* tale (*apud reges rex perhibebor*, 931). To him, the possibilities inside the trunk involve only wealth. But the trunk really belongs to the *leno* Labrax, who illegally purchased the *puella* Palaestra, daughter of Daemones (though he does not know this at the moment), from pirates who kidnapped her as a child. The *servus*

---

Stroup (2010, 77) and Young (2015, 61), who notes that Catullus' *aestimatio* simultaneously highlights the napkins' monetary value and rejects money as an appropriate form of valuation.

[40] On the functions of comic props, see Ketterer (1986a, 1986b, and 1986c) and Marshall (2006, 66–72).

[41] Suet. *Nero* 21.3 and Dio 63.9.5; see Bartsch (1994, 46–50) and Slater (1996).

[42] Marshall (2006, 71).

Trachalio, who knows the trunk is Labrax' and that the objects inside will prove the identity and free status of Palaestra, stops Gripus from taking it and convinces Daemones to arbitrate the claim. Trachalio explains that the value of the props is totally different for Gripus and Palaestra (1081–84):

> et ea quae olim parva gestavit crepundia
> istic in ista cistula insunt, quae istic inest in vidulo.
> hoc neque isti usu est et illi miserae suppetias feret,
> si id dederit qui suos parentes quaerat.


> And the trinkets she wore when she was little
> are inside that box there, which is inside that trunk there.
> This isn't of any use to that jerk and it would help that poor girl
> if he gave her it so she might look for her parents.

Gripus doesn't care, and his interest remains purely monetary. "What if they're made of gold?" (*quid si ea sunt aurea*, 1086). Even if they could mean a world of difference to Palaestra, that doesn't mean he should have to lose out, and Trachalio agrees to repay him the face value of the metal (*aurum auro expendetur, argentum argento exaequabitur*, 1087). And indeed, like Catullus' napkins, as their identity is revealed we learn their objective value is nothing to sneeze at, especially to a poor slave like Gripus: a miniature sword (*ensiculust aureolus*, 1156), a tiny ax (*securicula ... aurea*, 1163), and a locket (*bulla aurea*, 1172), all made of gold, and a silver sickle and charms in the shape of two hands clasping and a sow (*sicilicula argenteola et duae conexae maniculae et / sucula*, 1169–70). But the metal doesn't matter to Palaestra as much as the family connections the trinkets signify, the financially worthless but personally priceless names of her father and mother inscribed on the sword and ax (*mei nomen patris ... litterata: ibi matris nomen*, 1157–59) that wouldn't bring Gripus a penny more but could secure Palaestra her freedom and father. For a girl kidnapped from her family as a child, these mementos are the only parents she has, and when she sees the *cistella*, she exclaims, "o my parents, here I carry you shut in, here I have buried the means and hopes of recognizing you" (*o mei parentes, hic vos conclusos gero / huc opesque spesque vostrum cognoscendum condidi*, 1144–45). The tokens are stand-ins for her lost mother and father, the only remaining link between her and her family, not to mention her very identity. While her case represents an extreme example of the link between object and identity, it is essentially the same situation as is represented by Catullus' *mnemosynum*.

The napkins are more than a souvenir of his friends' travels or exotic present; they are a physical manifestation of the friendship, a form of comic recognition token adapted to the particular context of late Republican elite discourse.[43] Here and throughout his corpus Catullus shows that behind his nugatory aesthetics lies the mind of a stage property master, of the actor/playwright in whose hands everything can be imbued with new meaning.

One final example illustrates the comic flavor of Catullus' nugatory sensibility. In poem 25, the speaker's belongings have been stolen again, this time by a man named Thallus, who has taken not only napkins, but practically a whole chest of exotic textiles:[44]

> cinaede Thalle, mollior cuniculi capillo
> vel anseris medullula vel imula oricilla
> vel pene languido senis situque araneoso,
> idemque, Thalle, turbida rapacior procella
> 5   cum diva Murcia arbitros ostendit oscitantes,
> remitte pallium mihi meum, quod involasti,
> sudariumque Saetabum catagraphosque Thynos,
> inepte, quae palam soles habere tamquam avita.
> quae nunc tuis ab unguibus reglutina et remitte,
> 10   ne laneum latusculum manusque mollicellas
> inusta turpiter tibi flagella conscribillent,
> et insolenter aestues, velut minuta magno
> deprensa navis in mari, vesaniente vento.

> Thallus, you fairy, softer than a bunny's fur
> or a goose's marrow or the very tip of an earlobe
> or an old man's flaccid penis and cobwebbed decrepitude,
> but at the same time grabbier than a rough breeze, Thallus,
> when Murcia, goddess of sloth, shows witnesses who are yawning:
> give me back my Greek cloak, which you pilfered,
> and my Saetaban napkin and Bithynian embroideries.
> You're an idiot to keep flashing them like family heirlooms.
> Now, peel them out of your claws and give them back,
> or whips will write up shameful brands all over your
> woolly-soft tender flanks and your tiny manicured hands,

---

[43] Nappa (2001, 107–21) discusses the napkins' role in elite social discourse.

[44] The opening of line 5 is corrupt; I prefer Putnam's (1964) and Quinn's (1970) reading to Thomson's (1998), but neither figures significantly into my interpretation of the poem. The meaning of *catagraphos* in line 7, otherwise unattested, is obscure. The two most attractive guesses are figured cloths or writing tablets; see Ellis (1889, 86) and Thomson (1998, 267). For my purposes, it matters only that they seem insignificant but become props whose significance is contested by Thallus and Catullus.

and you'll froth like never before, just like a minuscule
boat caught by a raging wind in the wide-open sea.

The rhythm stands out: iambic septenarii "had a special association with
comedy . . . Varro called the meter a *comicus quadratus* (*De serm. lat.* fr. 39
Funaioli), and two late antique grammarians . . . described the meter as
especially appropriate to comic gestures."[45] So does the thief's unusual
name: Thallus, from θαλλός, "a young branch, switch" – an apt moniker
for someone so pliant and soft, as well as a springboard for Catullus'
imagination as he devises an ironic penalty for his theft. How better to
punish a "Switch" than to whip some shame into him? His menacing
carries extra degradation, because this is exactly the sort of punishment the
slaves of Roman comedy are subject to: Pseudolus tells his master Simo to
"write all over me with pens of elm-wood, just like when letters are written
in a book with a reed" (*quasi in libro [quom] scribuntur calamo litterae /
stilis me totum usque ulmeis conscribito*, 544a–45), and *Bacchides'* Chrysalus
fears his master "will right away make me a Cross-alus out of a Chrysalus"
(*facietque extemplo Crucisalum me ex Chrysalo*, 362), using his own name
against him as a torture device.[46] From its start, Catullus signals that
something funny is going on in this poem.

As in poem 12, the point of poem 25's comic humor centers on who
gets to control not just objects, but also their meaning. Like Marrucinus'
crime, Thallus' is principally a social one, because he has handled these
objects without tact (*inepte*, 8; cf. *hoc salsum esse putas? fugit te, inepte*,
12.4): he has the gall "to flash them out in the open, as if they were family
heirlooms" (*palam soles habere tamquam avita*, 8). But Catullus will not
allow another man to rewrite their significance. It was he, not Thallus, who
put up with Bithynia for those embroideries, and it was his pals Veranius
and Fabullus who trudged all over Spain with nothing to show for their
trouble except for those napkins, all three of them getting fucked over by
their commanders (28.4–10). What gives Thallus the right to wield them
or to imbue them with new backstories and meaning?

But what about the first item Catullus demands, "that Greek cloak of
mine that you swiped from me" (*pallium mihi meum, quod involasti*, 6)?
When did he get it? More to the point, why on earth does he have one?

---

[45] Moore (2012, 184–85); Ter. Maur. 2394–6 = Keil 6.396–97 and Mar. Vict. Keil 6.135.25–29.

[46] Fitzgerald (1995, 101–3) observes the ironic significance of Thallus' name and compares the threat
to "write" on Thallus with Pl. *Ps.* 544a–45 but does not argue these allude to Roman comedy.
Young (2015, 68) notes that "this threat of lashing, so familiar from Roman comedy, poses Thallus
as a slave whose body was typically subject to such tortures."

The *pallium* was the Greekest piece of fashion one could wear, and Elizabeth Young remarks that "the association between this article of clothing and the men who typically wore it was so strong that Greeks were often termed *homines palliati* (men who wear the *pallium*) in contrast with Rome's *homines togati*." By casually mentioning that he owns a *pallium*, Catullus "revels in posing himself as more Greek than the Greeks."[47] As Young adds, "Thallus' ancestors would, in fact, have worn the *pallium*, making it a legitimate heirloom for him, from a cultural perspective. We might understand his theft of Catullus's cloak as a scene of repatriation, a Greek's attempt to reclaim his rightful patrimony from a hellenizing Roman." Indeed, in the period between Plautus and Catullus, the *pallium* had become a powerful symbol of Romans' appropriation of Greek culture, a costume to playact as Greeks.[48] Nowhere is this more evident than in Roman comedy itself, the *fabula palliata* (literally, "a play that wears a Greek cloak"), for which the *pallium* was recognizable shorthand. Indeed, the cloak that Thallus is accused of stealing acts as a metapoetic marker Catullus winkingly deploys to corroborate his allusions to Roman comedy in poem 25.[49] Like the *libellus* of poem 1 or the *lintea* of poem 12, in Catullus' hands this little cloak can say more than inanimate objects normally do. It proclaims the poet's power to possess and to control imported culture and literature, to define who can use them and how, and to manipulate their significance for his own ends. Catullus' *pallium* is an assertion of Roman dominion over Hellenic culture.

At the same time, the fact that it is not only a prop but also a piece of clothing makes it especially powerful.[50] Clothes, after all, are costumes, and like all costumes the *pallium* has the power to transform its wearer into someone and something else. As a generic marker, it turns this poem into a miniature threat monologue from Roman comedy. And when Roman actors donned the *pallium*, they temporarily ceased to be either Romans or actors, transporting themselves to a fictional Greek setting and

---

[47] Young (2015, 71–72).

[48] Young (2015, 72). On *Romani palliati* during the late Republic, see Bieber (1959).

[49] On the Greek identity of the *pallium* and the origins of the name *fabula palliata*, see Barsby (1999a, 9) and Manuwald (2011, 131–33), as well as Varro fr. 306 Funaioli (*graecas fabulas ab habitu palliatas Varro ait nominari*). The *pallium* functions as a metapoetic marker in Roman comedy itself. Csapo (1993, 48) remarks, "the *pallium*, to Roman eyes the stereotypical Greek dress, was selected for overuse on the Roman stage as a signifier of Graecitude," and Pl. *Curc.* 280–98 shows the eponymous parasite complaining that he keeps bumping into *isti Graeci palliati*. See also Goldberg (1978, 84) and Sharrock (2009, 54) on Pl. *Epid.* 1.

[50] Ketterer (1986a, 1986b, 1986c) and Marshall (2006, 66–72) discuss the fuzzy lines between "prop" and "costume," which often perform the same or different, but complementary, functions.

becoming strangers to their own city and to themselves. Even inside the play, the *pallium* can transmute a character's stock type into another, and Plautus repeatedly uses it to mark this kind of metatheatrical performance. When the slave Epidicus wants to dupe his master, he realizes the best way is to dress up and pretend to be a *servus currens*, or "running slave," who in Roman comedy is stupid and guileless and thus trustworthy (*Epidicus* 192–95):[51]

> di hercle omnes me adiuvant, augent, amant:
> ipsi hi quidem mi dant viam, quo pacto ab se argentum auferam.
> age nunciam orna te, Epidice, et palliolum in collum conice
> itaque assimulato quasi per urbem totam hominem quaesiveris.

> By Hercules, all the gods help, bless, and love me!
> These guys here are actually giving me a way to take money from them.
> Come on now, Epidicus, get your get-up on, toss your little cloak on your neck –
> yeah, just like that, pretend like you've been looking for the man all over the city.

More than mere cloth, the *pallium* is invested with multiple significances that can be wielded by someone who understands the capacity of objects to mean other than they seem. This is the point *Curculio's choragus* makes in praising the parasite as *lepidus nugator* and *halophanta*: having gotten control of the troupe's props and costumes, the master of disguise can use them to play, perform, and manipulate. In poem 25, Catullus shows himself to be just as skilled at raiding the costume shop and at using these objects to construct, conceal, and reveal the backstories and identities of himself and others. Moreover, his choice of the *pallium* here signals his eagerness to borrow elements from the *fabula palliata* throughout his work.

In all these poems, Catullus calls attention to his role as the comic parasite of his world: props and costumes are his to use, and in the hands of a *lepidus nugator* worth his salt, they can be made to define, alter, and nullify identity and social relationships. We could run from object to object in the Catullan corpus and see proof of the myriad ways in which the poet can make physical things say, do, and mean more than they should be able: Flavius' chatty bed (*clamat* / . . . *tremulique quassa lecti* / *argutatio*, 6.7–11), books that poison good poets and others that punish

---

[51] On metatheater and disguise in this scene and in other places where characters use the *pallium* as a significant prop, see Csapo (1993, 46), Muecke (1986, 219), and cf. Pl. *Capt.* 778–79. Poem 55, discussed in Chapter 4, features a meaningful recurrence of the *servus currens* schtick.

thieves (poems 14 and 42), and bright teeth that scream social and sexual faux pas (poems 37 and 39).[52] Indeed, throughout this book I call attention to how Catullus' use of Roman comedy centers on the poet's manipulation of everyday materials to redefine elite Roman discourse and experiences in theatricalized terms. For now, though, these examples show how he uses physical objects to cast himself and those around him as characters in a drama playing out in his corpus' cosmopolitan setting – a setting, not coincidentally, in which Rome and the comic stage overlap.

## Domestic, Urban, and Local Perspectives
## (Poems 10, 31, and 51)

"However exotic or contrived the offstage settings, and whatever name the play happens to give to the town, the setting of the *fabulae palliatae* is, essentially, always the same street."[53] And this street runs through a sleepy neighborhood: almost all its traffic flows between the doors of two modest houses on stage. Two side entrances, "one from the forum, the other from foreign parts," provide the inhabitants of these upper-middle-class homes a conduit to the outside world, where they occasionally need to take care of some *negotium* and which sometimes lets in some outsider who sets the residents into a tizzy.[54] But everything that the audience observes takes place in this mundane urban space, where everyone's hopes and fears are decidedly homespun: petty rivalries and lovers' tiffs, births and marriages, misunderstandings and reunions, rows and reconciliations. In this respect, Roman comedy gives its audience an immediacy unmatched in most other genres. What they see is a kind of Mediterranean Main Street, USA, utterly ordinary and filled with little people like themselves and their neighbors, not consuls and cohorts. Roman comedy is preoccupied with its own business, shying away from the macrosocial concerns of the superpower that enabled its development and turning from forensic,

---

[52] On the bed as speaking object, see Stevens (2013, 19–46); on extra-material powers of books, see Roman (2006, 351–59) and Stroup (2010, 234–36); on Egnatius' smile, see Krostenko (2001b). Although it might seem odd to call teeth a "prop," Roman comedy regularly deploys body parts in ways that are similar to the treatment of props and costumes, as does Catullus; see Sharrock (2008) on eyes and guts in *Curculio*, as well as, e.g., the *lena*'s teeth (Pl. *Truc.* 224–26) and the backs of slaves (*As.* 276, *Men.* 275, and *Ps.* 1325), on which see Dutsch (2008, 124–26).
[53] Marshall (2006, 54).
[54] Vitr. 5.6.8 (*una a foro, altera a peregre*). See Duckworth (1952, 85–88) and Marshall (2006, 49–56) for Roman comedy's setting conventions, including the houses and entrances from the forum and harbor/countryside.

political, and military strife toward the dysfunctional home lives of private individuals and their friends, foes, and family.

If we were to replace "Roman comedy" with "Catullus" in the preceding paragraph, it would remain more or less accurate. Catullus' world is just as small and intimate as that of the *palliatae*, and he consistently calls attention to the domesticity of his poetry's setting: Flavius' bedroom (*tacitum cubile*, 6.7), Veranius' home (*domum ad tuos penates*, 9.3), Catullus' dining room (*cenabis ... apud me*, 13.1), and the private locales where he can canoodle and quarrel with Lesbia all speak to Catullus' obsessive interest in the private lives of well-off Romans. And these spaces are dominated by, even revel in, the most humdrum activities, chiefly flirting, gossip, and invective. Catullus' poems often seem like "snatches of conversation in a dramatic continuum" that could have been (and in some cases are) drawn from Roman comedy's everyday chatter. A case in point: Gaisser shows that the opening of poem 10 employs the staging conventions of Roman comedy to produce a comic scene in miniature (10.1–13):[55]

> Varus me meus ad suos amores
> visum duxerat e foro otiosum,
> scortillum, ut mihi tum repente visum est,
> non sane illepidum neque invenustum.
> huc ut venimus, incidere nobis                  5
> sermones varii: in quibus, quid esset
> iam Bithynia, quo modo se haberet;
> ecquonam mihi profuisset aere.
> respondi, id quod erat, nihil neque ipsis
> nec praetoribus esse nec cohorti,             10
> cur quisquam caput unctius referret,
> praesertim quibus esset irrumator
> praetor, nec faceret pili cohortem.

> Varus led me, while I was at my leisure,
> out of the Forum to see his lover –
> a little tart, as I saw right then and there,
> but not altogether unappealing or uncharming.
> When we arrived there, various topics fell into
> our conversation, including how it was with
> Bithynia and how it was getting along,
> and what sort of money had it made me.

---

[55] For "dramatic continuum," see Quinn (1970, 398); Gaisser (2009, 51–55).

> I responded just like it was: that there was no way
> that anyone – not the cohort and not the praetors
> themselves – came back with more oil on their heads,
> especially those of us who had a skull-fucker of a
> praetor who didn't care one lick about his cohort.

Here is a domestic tableau straight out of Roman comedy: the speaker plays an indolent young man (*otiosum*, 2), led onto the poem's stage from the entrance *a foro* to the house of a *puella* – or, as he suggests shortly, of a beguiling comic *mala meretrix* (*scortillum . . . non sane illepidum neque invenustum*, 3). We also learn he has recently returned to the city from abroad, gesturing toward the theatrical entrance *a peregre*. But he cares little for life in either direction. Catullus in fact represents his time in Bithynia as an unmitigated disaster that he is glad to have escaped for the urban domestic world where the battles are social, weapons are wit and charm, and prizes are self-satisfaction and admiration of one's peers.

The poem's theatrical setting paves the way for some comic *nugae* as Catullus introduces a group of Bithynian litter-bearers, whom he deploys as living props around which the tension of this little social drama revolves (10.14–27):

|    | "at certe tamen," inquiunt "quod illic |
| 15 | natum dicitur esse, comparasti |
|    | ad lecticam homines." ego, ut puellae |
|    | unum me facerem beatiorem, |
|    | "non" inquam "mihi tam fuit maligne, |
|    | ut, prouincia quod mala incidisset, |
| 20 | non possem octo homines parare rectos." |
|    | at mi nullus erat nec hic neque illic, |
|    | fractum qui veteris pedem grabati |
|    | in collo sibi collocare posset. |
|    | hic illa, ut decuit cinaediorem, |
| 25 | "quaeso" inquit mihi, "mi Catulle, paulum |
|    | istos commoda: nam volo ad Serapim |
|    | deferri." |

> "But still surely," they said, "you got ahold of
> what's said to be the native crop there, some
> men for a litter." Then to make out to the girl
> that I was exceptionally fortunate, I said,
> "It wasn't so dreadful for me that,
> though I got stuck with a bad province,
> I couldn't get together eight sturdy men."

> But I didn't have one, either here or there,
> who could put the broken leg
> of an old cot on his shoulders.
> Then she, like the fairy she was,
> said to me, "Please, my dear Catullus,
> lend me them a little while. See, I want
> to be conveyed to the Temple of Serapis."

The speaker has already admitted his time with the cohort won him nothing but pain, but when it becomes clear that he runs the risk of losing face in front of Varus and the *puella*, he lays claim to litter-bearers that he says he brought back as prizes from his foreign service. His boasts are idle talk, however, and Rüdiger Bernek shows persuasively that Catullus' speaker here mirrors the comic *miles gloriosus* or "braggart soldier," adducing parallels from Plautus' depiction of Pyrgopolynices in his *Miles Gloriosus* in particular.[56] His attempt to assimilate himself to the *miles gloriosus* stock type is made even more ridiculous by Catullus' repeated emphasis on the military roles of the expedition (*praetoribus ... cohorti*, 10; *praetor ... cohortem*, 13). But clearly he never performed as a soldier, and he reveals that any spoils he brought back were entirely dependent on the patronage of other men who actually performed military service, such as the praetor Memmius, whom he blames for hindering his acquisitions (9–12). The *lecticarii* he claims are, at best, the crumbs of provincial predation bestowed on him by other, more virile and martial men.[57] Moreover, like the comic soldier, Catullus tries to boost his own public image by exaggerating his success abroad (*ut ... me facerem beatiorem*, 16–17), but we quickly learn that he has nothing to back up his claim (*at mi nullus erat*, 21). In fact, the only reason we discover he is lying is that Catullus' speaker splits his persona and plays two comic characters at once: to Varus and the *puella* he shows off like a *miles gloriosus*, but to the reader he adopts the stance of the *parasitus*, the wry hanger-on who breaks the fourth wall to undercut the empty hyperbole of his boss.[58] Catullus' confession at 10.21–23 finds a neat parallel in the opening scene of Plautus' *Miles Gloriosus*. After the parasite Artotrogus puffs up the soldier's ego, he

---

[56] Bernek (2004); see also Kutzko (2006, 408).

[57] On the litter-bearers, military patron/client dynamics, and implications of virility and effeminacy in Catullus' insult *irrumator praetor*, see Skinner (1989), Braund (1996), Nappa (2001, 85–105), Cairns (2003), and Young (2015, 91–92).

[58] For the *parasitus* in Roman comedy, see Damon (1995) and bibliography there (esp. 181 n. 2).

confides in the audience that they shouldn't believe a word Pyrgopolynices
says (19–23):

> PYRG: "istuc quidem edepol nihil est."
> ART: "nihil hercle hoc quidem est
> praeut alia dicam ... quae tu numquam feceris.
> periuriorem hoc hominem si quis viderit
> aut gloriarum pleniorem quam illic est,
> me sibi habeto, ei ego me mancupio dabo."

> PYRG: "Why, that was nothing."
> ART: "By Hercules, it sure was nothing compared with other things
>       I could say" <aside> "... that you never did.
> If anyone ever sees someone who's a bigger liar than this guy
> or more full of his own boasting than that one there is,
> they can have me for themselves – I'll sell myself to them."

Moore notes that Artotrogus' aside is designed to build a rapport between
him and the audience, and Victoria Pedrick and Marilyn Skinner have
observed the same effect in Catullus' tattling on his *miles* alter ego in poem
10.[59] Catullus takes his parasitical identity a step further in the finale of the
poem (10.27–34):

> "mane," inquii puellae,
> "istud quod modo dixeram me habere,
> fugit me ratio: meus sodalis –
> 30   Cinna est Gaius – is sibi paravit.
> verum, utrum illius an mei, quid ad me?
> utor tam bene quam mihi pararim.
> sed tu insulsa male et molesta vivis,
> per quam non licet esse neglegentem."

> "Wait!" I said to the girl,
> "What I just said that I have,
> my mind wandered away. My buddy –
> Cinna, that is Gaius – he got them for himself.
> But really, whether they're his or mine, what's that to me?
> I use them just as if I got them for myself.
> But you're a really unwitty girl and a bother
> that a person isn't allowed be careless around!"

Catullus calls Cinna his *sodalis*, but he figures their relationship differently
from the *sodalitas* he claims with Veranius and Fabullus (12.13). Both are

---

[59] Moore (1998, 207 n. 8), Pedrick (1986), Skinner (1989).

defined by physical objects acquired during service abroad (*sudaria Saetaba*, 12.14; *ad lecticam homines*, 10.16), but the litter-bearers set up Catullus as Cinna's dependent rather than his peer, and Nappa shows that the speaker in poem 10 is playing the role of Plautine *parasitus* rather than an authentic friend.[60] Indeed, by resorting to "borrowing" Cinna's property in order to gain social capital, Catullus strengthens his connection to Veranius and Fabullus, whom "Catullus ironically censures [in poem 47] for snatching crumbs of recognition from the tables of the great."[61] The situation is much the same in poem 28, where he says Veranius' and Fabullus' lot in Piso's cohort in Spain mirrored his own under Memmius in Bithynia, with all three striving – and ultimately failing – to "seek noble friends" (*pete nobiles amicos*, 28.13) through whom they might improve their fiscal and social standing.[62] In poem 10, Catullus reminds us that he was a low man on more than one ladder. By any measure, Cinna was more successful than Catullus in political and military life: he is said to have brought Parthenius of Nicaea back to Rome as a war captive after participating in the campaign against Mithridates in 66 BCE and was a tribune in 44 BCE when the mob killed him in the aftermath of Caesar's death.[63] Whatever his precise role in the Bithynian campaigns of 57/56 BCE, Cinna was clearly in a position of superiority relative to Catullus and not all that different from Memmius, except – at least in Catullus' telling – more willing than the praetor to give Catullus a taste of provincial spoils. But Varus' *puella* catches Catullus' hand in Cinna's cookie jar, forcing him to confess that his attempt to wear the costume of an independent and triumphant *miles* is merely a delusion of comic grandeur.

Catullus' failure in poem 10 stems not so much from trying to deceive as from doing so poorly, like the *senex amator* of Plautus' *Casina*, and without his usual nugatory flair. His crime is more or less what he abuses Marrucinus for in poem 12, namely, assigning monetary worth to objects and failing to recognize their hidden social value. By appropriating the litter-bearers for himself, he erases Cinna from his social connections, with the aim of making his "head oilier" (*caput unctius*, 10.11), that is, himself wealthier. But this was Marrucinus' cardinal error: to steal Catullus'

---

[60] Nappa (2001, 91); see also Damon (1997, 17–19).    [61] So Skinner (1979, 141).

[62] On the parasitical stance of the speaker and his friends, see Skinner (1979) and Nappa (2001, 85–105).

[63] On Cinna's military and political career, see Clausen (1964), Wiseman (1974, 44–58), and Hollis (2007, 18–23).

napkins is to destroy the memory of friendships they embody, whose value cannot be counted in *talenta*. To top it all off, he elides Cinna's friendship merely to play *miles gloriosus*, comedy's grossest *alazon* (the uncouth impostor antagonist), leaving the space of the *eiron* (the clever underdog) open to be played by the *puella*, who performs the role *lepide*. Catullus admits at the poem's start that he erred in trusting appearances and so misreading her as merely a "little slut" (*scortillum, ut mihi tum repente visum est*, 3). He shouldn't have taken her at face value, as she turned out to be both *lepida* and *venusta* (4), that is, a master of props herself. Catullus tries to use the litter-bearers to gain the status of a wealthy *miles*, but she turns his props against him. Indeed, when she asks to borrow the litter-bearers, she transforms his grand prize into something ridiculous. Only the enfeebled or effeminate would bear to be borne by a litter, and her proposed destination caps her joke: the cult of Serapis had been banned and its altars ordered destroyed by the Senate in 59 BCE, but popular resistance restored them almost immediately and supporters heckled the consuls into temporary submission.[64] By directing Catullus' pretentious *lecticarii* to the temple of an eastern cult that elite Romans failed to control and emphasizing their traditional identity as a woman's conveyance, she matches the clever manipulation of props that Catullus performs elsewhere.[65] And just as in poems 12 and 25, although the objects whose significance is contested come from far-flung exotic lands, the location of that contest is domestic and urban. The Forum and Bithynia are left waiting in the wings as Catullus' drama plays out in an intimate comic space.

Catullus' gaze consistently points toward the local, bringing in the global only when it helps or harms his life at home. Memories of Bithynia reappear to weigh on him as he returns home to his beloved Sirmio in poem 31:[66]

---

[64] For litters as transport for the infirm, women, and sexually submissive men, see Nappa (2001, 90) and Skinner (1989, 12–14); on Serapis in Rome and the attempts to suppress the cult, see Orlin (2010, 204) and remarks by Varro preserved in Tertull. *Apol.* 6 and *Nat.* 1.10.17–18, as well as Arnob. 2.73.

[65] Skinner (1989, 18) argues that "the message of C. 10 is that the game will be won by the side that has usurped the prerogative of defining the rules. Such a postulate is inherently opposed to the spirit of comedy; yet it is present in the subtext, which identifies the very jargon of *urbanitas* as one prominent dialect of the controlling discourse." While I certainly agree with her assertion, I disagree only with the division of comedy and *urbanitas* into mutually exclusive spheres. The woman's *urbanitas* (in the form of *venustas* and *lepos*) and comic traits mirror anti-traditional values espoused by Catullus throughout his corpus. Note, though, that Catullus retains control of the narrative and reasserts his power to define what counts as *sal* when he ends by calling her *insulsa* (33).

[66] Ellis' (1889) reading of line 13, followed by most editors, is more persuasive than Thomson's (1998).

paene insularum, Sirmio, insularumque
ocelle, quascumque in liquentibus stagnis
marique vasto fert uterque Neptunus,
quam te libenter quamque laetus inviso,
vix mi ipse credens Thyniam atque Bithynos                    5
liquisse campos et videre te in tuto.
o quid solutis est beatius curis,
cum mens onus reponit, ac peregrino
labore fessi venimus larem ad nostrum,
desideratoque acquiescimus lecto?                             10
hoc est quod unum est pro laboribus tantis.
salve, o venusta Sirmio, atque ero gaude
gaudente, vosque, o Lydiae lacus undae,
ridete quidquid est domi cachinnorum.

Sirmio, darling eye of headlands and of
islands too – every one that either Neptune
holds in limpid lakes and on the vast sea –
how gladly and how happily do I look upon you,
barely believing myself that I have left behind Thynia
and Bithynia's fields and that I see you safe and sound.
What is more blessed, when we've cast off our cares,
and our mind puts off its burden, and worn by foreign
labor we come home to our hearth and
lay ourselves on the bed we had missed?
This is the only thing that is consolation for such labors.
Greetings, charming Sirmio, and rejoice in your joyous
master. And you, lake of the Lydian wave, beam with
all the laughter you have in store at home.

Francis Cairns and others identify this poem as an *epibaterion*, defined by
Menander Rhetor as "the speech of a man who wishes to address his native
land on arrival from abroad," and assert that the allusion here is primarily
Homeric.[67] Some details in poem 31, however, should give us pause before
we read Catullus as a Transpadane Odysseus. Indeed, Cairns admits that
Catullus' version lacks many of the formal public aspects of the Homeric
eulogy of return, noting that the whole poem is far more personal and
intimate in its choice of *topoi*.[68] The poem's meter suggests a far more
mundane register: the limping iambic is a humorous meter that Catullus

---

[67] Cairns (1974, 13–14), Moore-Blunt (1974), Baker (1983). Haywood (1984) provides the most
comprehensive study of the *epibaterion*.
[68] Griffin (1981) broadly criticizes Cairns' reliance on the precise rhetorical subcategories and their
filiation; cf. remarks by Vessey (1985)

uses, outside poem 31, exclusively to mock people, including his
own speaker in the highly comic poem 8.[69] Particularly striking is how
he imagines the response to his return. Town and lake are to rejoice,
smile, and laugh (*gaude*, 12; *ridete quidquid ... cachinnorum*, 14). The
occasion is festive, more comedy than epic. Catullus' celebration of Sirmio
as *venusta* can be seen to reinforce its comic affinity. Susan Wiltshire
observes, "Catullus alone of the Latin love poets uses in his poetry
the derivatives of the love goddess's name. With the exception of
comedy, the terms *venustas* and *venustus* appear elsewhere only rarely in
extant Latin poetry of any type."[70] Both in Catullus and in Roman
comedy it signifies not merely physical beauty, but a special sort of
cultivated urbanity and ability to conduct oneself with wit and humor,
as we saw above with Varus' *puella*.[71] Sirmio is *venusta* because it presents
the playful, intimate, and urbane setting in which Plautus, Terence, and
Catullus all thrive and which stands in contrast to the bothersome world
abroad.[72]

  While Homer may represent part of the allusive texture of the poem,
comic allusion can be seen to overlay and refract the epic effects. Plautus'
*Trinummus* – a familiar play in Catullus' time, O'Bryhim notes – presents
a noteworthy parallel to Catullus' homecoming to Sirmio in a pivotal scene
where the *senex* Charmides arrives on stage from the harbor entrance
(820–24):[73]

salsipotenti et multipotenti Iovis fratri et Nerei Neptuno
laetus lubens laudis ago et gratis gratiasque habeo et fluctibus salsis,
quos penes mei <fuit saepe> potestas, bonis meis quid foret et meae vitae,
quom suis med ex locis in patriam urbem usqu' columem reducem faciunt.

Lord of the briny deep and mighty ruler, Neptune, brother of Jove and Nereus,
gladly and gratefully I give you my gratitude and praise and proffer my thanks,
and to the briny waves that held power over me – that is, over my property and
my life –

[69] Morgan (2010, 128), Lavigne (2010).     [70] Wiltshire (1977, 319).
[71] Wiltshire (1977); cf. Krostenko (2001a, 234–41) on *venustas*. This connection to comic play may
    also be reinforced by Catullus' address to the water as "Lydian wave" (*Lydiae ... undae*, 13), which
    Cairns (1974, 11) argues represents an etymological joke tying *Lydius* (Lydian, Etruscan) to *ludius*
    (actor) and *ludere* (play, perform).
[72] Sirmio is no Rome, of course, and Wiltshire (1977, 322) notes the oddity of using an urban term to
    describe this setting, remarking that it emphasizes the promontory's role as home of a "cosmopolite"
    in contrast to that of the rustic laborer, not to mention of the foreign *barbarus*.
[73] O'Bryhim (2007, 137). Cicero quotes it offhandedly at *De orat.* 2.39.17 and *ad Brut.* 1.2a.2.8; cf.
    Var. *L.* 7.3.57 and 7.4.78.

since from their realms they make me returned safely back into my country and my city.

The reference to Neptune, the direct address to the waves, and even some of the alliteration and wordplay (e.g., *laetus lubens laudes ago*, 821; cf. *quam te libenter quamque laetus inviso*, 31.4; *grates gratias habeo*, 821; cf. *ero gaude / gaudente*, 31.12–13) are suggestive.[74] There are also potential ties near the end of Charmides' speech, where he explains why he has been away from home and what he plans now that he has returned (838–39):

apage a me sis, dehinc iam certum est otio dare me; satis partum habeo
quibus aerumnis deluctavi, filio dum divitias quaero.

Please, let me be; from now on I've decided to give myself to leisure. I've gotten enough.
What labors have I wrestled with while I sought riches for my son.

Charmides and Catullus both lament their weary labors abroad (*quibus aerumnis deluctavi*, 930; *ac peregrino / labore fessi*, 31.8–9), and Charmides' equation of homecoming with delight and *otium* finds echoes in Catullus (*larem ad nostrum / desideratoque acquiescimus lecto*, 9–10). Though different, the meters reinforce this juxtaposition of foreign labor and domestic reprieve. Morgan argues that limping iambics convey the joyful fatigue of the traveler who can finally stagger into bed, while Moore notes that Charmides' long, stichic string of anapestic octonarii communicate calm reflection, in keeping with his relief to disembark at home finally.[75]

Significantly, as much as they associate their return to their home city with *otium*, both Catullus and Charmides also identify travel abroad with the troubles of money. Indeed, beyond poem 31, in which the speaker tries to keep his journey as much in his rear view as possible, the Bithynia poems put financial concerns front and center. Wiseman documents well how Catullus and Roman men of his class saw service abroad as a path to self-enrichment, and he persuasively suggests that Catullus' time in Bithynia was meant to build his financial fortunes. In poem 10, Catullus implies he went for this reason (*mihi profuisset aere*, 8), and he contrasts *otium* he now enjoys in his urban setting at home (*e foro otiosum*, 2) with his hunt for money abroad to enable that leisure.[76] Charmides, too, says he

---

[74] See Haywood (1984, 50 n. 28).

[75] Morgan (2010, 124–30); cf. Thomson (1998, 284). On Charmides' anapestic octonarii, see Moore (2012, 202 and 211).

[76] Wiseman (1985, 101–7); cf. Forsyth (1986, 46): "the poet's leave-taking of Bithynia and its related *negotium* in order to resume the life of *otium* at home." Skinner (1979 and 1989), Braund (1996),

left the city to seek a fortune (*dum divitias quaero*, 839), and the mercantile adventures of both men have the same goal: the maintenance of an *adulescens* with a taste for the high life and weakness in love. For Catullus, of course, that meant Catullus himself, and Charmides says that his foreign money is meant to support his son (*filio*, 839), the *adulescens amator* Lesbonicus, who earlier laments his prodigality (655–58):

> omnia ego istaec quae tu dixti scio, vel exsignavero,
> ut rem patriam et gloriam maiorum foedarim meum:
> scibam ut esse me deceret, facere non quibam miser;
> ita vi Veneris vinctus, otio captus in fraudem incidi.

> I know everything you just said. I'd even set my seal on it.
> How I spoiled my father's estate and the glory of my ancestors!
> I knew how I should've behaved, but poor me, I just couldn't do it.
> Bound by Venus' power, captured by leisure, I fell into a trap.

Rosivach notes that Lesbonicus' speech finds parallels in Catullus' poetry, particularly in poem 51, "written from the point of view ... of a repentant *adulescens* seeking to pull himself together and behave in an apparently adult fashion."[77] Indeed, I think the comic lover's name (derived from Λέσβος, "Lesbos" + νίκη, "victory"), would have been especially significant to Catullus when considering his relationship with Lesbia.[78] Lesbonicus recognizes that he is a victim of his own *otium*, which has been enabled only by his father's foreign bounty. The situation is similar for Catullus, who ends poem 51 (*ille mi par esse deo videtur*) by lamenting his own destructive *otium* (13–16):

> otium, Catulle, tibi molestum est;
> otio exsultas nimiumque gestis;

---

Nappa (2001, 85–106), and Cairns (2003) examine Catullus' financial concerns and the regular practice of extracting money from provincial service by elite Romans.

[77] Rosivach (1986, 183). Note the prominent placement of Lesbia's name at 51.7 and cf. *miser* at 656 and *misero* at 51.5 (a descriptor strongly associated with the comic *adulescens*; see Newman [1983, 36]), as well as *otio captus* at 658 and the *otium* stanza at 51.13–16. Baehrens (1876, 260) and Woodman (1966, 226) observe the parallel but leave it unexplored. Hunter (1980, 225–26) argues that Lesbonicus' apologia recalls Phaedra's speech at Eur. *Hipp.* 380–85, to which Segal (1989, 818–19) argues the *otium* stanza of Catullus' poem 51 also alludes. The shared Greek source and other allusions to Pl. *Trin.* in Catullus suggest he is here reading Euripides' Phaedra through the "window reference" (on which, see Thomas [1986, 188]) of Plautus' Lesbonicus. On further comic allusions in poem 51, see Newman (1983)

[78] Schmidt (1902, 372) suggests Lesbonicus' name is apt for his situation because the inhabitants of Lesbos had a reputation for luxury, inebriation, and lawlessness, not to mention what Fantham (1977, 407 n. 5) calls "the comic tradition of Lesbian profligacy (cf. λεσβίζειν, λεσβιάζειν)." Cf. Ernout (1961, 8), who interprets it, "le vainqueur à Lesbos, ou le roi des amoureux," which Segal (1974, 263) follows by translating as "passion triumphant."

> otium et reges prius et beatas
>> perdidit urbes.

> Leisure, Catullus, is bothersome to you.
> In leisure you exult and are too restless.
> Leisure has before now destroyed kings
>> and blessed cities.

This stanza has presented numerous puzzles for Catullan scholarship, but here I want to focus on the hyperbole of the final two lines. What does the messy love affair of a dissolute young Roman have to do with "kings and blessed cities," and why should his *otium* pose a threat to anyone but himself? Elizabeth Young has recently offered a persuasive answer: "*Otium* was frequently used as a catchall term for the forms of luxurious living that gained popularity at Rome in the wake of its military incursions into the East. This series of campaigns reputedly 'converted the Roman citizenry from labor (*negotiis*) to leisure (*in otium*)' and transformed a citizen body of stalwart soldiers into 'lazy little Greeks' (*graeculi otiosi*)."[79] In other words, *negotium* performed abroad extracts resources from other cities and enables a lifestyle of *otium* at home; this domestic *otium* in turn creates time and opportunity for young men to spend this acquired wealth to, among other pursuits, impress women.[80] As Cairns observes, "Bithynia was rich in natural resources.... Under its earlier Hellenizing kings it had been very prosperous, as it was again to be under the Roman Empire. But under its later kings and for the half-century after its annexation by Rome in 74 BC it was in decline," and one of the prime causes was "the growing impact of Roman power." The comic allusions to Plautus' *Trinummus* here and in poems 10 and 31 clarify that Catullus' *reges et beatae urbes* are not simply proverbial, but specifically the sources of wealth whose sacrifice Roman domestic *otium* demanded, as Catullus knew firsthand.[81] The spoils of distant lands are thus redirected toward social and erotic use. The global is

---

[79] Young (2015, 179); the quotations are from Vell. Pat. 2.1.1–2, who identifies the campaigns of Scipio Aemilianus with the dissolution of Roman *virtus* into Greek *otium*. It may be significant that the rebuke Lesbonicus' upright friend Lysiteles delivers directly before the passage quoted (*Trin.* 642–51) mirrors this same Scipio's defense against criticisms of his own un-Romanness at Polyb. 31.23; see Earl (1960, 236) and Segal (1974, 257).

[80] See also Newman (1983, 1), who argues that Diniarchus' lament at Pl. *Truc.* 74–76 makes a similar point that the conquest of foreign enemies has led to *otium* and supplied young men the resources necessary to become lovers.

[81] Cairns (2003, 177–78); additionally, Baehrens (1876, 261) remarks that "*urbesque beatae = divites et potentes.*" I wonder whether it is significant that the prologue of *Trinummus*, delivered by Luxury anthropomorphized, summarizes the play's situation thus: *adulescens quidam est, qui in hisce habitat aedibus; / is **rem paternam** me adiutrice **perdidit**,* 12–13.

made local, the direction of Roman comedy and of Catullus always the same: back to their country, their city, their home.

## Greco-Roman Hybridity and Translation (Poems 70 and 68)

This is not to say that Roman comedy's ostensibly ordinary setting does not also contain elements of the extraordinary. A Roman audience member would likely not find a Pseudolus or Pamphilus or Pyrgopolynices living next door. Roman comedy, *fabula palliata* – a paradoxical collocation. Although an essential, even foundational genre of Roman literature, its Latin name (a play in a Greek cloak) reveals that it is anything but straightforwardly Roman.[82] Plautus and Terence alike set their plays in ostensibly Greek cities populated entirely by people with Greek-sounding names.[83] Nevertheless, the Greek world of Roman comedy is not consistently Greek: its characters invoke laws, cultural practices, and places that are specific to Rome.[84] The result is a bizarre amalgamation, neither wholly real nor wholly fictional, Greek or Roman, but endowed with the "exoticism and prestige of Greek culture" and "an escape from the constraints of Roman morality" at the same time that it enables playwrights to point directly and mockingly at Roman culture behind the protection of plausible deniability.[85] And the playwrights revel in the fact that they are creating something not simply derivative of the traditions before them or isolated from them, but an interesting new construct that could come about only by adapting, combining, and reshaping: Terence frequently calls attention to the novelty of his *contaminationes*, and Plautus proudly asserts in the prologue to the *Asinaria* that he has taken a Greek script and "is adapting it barbarously" (*vortit barbare*, 11) – that is, into Latin, a *lingua barbara* as far as comedy's Greek characters are concerned, but also into something foreign to Romans as well.[86]

An analogous interest in translation and hybridity also permeates Catullus' work. We have already seen hints of it above: poem 51 is a Latin adaptation of a poem by Sappho (fr. 31), but one that is overlaid

---

[82] See above on the Greek identity of the *pallium* and the origins of the name *fabula palliata*.

[83] The Greek names are often fanciful and suggestive of character rather than reflective of actual naming practice; the only exceptions to the exclusively Greek names are those of Punic visitors, i.e., Hanno and Gidennis in *Poenulus*; see Fontaine (2010, 63).

[84] Bibliography on the Greek and Roman elements and their shifting significance in Roman comedy is massive. Fraenkel (2008 [1922]) remains the standard for Plautus, but Moore (1998, 50–66) offers a more careful and nuanced introduction; on Terence, see Starks (2013).

[85] So Moore (1998, 51).     [86] Gilula (1989) and Moore (1998, 54).

with elements from Roman culture and Roman comedy that reshape the significance of the Greek source for a Roman audience. The speaker of Sappho, the *ipsissima Lesbia poetria*, finds herself recast to address Catullus' Roman Lesbia (*nam simul te, / Lesbia, aspexi, nihil est super mi*, 51.6–7). In the process, Catullus ventriloquizes the feminine voice of Sappho, but in the final stanza he begins speaking thoughts reminiscent of Plautus' Lesbonicus, helplessly lamenting Lesbia's erotic conquests. As with the *epibaterion* of poem 31, Sappho's Greek lyric takes on new meaning as Catullus' comic allusions ground it in specifically Roman social anxieties and the financial and political scene of the late Republic.

This process of layering Roman comedy over non-dramatic Greek sources and refracting them through a comic lens appears frequently in Catullus' poetry. Poem 70, the first explicitly erotic poem in the epigrammatic part of the Catullan corpus, offers a clear example of Catullus' appropriation of comic hybridity. The speaker says that his *mulier* claims to prefer no one before him, but he has his doubts:

> nulli se dicit mulier mea nubere malle
>     quam mihi, non si se Iuppiter ipse petat.
> dicit; sed mulier cupido quod dicit amanti,
>     in vento et rapida scribere oportet aqua.

> My woman says that she prefers to marry no one
>     other than me, not even if Jupiter himself should ask.
> She says; but what a woman says to a desirous lover
>     should be written in the wind and rapid water.

As has long been noted, the poem draws strongly on Callimachus *Epigrams* 25 Pfeiffer:

> ὤμοσε Καλλίγνωτος Ἰωνίδι μήποτ' ἐκείνης
>     ἕξειν μήτε φίλον κρέσσονα μήτε φίλην.
> ὤμοσεν· ἀλλὰ λέγουσιν ἀληθέα τοὺς ἐν ἔρωτι
>     ὅρκους μὴ δύνειν οὔατ' ἐς ἀθανάτων.
> νῦν δ' ὁ μὲν ἀρσενικῷ θέρεται πυρί, τῆς δὲ ταλαίνης
>     νύμφης ὡς Μεγαρέων οὐ λόγος οὐδ' ἀριθμός.

> Callignotus swore to Ionis that he would never hold
>     either a boy or a girl more dear than her.
> He swore: but what they say is true, that oaths given
>     in love do not reach the ears of the gods.
> But now he burns with fire for a youth, and of that wretched
>     girl, as of the Megarians, there is neither word nor reckoning.

The poems share the broad theme of erotic deception, as well as a number of formal and lexical elements (e.g., *dicit ... dicit* and ὤμοσε ... ὤμοσεν in lines 1 and 3), which have been discussed at length by others.[87] But Catullus also departs from Callimachus in some striking ways. Whereas Callimachus' epigram is spoken by an omniscient external narrator, the Catullan speaker inserts himself directly into the situation. As a result, Catullus also ventriloquizes the female Ionis and assumes her role as victim of her beloved's deception, much as he does in poem 51's adaptation of Sappho fr. 31.[88] The deviation that most catches my eye, though, is his inclusion of Jupiter in Lesbia's oath (*non si se Iuppiter ipse petat*, 2). While commentators have generally understood the phrase "not even if Jupiter himself should ask" as proverbial, this expression is quite rare, appearing only once before Catullus, in Plautus' *Casina*.[89] If we consider the context in which that previous oath appears, we can understand Catullus' addition in a new light as a meaningful comic allusion that reinterprets Callimachus' epigram.

The plot of *Casina* centers on a basic, if disturbing, conflict: the *senex* Lysidamus wants to have sex with Casina, an orphan girl who has been raised from a baby to adulthood by his wife Cleostrata; she wants Casina to marry her son, who is currently away from home, but Lysidamus plots to have her marry his slave Olympio so that Casina will become his property as well and he can do as he pleases with her. In an exchange between Lysidamus and Olympio, the latter reveals that he has been falsely telling Cleostrata that he is unshakably in love with Casina and refuses to give up his chance to marry her for anyone, including Jupiter himself (317–24):

> LYS: "quid istuc est? quicum litigas, Olympio?"
> OLYM: "cum eadem qua tu semper." LYS: "cum uxoren mea?"

---

[87] Among several other sources; cf. Meleaeger *AP* 5.8 (χὠ μὲν ἐμὲ στέρξειν, κεῖνον δ᾽ ἐγὼ οὔ ποτε λείψειν / ὠμόσαμεν· κοινὴν δ᾽ εἴχετε μαρτυρίην. / νῦν δ᾽ ὁ μὲν ὅρκια φησὶν ἐν ὕδατι κεῖνα φέρεσθαι). Konstan (1972, 103) remarks, "This apparently simple, straightforward poem is, as it happens, indebted for almost every thought and phrase to some Greek model or other"; see also Laurens (1965).

[88] Skinner (2003, 64) discusses the speaker's self-insertion into the poem; for the poem's gender inversions, see Miller (1988).

[89] Fordyce (1961, 362) and Thomson (1998, 493) claim the phrase is proverbial. Otto (1890, 179) cites the *Casina* passage as a type of argument a fortiori that invokes Jupiter, but none of the examples he adduces (which do not include Catullus' poem 70) offers a close parallel; similar phrases appear only two other times in extant Latin, at Ov. *Her.* 4.36 and *Met.* 7.801. I lack space to explore the issue here, but I suspect both represent allusions to Catullus' poem.

OLYM: "quam tu mi uxorem? quasi venator tu quidem es:
dies atque noctes cum cane aetatem exigis."

320

LYS: "quid agit, quid loquitur tecum?" OLYM: "orat, opsecrat
ne Casinam uxorem ducam." LYS: "quid tu postea?"
OLYM: "negavi enim ipsi me concessurum Iovi,
si is mecum oraret."

LYS: "What's up over there? Whom are you litigating with, Olympio?"
OLYM: "The same woman you always are." LYS: "With my wife?"
OLYM: "What wife are you talking about? You're really more like a hunter:
day and night you spend your life with a bitch."
LYS: "What's going on, what did she say to you?" OLYM: "She's begging,
 pleading that I not take Casina as my wife." LYS: "What did you say then?"
OLYM: "I denied that I would even yield to Jove himself,
if he were to beg me."

Olympio is lying, of course. As Lysidamus' coconspirator, he plans to surrender his erotic place to his master the moment they are married. His false a fortiori oath to Cleostrata takes on further meaning a few lines later, when Olympio complains about the trouble he is in with the rest of the family, and Lysidamus reminds him who wears the divine pants around here (328–39):

OLYM: "verum edepol tua mihi odiosa est amatio:
inimica est tua uxor mihi, inimicus filius,
inimici familiares." LYS: "quid id refert tua?     330
unus tibi hic dum propitius sit Iuppiter,
tu istos minutos cave deos flocci feceris ...     332
opinione melius res tibi habet tua,     338
si hoc impetramus, ut ego cum Casina cubem."

OLYM: "By Pollux, your love affair's become hateful to me:
your wife's my enemy, your son's my enemy,
your family are enemies." LYS: "What's that to you?
As long as this Jupiter alone smiles upon you,
you don't have to care one lick about those mini-gods ...
Your situation's better than you think,
if we manage it so I get to bed with Casina."

This sacrilegious joke runs throughout the play, and Lysidamus regularly equates himself with Jupiter – and, by extension, his wife with Juno. One hundred lines earlier, he tries to soothe the angry and suspicious Cleostrata, telling her, "Aww, my Juno, you shouldn't be so grumpy with your Jove" (*heia, mea Iuno, non decet / ess' te tam tristem tuo Iovi*, 230–230a). And about fifty lines later, Lysidamus and Cleostrata employ

their respective slaves, Olympio and Chalinus, as proxies in a fistfight over
Casina's fate (406–8):

CLEO: "quid tibi istunc tactio est?" OLYM: "quia Iuppiter iussit meus."
CLEO: "feri malam, ut ille, rursum." OLYM: "perii! pugnis caedor, Iuppiter."
LYS: "quid tibi tactio hunc fuit?" CHAR: "quia iussit haec Iuno mea."

CLEO: "Why did you touch him?" OLYM: "Because my Jupiter ordered me."
CLEO: "Hit him back." OLYM: "I'm dead! I'm being slaughtered by punches,
Jupiter!"
LYS: "Why did you touch him?" CHAR: "Because my Juno here ordered me."

By acknowledging Lysidamus' appropriation of Jupiter's identity,
Olympio reveals that his oath to Cleostrata was doubly duplicitous: not
only was he willing to give up Casina to someone else, but he was planning
from the beginning literally "to yield to Jove" (*concessurum Iovi*, 323) – at
least, to the human "Jove" whose desires most directly affect his life.

Catullus' evocation of these Plautine exchanges can be seen to produce
several effects in our reading of poem 70. First, the speaker's representation
of Lesbia's promise through the semi-quotation of Olympio strengthens
the poem's gender inversions. Lesbia becomes the male comic slave antagonist, while Catullus' speaker identifies not only with Callimachus' female
Ionis, but also with Plautus' Casina. In the process, he becomes a divided
*puella*, simultaneously Ionis and Casina, desirous and desired, willing and
unwilling. That neither Ionis nor Casina actually speak in their respective
texts is also significant, mirroring and emphasizing the feminine passivity
that the Catullan speaker displays elsewhere in the corpus.[90] At the same
time, as the addressee of the false oath, Catullus' speaker takes on the role
of Cleostrata the *uxor*, the comic stock type whose husband is perennially
faithless. Her status as wife – and, indeed, the *Casina*'s entire focus on
marriage and the creation and control of a new bride – are especially
significant for poem 70 and clearly inform several meaningful deviations
from Callimachus' epigrammatic model.

First, *nubere* (1): both poets say that their duplicitous lovers claim not to
prefer anyone to their beloved (*malle*, 1; κρέσσονα, 2), but whereas
Callimachus' Callignotus swears merely that he would not rather "have"
(ἕξειν, 2) someone else, Lesbia promises "to have and to hold" no one else.
Moreover, Lesbia is represented not as a young unmarried woman like

---

[90] Clark (2008, 272): "Being unable to speak could mark someone as unmanly, given the high value
put on speech in Roman male culture." On the effeminacy of silence in Catullus, see, e.g.,
Fitzgerald (1995, 64–72) and Stevens (2013, 47–81 and 203–56).

Callimachus' Ionis (νύμφης, 25.6) but as a *mulier*, both "woman" and "wife."[91] Marriage, Ross and Konstan note, is largely foreign to ancient erotic poetry, and is certainly absent from any of the Greek sources to which Catullus' poem 70 points.[92] Catullus' comic allusion allows him to conceptualize a new kind of erotic relationship, one that is not formally a marriage but nevertheless expresses a depth of emotion and interdependence that surpasses the forms of love found in other erotic literature.[93]

In fact, Catullus' and Lesbia's relationship is more meaningful than an everyday marriage: poem 70's mention of Jupiter and ensuing allusion to the competition between Lysidamus-as-Jove and Cleostrata-as-Juno in Plautus' *Casina* elevates it to the status of a *hieros gamos*. It is notable that Catullus omits Callimachus' assertion that lovers' oaths "cannot reach the ears of the gods" (μὴ δύνειν οὔατ' ἐς ἀθανάτων, 25.4). Catullus' hybridization of his Greek epigram with Roman comedy has turned the speaker and Lesbia into the very gods that Callimachus says are deaf to lovers' words.

Poem 70's divinization of Lesbia mirrors a theme that recurs throughout Catullus' work, which, Janan argues, represents her paradoxically as both whore and goddess.[94] Indeed, only two poems before, Catullus presages the divinity and infidelity that play out in the comic allusion we have just examined. After calling Lesbia *candida diva* (68.70), he confesses she is not an *univira*, but he finds consolation in comparing their situation to that of Jupiter and Juno (68.135–40):[95]

> quae tamen etsi uno non est contenta Catullo,
>> rara verecundae furta feremus erae,
> ne nimium simus stultorum more molesti;
>> saepe etiam Iuno, maxima caelicolum,
> coniugis in culpa flagrantem contudit iram,
>> noscens omnivoli plurima facta Iovis.
>
> Even if she is not content with Catullus alone,
>> we'll endure the occasional trysts of a modest mistress,
> so that we don't become too much a bother, like stupid men.
>> Even Juno, the greatest of those who dwell in heaven,

---

[91] On the semantic range of *mulier*, see Adams (1972) and Deuling (1999, 189 and 193 n. 4).

[92] See Ross (1969, 90); Konstan (1972, 104) notes that "the idea of marriage (*nubere*), which is here proposed to the *cupidus amans*, the victim of passionate infatuation, again appears to be Catullus' contribution: marriage is a notion generally foreign to the erotic tradition."

[93] Williams (1968, 404), who does not notice the *Casina* allusion but astutely observes that both Roman comedy and Catullus use the language of marriage to this end.

[94] Janan (1994); for Lesbia as goddess, see also Skinner (1997 and 2003, xxxv).

[95] Skinner (2003, 65) and Miller (1988, 131) discuss this link between poems 68 and 70.

often beat down her seething anger at her husband's sins,
knowing the many outrages of all-willing Jove.

By equating Jupiter's indiscretions with Lesbia's and appropriating Juno's
identity as wronged woman for himself, Catullus further upends the
traditional boundaries that restricted Roman social behavior, blurring the
lines between god and human, lover and wife, and man and woman. His
allusions to Plautus' *Casina* in poem 70 situate this blending in the
domestic setting of Roman comedy and highlight the precarious nature
of the speaker's identity. He views himself as the spurned girl of Hellenistic
epigram's usual love-'em-and-leave-'em relationships, but also as comedy's
vulnerable *virgo intacta* and long-suffering *uxor*, whose identities are
defined by the bonds of marriage that take center stage in Plautus and
Terence, though in opposite terms: comic *virgines* are objects of desire, and
their perennial end in the dramatic script is to become an *uxor* married to a
desirous *adulescens*; the *uxor*, however, is always already a henpecking
obstacle to her husband, who yearns for another woman outside their
marriage. As Susanna Braund remarks, this is "the essential paradox of
Roman comedy: while marriage is the objective of the essential comic plot,
already-established marriage is portrayed as a negative experience."[96] By
invoking these recognizably distinct but readily changeable figures,
Catullus uses Roman comedy's preexisting hybridity to convey both how
familiar and how unstable his own position is within his relationship with
Lesbia. This approach parallels what we saw above in his appropriation of
the *senex* Charmides and *adulescens* Lesbonicus as he examines the insep-
arability of *negotium* and *otium*. The ultimate goal of Plautus' *Trinummus*
is for the *adulescens amator* to settle down and eventually become a *senex*,
who will in turn produce an *adulescens*, continuing the comic cycle.
Today's *virgo* is tomorrow's *uxor* (or *meretrix*, depending on luck and
circumstance), and every *adulescens* is destined to be a *senex*. Recognizing
that Roman comedy's stock types are part of a social continuum, Catullus
puts on multiple roles – sometimes within the same poem, sometimes in
different poems spread across the collection – to express the paradoxes that
are inherent in the Roman experience. This is one of the most important
parts of the Catullan comic project: stock type shifting, which is a feature
of comic hybridity, enables him to use characters that seem static and easy
to grasp to explore identity as a dynamic and fluid concept. Indeed,

---

[96] Braund (2005, 40).

Catullus' ability to manipulate comic stock types and combine them not only with one another but also with "real" people to produce new hybrids represents one of his most significant achievements in developing what Plautus and Terence had begun and what would become key later for the Latin elegists.

All three of the comic qualities I have discussed are interrelated: the *nugator* is a chameleon, using his powers to infuse objects and people with new, hybrid identities and deploying them within the local world of the Roman elite. Likewise, all three are deeply embedded in Catullus' use of Roman comedy throughout his corpus, and over the course of this book I will show how he deploys them as he takes on the roles of various Plautine and Terentian characters, as well as imbues other people in his poetry with these same stock types. Before we begin looking at them in detail, though, I want to end this introduction with a few remarks on why it is the *characters* of Roman comedy that serve as Catullus' primary focus of allusion to the genre rather than, say, its particular props, idioms, or style. Even when these last elements offer significant moments of allusive contact, they become legible only when read against the stock characters that use them. We saw above, for example, that Catullus manipulates the meanings of a range of objects in his work, and that other people regularly either fail to perceive what he does or misstep in trying to pull off the same effects. Behind each of these interactions lies the comic *parasitus*, whose dual role as agent of deceit and as subservient dependent informs our interpretation of that success or failure. Likewise, Catullus' portrayal of his relationship with Lesbia in poem 70 depends on his hybrid use of the comic *adulescens* and *senex*, and of the *servus* and *uxor*.

So why comic stock characters? They are, first and foremost, familiar and regular – that is, they are *stock* characters. Catullus and his readers can see and use them as shorthand, ethical touchstones that carry built-in meanings, expectations, thoughts, and behaviors. Still, while regular, they are also tractable and endlessly variable. Plautus and Terence reveal the almost infinite variations on the individual themes of their characters that are possible, and the same quality offers Catullus the ability to conform people in his poetry to stereotypes while also making them distinct. Moreover, this variety is manifest in the whole system of interrelations between the individual stock types. The "clever slave" cannot exist when there's no one else. He needs someone who can benefit from his *calliditas* (the *adulescens*), someone to acquire (*virgo, meretrix*), someone to embarrass (*senex*), someone to cheat (*leno, miles gloriosus*), and – every once in a while – someone who's a match for him (*meretrix mala*). We might be tempted by the basic sameness of Roman comic plots to see these relations as simple, but they are quite the opposite: the complexity of innumerable iterations of collaboration and competition between the comic cast of characters is what allows the plot to be simple, since the audience derives enjoyment from a combination of both knowing that everything will turn out "all right in the end" but not really knowing the particular paths by which the play will wend its way. Something similar can be said of Catullus' "real" Roman, which is the final reason why I think comic stock characters and their relationships offered an especially appealing target of allusion. Rome and Roman society were imbued with a sense of inevitability – that is, social mobility was at best an ominous exception to the conservative norms of the day, just as in comedy. A practicing *meretrix* will never become a *virgo*, a *servus* will remain socially inferior, and so on. Even if change occurs within the play, it is still inevitable that eventually the applause will die down and everything will revert to normal. But Roman comedy offers a vivid snapshot of many people from different segments of society stretching and pressing against one another, competing for control and engaging in temporary play, some celebrating and others rejecting the traditional mores. For a Roman like Catullus, who was neither a cultural dope nor a man living outside his own time, it offered a tool to experiment within and to push against those boundaries, to try on roles both familiar and strange as he and others worked out their place inside the Play of Life, the topic of my next chapter.[97]

---

[97] For "cultural dope" and this basic sentiment, see remarks by Janan (1994, 34) and Nappa (2001, 28–29).

CHAPTER I

# Through the Comic Looking Glass

Although Catullus is often considered a literary and social revolutionary, he nevertheless was a product of his place and time, and his approach to Roman comedy in his work is informed by a broad set of cultural ideas about the theater and its connection to "real" life that permeated Rome during the late Republic. Nearly two centuries after the first play was performed in Rome, the city in the first century BCE was undergoing something of a renaissance in theatrical interest. When Catullus was a toddler, with Rome still reeling from the bloody civil war between Marius and Sulla, a set of significant theatrical events was unfolding. To celebrate his eventual triumph, Sulla inaugurated in 81 BCE the *ludi Victoriae Sullanae*, the first new annual *ludi scaenici* since the *ludi Megalenses* were established more than a century before in 191 BCE.[1] The dictator was fond of the theater broadly, trying his hand at writing Atellan farce (a relative of Roman comedy) and incorporating it into everyday life: when brought the head of Marius' son, his last major foe, he sardonically chided the dead boy for his arrogance by quoting Aristophanes' *Knights*: "First learn to row before you try to steer." He also counted all manner of stage-folk among his closest friends, including Quintus Roscius Gallus, the most famous comic actor in Rome, who would go on to become an important mentor of Cicero, who incorporated the theater into his life and all manner of his works, from public orations to philosophical writings to private correspondence.[2] In Cicero we can see glimpses of a peculiar Roman mindset, an ability to see and engage with the world in terms taken from

---

[1] On the *ludi Victoriae Sullanae*, see Bernstein (1998, 313–26).

[2] Arist. *Kn.* 542 (ἐρέτην χρῆναι πρῶτα γενέσθαι πρὶν πηδαλίοις ἐπιχειρεῖν). For Sulla's theatrical interests, Garton (1972, 141–68) remains indispensable, if somewhat fanciful. On Roscius, see Duncan (2006, 160–87). A comprehensive treatment of Cicero's engagement with the theater, though a *desideratum*, is beyond the scope of this book; for outlines of his use of the theater, see references in the Bibliography, as well as Wright (1931).

45

the theater, which he seems to have shared with many elite Romans of his day, Catullus included.

In this chapter, I examine two interrelated concepts – "metatheater" and "theatricality" – that undergird Catullus' and other Romans' understanding of their society and the roles that they play in it. As we will see, Romans of the first century BCE imagined themselves living in a world that could often seem interchangeable with that of their literary and popular dramas, especially Roman comedy, whose boundary between fiction and reality is thin at the best of times. In the process, we will explore the attitudes that make possible not merely theater that is self-conscious of its status as theater, but the underlying ideas that allow self-conscious theater to be legible. In particular, we will consider metaphors of life as theater and points of contact between notions of self and of performance – *persona* in the sense of "unique individual" and in the sense of "mask that superimposes its identity on the wearer," both of which definitions were operant in the late Republic. We will also see that Romans often represented themselves playing a series of shifting roles and improvising their lives as they lived them.

Most of this chapter is not about Catullus, but I believe it sets the stage for the theatrical allusions that make up the remainder of this book, not least because so many of the moments in which "reality" and comedy merge in Rome appear in sources written by his contemporaries or about them in hindsight. Two of these prominent theatricalized moments book-end Catullus' life, appearing in Cicero's defense of Roscius of Ameria in 80 BCE and then his defense of Marcus Caelius Rufus in 56 BCE, and so they also bookend this chapter. Let us begin with a snapshot of everyday theatricality in Rome from when Catullus was still a young child.

## Theatricality and Metatheater in the Late Republic

Sextus Roscius Jr. was on trial in 80 BCE for the murder of his father and, according to Cicero, the prosecutor Gaius Erucius tried to paint the defendant as a rustic misanthrope whom his father kept banished on his farm while he doted on his more refined son in the city.[3] Erucius was retreading an old tale about a son driven to patricide by jealousy and his

---

[3] Roscius Jr. depicted as a rustic misanthrope: *vitam huiusce depinxeris, hunc hominem ferum atque agrestem fuisse, numquam cum homine quoquam conlocutum esse, numquam in oppido constitisse* (*S. Rosc.* 74); relegation to the country: *cum duos filios haberet, illum alterum qui mortuus est secum omni tempore volebat esse, hunc in praedia rustica relegarat* (*S. Rosc.* 42).

father's favoritism. But Cicero saw an opportunity here to play up the same farm-boy angle to his client's advantage by spinning a different story that his listeners would find familiar and more agreeable. The country was where Romans got their moral fiber from, after all, and what father wouldn't be proud to have a sturdy lad who knew the value of toiling in the fields?[4] And Roscius Jr. was the spitting image of the honest and devoted *adulescens rusticus*, a stock character type from Roman comedy everyone in the jury would have recognized. Cicero cites one example of this stereotype, the young Eutychus from Caecilius Statius' *Hypobolimaeus*, to remind the jurors of what they all knew well: a farmer with two sons and business away in town puts his lands in the hands of the boy he trusts most (*S. Rosc.* 46–47):

> ecquid tandem tibi videtur, ut ad fabulas veniamus, senex ille Caecilianus minoris facere Eutychum, filium rusticum, quam illum alterum, Chaerestratum? – nam, ut opinor, hoc nomine est – alterum in urbe secum honoris causa habere, alterum rus supplici causa relegasse? "quid ad istas ineptias abis?" inquies. quasi vero mihi difficile sit quamvis multos nominatim proferre, ne longius abeam, vel tribulis vel vicinos meos qui suos liberos quos plurimi faciunt agricolas adsiduos esse cupiunt. verum homines notos sumere odiosum est, cum et illud incertum sit velintne ei sese nominari, et nemo vobis magis notus futurus sit quam est hic Eutychus . . .

> And finally to take an example from the theater, surely you don't suppose that old man in Caecilius' play thinks any less of Eutychus, his country son, than Chaerestratus (I believe that's his name), his other one? That he keeps the latter with him in the city as a badge of honor but banished the former to the country as a punishment? You'll ask, "Why are you going off on these silly excursions?" Really, as if it'd be hard for me without "going off" very far to trot out however many names you please of my tribesmen or neighbors who by and large long for their children to be hardworking farmers! But it's obnoxious to use as examples people who are well known, since we don't know whether they'd want to be named here, and no one is going to be better known to you than Eutychus . . .

Already here in his first criminal case, Cicero reveals he appreciates the value of the theater for sketching character, both because plays were memorable and because playwrights were masters of *ethopoeia*, and Ann Vasaly and others have shown how effectively Cicero deploys theatrical

---

[4] Cicero expresses this point at *S. Rosc.* 43 (*hoc patres familiae qui liberos habent . . . nonne optatissimum sibi putant esse filios suos rei familiari maxime servire et in praediis colendis operae plurimum studique consumere?*); on the countryside as the source of traditional Roman values, see Vasaly (1985 and 1993, 157–62) and Kronenberg (2009, 94–107).

stereotypes in this speech to manipulate his audience.[5] Roscius as an
individual was unknown to the jurors, so Cicero had either to convey his
actual life and manners to them or, better yet, to tie his story in to one they
already knew, drawn in this case from the stage. The result is a vivid and
familiar picture of Roscius as an amiable character from Roman comedy
who could never have done wrong by his father, let alone murder him.
Vasaly astutely observes, "Once the orator has led his audience to see the
defendant as a typical *rusticus bonus* he need only place him, the chief
character in his drama, in the pathetic circumstances to which he has fallen
victim in order to wring the hearts of the jury."[6]

Blending his living, breathing defendant and the fictional Eutychus into
one and the same figure needs careful rhetorical brushwork on the orator's
part, to be sure. But his listeners play the determinative role in Cicero's
success or failure, and ultimately this defense depends on their readiness to
believe a real person can be enough like a fictional *persona* for their morals
and motivations to be equivalent. In other words, Cicero's audience has to
accept that the boundaries between the stage world and the world they
experience everyday are thin and that individuals and situations from the
one can – and habitually do – appear in the other. Cicero makes this
assumption explicit directly after he invokes Eutychus as his ethical *comparandum* (S. Rosc. 47):

> ... et certe ad rem nihil intersit utrum hunc ego comicum adulescentem an
> aliquem ex agro Veienti nominem. etenim haec conficta arbitror esse a
> poetis ut effictos nostros mores in alienis personis expressamque imaginem
> vitae cotidianae videremus.

> ... and certainly it makes no difference at all in this case whether I name
> this young man from comedy or someone from the fields of Veii. For in
> fact, I think the poets portrayed them so we might see the image of everyday
> life reproduced and our manners represented in characters other
> than ourselves.

Whether Cicero uses as his example an actual person or some fictional
character from a comedy, *nihil intersit* – "it makes no difference." To our
modern eyes, this may seem an odd assertion for an advocate to make in a
court of law: "It doesn't matter if my evidence is real or made-up." But
from the late Republic onward, Romans would not bat an eye at Cicero's
equation between their lived experience and whatever played out on the

---

[5] Vasaly (1985 and 1993, 157–62), Hughes (1997), Harries (2007), Dyck (2010, 114–17 and
140–46).
[6] Vasaly (1985, 13).

stage. Any lines drawn between reality and the theater represented a false dichotomy, because these were not two mutually exclusive frames of reference. Cicero's last statement, that playwrights reproduce their audience's selves in the stage lives of their characters, points to a pervasive notion undergirding this Roman tendency toward a theatricalized worldview. Whatever a comedy revealed about father–son relations was no less real than what Romans got from witnessing their own families. In fact, plays were better, since they offered universal truths that come only from ordinary experience joined with objective distance: "the image of everyday life reproduced and our manners represented in characters other than ourselves."

Cicero's remark here is merely one instance of an old tradition, dating back at least to the third century BCE, that sees an uncanny similarity between comedy and "reality." This idea finds its earliest voice in a famous apostrophe by the scholar Aristophanes of Byzantium to the preeminent playwright of Greek New Comedy: "Menander and life, which of you has imitated the other?" (Ὦ Μένανδρε καὶ βίε, πότερος ἄρ' ὑμῶν πότερον ἐμιμήσατο;).[7] Around the same time, Rome's first playwright Livius Andronicus made much the same observation, expanding it beyond Menander to encompass his entire genre (Evanthius, *Excerpta de Comoedia* 5.5):

> aitque [sc. Livius] esse comoediam cotidianae vitae speculum, nec iniuria. nam ut intenti speculo veritatis liniamenta facile per imaginem colligimus, ita lectione comoediae imitationem vitae consuetudinisque non aegerrime animadvertimus.

> Livius asserts that comedy is the mirror of, not a detriment to, everyday life. For just as we, gazing into a mirror, easily gather the outlines of truth through its image, so too by reading comedy we contemplate, without very much difficulty, an imitation of life and custom.

This was likewise the view of Cicero, who Evanthius asserts called comedy "an imitation of life, a mirror of custom, an image of truth" (*comoediam esse Cicero ait imitationem vitae, speculum consuetidinis, imaginem veritatis*).[8] Mirrors can distort or color, but they fundamentally cannot

---

[7] Menander K-A test. 73 = Syrianus' *Hermogenes* 2.23 Rabe; see similar remarks at Quint. 10.1.69: *ita omnem vitae imaginem expressit*; Mallius Theodorus (GrL VI 594 21): *hoc* [*sc. metro iambico*] … *Menander atque Aristophanes omnem humanae vitae imitationem persecuti sunt.*

[8] Evanthius *Excerpta de Comoedia* 5.1. On other instances of the metaphor of theater as mirror of everyday life, see Lada-Richards (2005, 344–55) and Hanses (2015, 295–312); *pace* Goldberg (2005, 91–92), the image is not a "bookish conceit," but represents comedy as an active and vital way Romans understood themselves and their world.

help but reflect back what is in front of them. Something similar can be said of Roman comedy, which shows us ourselves, maybe slightly warped, but nevertheless at our most essential. "When a mirror transmits reality on the rebound, it does so as a cognitive filter. The background noise of chaotic reality is stripped away, and the specular image, sometimes banal, sometimes beneficial, returns with concentrated force."[9] Cicero's case for Roscius thus was not about specific people or events, but rather about a universal form of filial piety, simplicity, and innocence that country life instills and that everyone dwelling in the city had so often seen on the stage. Roscius Jr. and Cicero's Veiientine acquaintances alike were comic characters made manifest, busily performing essentially the same lives as *adulescentes rustici*. And no comedy has goodhearted, naive farm boys like Eutychus killing their fathers. If the script doesn't fit, you must acquit – and that's just what the jurors did.

The idea that the world of drama can break into and meaningfully interact with the world offstage stands at the heart of two connected literary and cultural phenomena, "metatheater" and "theatricality." At its most basic, metatheater is "theatrically self-conscious theatre, i.e., theatre that demonstrates an awareness of its own theatricality," as Niall Slater defines it.[10] Metatheater occurs when characters in a play appear to recognize their status *as such* and acknowledge their own fictionality, often by moving between the world inside the (otherwise illusory) drama and that of the spectators looking in on that world from outside. For a superlative illustration of such metatheaterical awareness, we need only look at the eponymous hero of Plautus' *Pseudolus*, who repeatedly breaks into the audience's world to play as several "real" people who exist among the spectators, including the playwright, the actor, and a fellow audience member. Pseudolus needs to find money to help Calidorus, his master and the play's "young lover," purchase the *meretrix* Phoenicium from the pimp Ballio, and though he confidently promises to pull this off, he reveals that he has no idea how. He reassures the audience, however, by taking on the role of playwright, who has the power to will into existence anything he needs to keep the plot moving and reshape the fabric of the play's reality (401–5):[11]

---

[9] Taylor (2008, 6).
[10] Slater (1985, 10–11); for similar formulations of Roman metatheater, see, e.g., Moore (1998), Sharrock (2009, 96–162), Manuwald (2011, 301–9), and Curley (2013, 2–7).
[11] My reading of metatheater in Plautus' *Pseudolus* is indebted to Slater (2000, 97–120), Moore (1998, 92–107), Sharrock (2009, 96–162), Bungard (2014), and Christenson (2019).

sed quasi poeta, tabulas quom cepit sibi,
quaerit quod nusquam est gentium, reperit tamen,
facit illud veri simile quod mendacium est,
nunc ego poeta fiam: viginti minas,
quae nusquam nunc sunt gentium, inveniam tamen.

But just as the poet, when he's picked up his tablets,
looks for what has never existed anywhere but still finds it
and makes what is a falsehood look like the truth,
now I'll become a poet: those twenty minae
as of now never existed anywhere, but I'll still find them!

Pseudolus begins to script the actions of those around him, developing his plotting into what will become both the plot of the fictional play the audience is watching and the "real" experiences of the characters around him whose lives play out inside the comedy. This slave-as-playwright thus wields enormous power, dictating what the audience gets to see as well as how his fictional peers behave, in the process morphing into "the god of his fictive world."[12]

But Pseudolus' power is still limited, and while his metatheatrical awareness allows him to assert control over other characters who do not know they are imaginary and living according to a script, his ability to perceive the audience puts him in the difficult position of both knowing how to manipulate the play and recognizing that he is still part of it. Alison Sharrock notes, "The relationship [between slave-as-playwright and audience] is neither straightforward subservience nor simple power, but rather an odd mixture of the two, in equilibrium. He deceives us, because we give him power to deceive. We are ... happy to put aside our work and watch the slave's antics all day – in admiration, yes, but also insisting that he perform."[13] Pseudolus must still play his assigned part, since his powers as playwright are internal to the play and necessarily end at the stage's edge. He cannot directly script the external audience's reactions to him, but his special knowledge that he is a fictional character living in a world with generic rules grants him another type of power: besides playwright, he also becomes an actor, adapting his character to whatever role suits his needs through improvisation and playacting. Soon after he promises as play-wright to write twenty minae into reality from nothing, he reassures the audience in his capacity as an actor that he is still playing the role expected of him (562–73a):

---

[12] Sharrock (2009, 132).     [13] Sharrock (2009, 134).

suspicio est mi nunc vos suspicarier,
me idcirco haec tanta facinora promittere,
quo vos oblectem, hanc fabulam dum transigam,
nec sim facturus quod facturum dixeram.
non demutabo. atque etiam certum, quod sciam,
quo id sim facturus pacto nil etiam scio,
nisi quia futurum est. nam qui in scaenam provenit,
novo modo novom aliquid inventum afferre addecet.
si id facere nequeat, det locum illi qui queat.
concedere aliquantisper hinc mi intro lubet,
dum concenturio in corde sycophantias.
<sed mox> exibo, non ero vobis morae;
tibicen vos interibi hic delectaverit.

I have a suspicion that you now suspect
that the reason I'm promising to pull off such feats
is to gratify you while I'm acting out this play,
and not to accomplish what I'd said I would accomplish.
I'm not changing the terms. But still, I know for sure that
I don't know at all how I'll accomplish this, except that it's
going to happen. See, when someone comes onto the stage,
he should bring something newly done in a new way;
if he can't do that, he should give way to someone who can.
I'd like to step away for just a little bit
while I assemble some trickeries in my heart.
I'll come back out soon, but I won't hold you folks up:
this here flautist will keep you entertained in the meantime.

As Timothy Moore rightly observes, "what Pseudolus thinks the audience suspects is in fact true: he is making promises only in order to delight them," and much of this metatheatrical play seems designed by him to convey his eagerness as an actor to entertain.[14] Pseudolus has promised to trick someone out of the money and get the girl, a common routine of the *servus callidus,* and he means to keep that promise and conform his performance to the norms of his character's stock type and the audience's expectations. His claim that actors "should bring something newly done in a new way" when they come on stage, though, suggests the situation is more complicated: Pseudolus-as-actor is only predictable inasmuch as he wants to be, and indeed he entices the audience with the prospect of the unexpected. Sharrock's observation that Pseudolus is both free to play and subservient to the spectators' desires applies equally to the audience, as William Fitzgerald points out in his remarks on this scene: "But if

[14] Moore (1998, 99 and passim).

entertaining is a slavish occupation, catering to the pleasures of others, it is one in which the entertained are in the ambiguous position of both passing judgement and suspending their authority in the throes of aesthetic fascination."[15] Pseudolus' skills as an actor capable of improvising himself give him power to manipulate those watching, in the play or out, and soon after this scene he resets the audience's perceptions. Moore shows that Pseudolus' summoning of the *tibicen* marks the beginning of what is essentially a whole new play, since evidence suggests it was standard practice for the *tibia* player to provide an overture at the start of a performance.[16]

For nearly half of the play, Pseudolus has been acting as the archetypal "clever slave," but when his plans finally begin coalescing, he cedes his position as both "clever slave" and the comedy's chief improvisational actor to a different character brought onstage to fill those roles in another incarnation of metatheater. Pseudolus asks Calidorus and his friend Charinus to find an assistant who is "bad, clever, and smart" (*malum, callidum, doctum*), preferably a slave (724–28), all distinctive characteristics of the *servus callidus*, to help him put on a show to trick Ballio. They deliver Simia, whom Pseudolus dresses in the costume (*ornatus*, 935) of Harpax, another character in the play, and instructs him to act like this man to whom the pimp expects to give Phoenicium.[17] Pseudolus thus reverts to his role as playwright, but only up until the start of the performance. As the play-within-the-play begins, Pseudolus takes his position on the side of the stage as a spectator (959). He proceeds to offer running commentary on Simia's acting, praising his strong start (969–70) and wordplay (974), worrying about a near misstep in the performance (984–85), and applauding his superior improvisation by remarking, "I have never seen a worse person or anyone more adaptably bad than this guy Simia is!" (*peiorem ego hominem magisque vorsute malum / numquam edepol quemquam vidi quam hic est Simia*, 1017–18).

In withdrawing from the play's action and merely observing, Pseudolus effectively joins the external audience and partakes in the kind of banter we can easily imagine those in the *cavea* sharing, commenting on points of

---

[15] Fitzgerald (2000, 46).

[16] Moore (1998, 93–94), with Moore (2012, 17–22) on the *tibicen*'s overtures and interludes; see also Bungard (2014) on Pseudolus' improvisational power.

[17] *Ornatus* and its cognates are semi-technical terms for theatrical costume; see Muecke (1986) and Hardy (2005, 27). On the doubled *servus callidus* role in Simia's performance, see Moore (1998, 94–95), and for *malus*, *callidus*, and *doctus* as signifiers of the "clever slave," see Anderson (1993, 60–87).

humor, anxiety, and successful completion of the performance. Despite remaining onstage, his separation from the action and ability to watch and speak while going unseen and unheard by the performers effectively transposes him into the "real" world of the Romans watching. Indeed, while Pseudolus represents the clearest example of someone in the comedy stepping aside to join the audience as fellow spectator and commentator, many of the play's characters metatheatrically praise the performance of the other characters: Pseudolus and Calidorus, unseen by Ballio, commend the pimp for playing his part well, and later Ballio calls their *flagitatio* of him "theatrical nonsense, just the sort of words said to the pimp in comedies" (*nugas theatri, verba quae in comoediis / solent lenoni dici,* 1081–82); likewise, while Pseudolus admires Simia as his stand-in *servus callidus,* Pseudolus is praised by his old master Simo (458, 1288) and Charinus (707) for his over-the-top performance skills.[18] Although Pseudolus asserts to Calidorus that "these spectators here are the reason we're performing this play" (*horum causa haec agitur spectatorum fabula,* 720), many of the comedy's dramatis personae are just as eager to entertain their fellow characters through their performances as they are to please the voyeurs in the *cavea.* The entire cast, then, possesses some degree of metatheatrical awareness and shifts variously between fictional characters, actors, playwrights, and members of the audience.

Slater, Moore, and others have done much to highlight metatheater as an important aspect of comedy worthy of our attention, showing that it is a crucial tool Roman playwrights can use to create humor and strengthen the audience's engagement with the comedy and sympathy with the characters/actors. But is metatheater simply a theatrical tool, some "autonomous creation of the theatre," as Slater puts it, that exists only in and for drama itself?[19] Or, if we recall the metaphor of Livius Andronicus and Cicero we examined above, is metatheater at least partly a reflection of something offstage that we see more clearly in the comic *cotidianae vitae speculum,* the "mirror of everyday life"? Recently, William Batstone has argued cogently that metatheater is an artifact of ancient culture that preexists its theatrical counterpart and presents a means by which Romans approach and interact with their "real" world. He suggests that "one of the claims being made by the Plautine play is that farce is the truth: Rip off the façade, undo convention, stop action, and this is what you are, what you really are. Life's a stage; it's all an act; and we improvise ourselves in the face of power and desire."[20] That is, while Roman comedy's

---

[18] Moore (1998, 97–98).    [19] Slater (2000, 10).    [20] Batstone (2005, 28).

metatheatrical moments can be seen as examples of dramatic artfulness and poetic play, they also represent a view of the world itself as fundamentally a stage and Romans as players upon it. If the mirror of comedy reflects an image of ourselves, what else can it mean when in that very mirror we glimpse characters who realize that they are, in fact, *characters*? Like the fictional Pseudolus, Romans in the audience recognize themselves as the playwrights and improvisational actors of their own lives, as well as audience members observing the drama of the world around them and assessing how compliant or creative other Romans were in playing their respective roles. Metatheater, in other words, is another component of quotidian experience to which comedy draws our attention. It offers the Roman audience member the objective distance necessary to recognize "his *world* a stage, his *life* already theatricalized, and his own *identity* just another role to be played."[21]

Batstone's formulation brings us to the second important phenomenon that underlies the interchangeability of on- and offstage realities, namely, "theatricality," for which Shadi Bartsch offers a succinct explanation: "As a descriptive model, 'theatricality' makes actors out of human beings placed in situations in which they feel themselves watched, in which their performance is subject to the evaluation of a superior who must be watched in turn to gauge his reactions."[22] Her study of theatricality during the Empire demonstrates just how pervasively Romans seem to have felt that they were both actors and audience members within their society, and indeed this notion of theatricalized life finds a special representative in the emperor Nero, whose actions thoroughly blurred the lines between reality and drama. Bartsch traces how Nero, who earned the nickname *imperator scaenicus*, was seen to have enacted at key moments during his life the roles he either saw or played himself in tragedies on the stage.[23] Indeed, our sources constantly link Nero's most egregious crimes with the experiences of tragic characters. Cassius Dio states that he set the fire in 64 CE to feel what Priam felt while watching his country burn to the ground, while "after he put on the costume of a lyre-player he sang 'The Capture of Troy,' as he dubbed it, though to those who watched it was 'The Capture of Rome.'"[24] Suetonius similarly suggests that Nero's murder of his stepson Rufrius Crispus was modeled on another tragic role he had played,

---

[21] Batstone (2005, 15).    [22] Bartsch (1994, 10).

[23] Nero is referred to as *imperator scaenicus* at Plin. *Pan.* 46.4 and Tac. *Ann.* 15.59.

[24] D. C. 62.16.21. Dio describes Nero's singing at 62.18.1; cf. Suet. *Nero* 38.2. For this role and the others discussed below, see remarks by Bartsch (1994, 61) and Frazer (1966).

that of Nauplius, since he reports Isidore the Cynic implied the former had been practice for the latter (*Nero* 39.3). And perhaps in his clearest mixing of reality and tragedy, Nero played the role of Orestes onstage and later emulated his murder of his mother Clytemnestra by killing his own mother Agrippina. As Bartsch documents, Nero's Orestes-like matricide became one of the dominant associations between Nero and the theater, appearing in graffiti, historical records, and even in a humorous metatheatrical jab by Juvenal, who commends Orestes for at least having the decency to not perform on the stage (*Satires* 8.215–20).[25] In the standard traditions of illusory Roman tragedy, Orestes was never more than a fictive character. By becoming both the character and the actor, however, Nero showed off his mastery over theatricalized reality and his ability to move between on- and offstage reality at will.

At the very end of his life, as he hides in a reedy swamp, Nero further blurs the theatrical line by abandoning his past roles and seeing his own self as a tragic role that he was performing (D. C. 63.28.3–5):[26]

> τοιοῦτον γὰρ δρᾶμα τότε τὸ δαιμόνιον αὐτῷ παρεσκεύασεν, ἵνα μηκέτι τοὺς ἄλλους μητροφόνους καὶ ἀλήτας ἀλλ᾽ ἤδη καὶ ἑαυτὸν ὑποκρίνηται· καὶ τότε μετεγίνωσκεν ἐφ᾽ οἷς ἐτετολμήκει, καθάπερ ἄπρακτόν τι αὐτῶν ποιῆσαι δυνάμενος. Νέρων μὲν δὴ τοιαῦτα ἐτραγῴδει, καὶ τὸ ἔπος ἐκεῖνο συνεχῶς ἐνενόει·
>   "οἰκτρῶς θανεῖν μ᾽ ἄνωγε σύγγαμος πατήρ."

> Such, then, was the drama that his Fate prepared for him, that he no longer played the roles of other matricides and beggars, but at last played the role of himself. And at that point he knew regret for the outrages he committed, as if he could make any of them undone. This was the tragic part that Nero was playing, and the following verse kept running through his mind:
>   "Pitifully my spouse and father command me to die."

The line Nero keeps bringing to mind belongs to an unknown tragedy, but Suetonius reports that it belongs to Oedipus and came from the play in which the emperor had most recently performed (*Nero* 46.3). In seeing himself as no longer playing other characters and yet speaking lines from a tragic script, Nero confounds his experiences qua fictional

---

[25] On Orestes, see Bartsch (1994, 46–50). Bartsch (1994, 61) and Baldwin (1979) discuss the connections between Nero mourning his mother's death and Agave mourning her slaying of her son Pentheus; D. C. 62.60.2 claims a lyre performance of *Bacchae* was one of Nero's earliest theatrical forays.

[26] On this theatricalized moment, see Bartsch (1994, 38–46); for σύγγαμος as "spouse" in the tragic fragment here, see Rollo (2017) and cf. Suet. *Nero* 46.3, where the line is quoted as θανεῖν μ᾽ ἄνωγε σύγγαμος, μήτηρ, πατήρ.

Oedipus with his experiences qua Nero, merging the realms of theater and reality. Indeed, this idea he was playing the role of Nero *tragicus*, which might seem odd and almost psychotic at first, represents a surprisingly common worldview we will explore in greater depth shortly: while Romans do not usually see themselves as actually becoming Oedipus or another fictional character, they do view themselves and their real-life personas as roles that they must perform – often, as we will see, in the mold of theatrical models – according to their individual circumstances and needs.

Tragic theatricality was well suited to Imperial Rome, with its larger-than-life tyrants and deified emperors, but in many ways Nero and other tragically minded *principes* were building on a tradition already underway in the Republic. Pompey, one of the leading public figures of the first century BCE, seems to have seen himself as Agamemnon reborn on Roman shores. The first- or second-century CE mythographer and historian Ptolemy Hephaestion (also called Chennus, "the Quail") reports that "Pompey the Great never set off for battle before reading Book 11 of the Iliad, since he was a steadfast admirer of Agamemnon," and several sources confirm that others compared him (sometimes favorably, sometimes not) with the Greek leader.[27] Indeed, praise of Pompey-as-Agamemnon bookends his involvement in the war with Caesar. At its outbreak, in a version of his oft-repeated "ship of state" metaphor, Cicero equates Pompey with Agamemnon as the true steersmen of their respective forces.[28] And after Pompey's death, Cassius Dio remarks on his great downfall: "Once master of a thousand ships, as the saying goes," nodding to the fleet that set out for Troy, ". . . and previously considered the most powerful of the Romans, so that he was even nicknamed 'Agamemnon' . . . he was slaughtered on the anniversary of the day on which he celebrated his triumph over Mithridates and the pirates."[29] At the height of the war, however, his detractors used this tragic likeness to attack Pompey for delaying after Dyrrhachium "so that he might rule over men of his same

[27] Ptol. Heph. *ap.* Phot. *Bib.* 190.151a.16–18 (ὁ δὲ Πομπήιος ὁ Μάγνος οὐδ᾽ εἰς πόλεμον προίοι, πρὶν ἂν τὸ λ Ἰλιάδος ἀναγνώσειε, ζηλωτὴς ὢν Ἀγαμέμνονος;). For the identification of Pompey with Agamemnon, by himself and others, see Champlin (2003, 297–300) and Berno (2004). On Ptolemy the Quail, see Bowersock (1994, 23–27) and O'Hara (1996).

[28] Cic. *Att.* 7.3.5. Cicero is responding to Atticus, who (mis)quotes a line from Eur. *Tr.* 455 (ποῦ σκάφος τὸ τοῦ στρατηγοῦ, "Where now is the ship of the general?").

[29] D. C. 42.5.3–5 (χιλίων ποτὲ νεῶν, ὡς ὁ λόγος ἔχει, ἄρξας . . . Πομπήιος μὲν δὴ κράτιστος πρότερον Ῥωμαίων νομισθείς, ὥστε καὶ Ἀγαμέμνονα αὐτὸν ἐπικαλεῖσθαι . . . ἐν τῇ ἡμέρᾳ ἐν ᾗ ποτε τά τε τοῦ Μιθριδάτου καὶ τὰ τῶν καταποντιστῶν ἐπινίκια ἤγαγεν, ἐσφάγη).

rank, and for this reason his critics calls him 'King of Kings' and
'Agamemnon.'"[30]

Pompey clearly preferred the positive usage, actively cultivating the
image of himself as Agamemnon, and no episode illustrates his theatricalized self-presentation better than the games he held for the opening of his
theater in 55 BCE. The inauguration of the city's first permanent venue
for drama offered a unique opportunity for blending theater and real life,
and Erasmo and others have shown that Pompey took full advantage with
the day's program.[31] Cicero provides an unusually clear glimpse of what
the Roman audience saw at the games, including "six-hundred mules in a
performance of the *Clytemnestra*, three-thousand bronze kraters in that of
*The Trojan Horse*, and assorted infantry and cavalry armor" (*sescenti muli in
"Clytaemestra" aut in "Equo Troiano" creterrarum tria milia aut armatura
varia peditatus et equitatus*, Fam. 7.1.2–3). It is no coincidence that the
plays Pompey produced to dedicate his theater feature the victories of
Agamemnon, and the significance of shows sponsored by *Agamemnon
Romanus* that glorify his Greek counterpart surely was not lost on those
present. But what most cinches the equation of the two figures are the
lavish props deployed for these stagings. Erasmo observes, "The plays
presented were carefully selected for the occasion. The triumphant return
of Agamemnon in the *Clytemnestra*, signaled by Cicero's reference to 600
mules, and the staging of a sacked city in the *Equos Troianus* not only
recall, but actually recreate, Pompey's own triple triumph held only six
years before the opening of his theatre."[32] The bowls and armor featured
in the performances were not merely props made for this occasion to
invoke Pompey's triumph; they must have been the very spoils he displayed during his triumphal parade in 61 BCE, brought out of dedicatory
retirement both to serve as aggrandizing reminders of Pompey's successes
and to combine him all the more closely with the figure of Agamemnon.
While our sources do not explicitly name these props as spoils from the
triumph six years earlier, Mary Beard astutely notes: "It may be fanciful to
imagine that Pompey's Mithridatic booty came back on stage to act the
part of Agamemnon's spoils. But where else did those 'three-thousand
kraters' come from?" Moreover, Amy Russell points out that there is

---

[30] App. *BC* 2.67 (ἵν' ἀνδρῶν ὁμοτίμων τοσῶνδε ἄρχοι, καὶ ἐπὶ τῷδε αὐτὸν βασιλέα τὲ βασιλέων καὶ
Ἀγαμέμνονα καλούντων); for the same attack, attributed to Domitius Ahenobarbus, cf. Plu. *Pomp.*
67.3, *Caes.* 41.1, and *Comp. Agesilai et Pompeii* 4.

[31] For propaganda and theatricality in the inauguration of Pompey's theater, see Beacham (1999,
61–71), Erasmo (2005, 83–91), Boyle (2006, 155–56), and Beard (2007, 26–29).

[32] Erasmo (2005, 87).

significant overlap between the specific items we know were used at both events: in his account of the triumph, Appian states that Pompey had "a countless number of wagons carrying armor" (ἁμάξας δὲ ὅπλων ἀπείρους τὸ πλῆθος, *Mithr.* 116), while Pliny the Elder relates that he had many spectacular vessels of gold, not to mention kraters such as the bronze example with an inscription from Mithridates currently on display in the Capitoline Museum, which Beard suggests came from these spoils.[33] When the characters in these plays referred to these objects as booty Agamemnon brought back from Troy, they imbued Pompey's own victories with an aura of theatrical continuity: if the spoils that belonged to the Greek "King of Kings" and those belonging to the Roman general were identical, the two men themselves also overlapped.

One could view Pompey's identification with Agamemnon as nothing more than an act of self-promotion, an attempt to emulate publicly the successes of a famous mythological model for political gain. But there is good reason to believe his appropriation of Agamemnon represented a theatricalized worldview in line with Nero's tragic performances of himself, albeit with far more restraint and stronger grounding in reality. Suetonius reports that Pompey "had been in the habit of grumbling and calling Caesar 'Aegisthus'" for allegedly sleeping with his wife Mucia, whom he divorced on returning from his campaigns in 61 BCE.[34] Pompey must have been selective in which aspects of Agamemnon he chose to put on display in celebrating his victories, but he and others saw the negative associations of the myths that this comparison inevitably brought with it. As with Nero, Pompey outfitted himself and those around him in theatrical garb to convey how he viewed his relationships with them, employing tragedy to comprehend his personal betrayal by his wife and Caesar.

As usual, our sources are skewed toward the elite and may not be fully representative, but it does seem that tragic theatricality was especially appropriate for public figures who were extraordinary and stood out from the mass of the Roman populace. After all, Aristotle identifies tragedy's defining feature as the presence of σπουδαῖοι, "weighty characters," who are βελτίονες ἢ καθ᾽ ἡμᾶς, "better than us," in the audience, such as kings, heroes, and gods.[35] And Plautus' *Amphitruo* confirms that Roman audiences recognized Aristotle's

---

[33] Beard (2007, 28) and Russell (2016, 163–64); cf. Rudd (1989, 108) on Hor. *Epist.* 2.1.193, who says the kraters were "presumably part of Pompey's Asian loot," as well as Champlin (2003, 297–98) and Manuwald (2011, 73). For the krater of Mithridates, see Beard (2007, 10–11).

[34] Suet. *Jul.* 50.1 (*nam certe Pompeio et a Curionibus patre et filio et a multis exprobratum est, quod cuius causa post tres liberos exegisset uxorem et quem gemens Aegisthum appellare consuesset, eius postea filiam potentiae cupiditate in matrimonium recepisset*). Beard (2007, 29).

[35] Arist. *Po.* 1448a16–18.

character rule: after noting the spectators' disappointment at the prospect of watching a tragedy, Mercury jokingly responds that he will change the play into a comedy – that is, until he realizes that there is a hitch in his plan: "See, I don't think it's right for me to make it a comedy through and through, because kings and gods are coming out onstage" (*nam me perpetuo facere ut sit comoedia, / reges quo veniant et di, non par arbitror*, 60–61).[36] With their theatricalized self-presentation as *reges* like Priam and Agamemnon and their outsized egos and standing in Roman society, Nero and Pompey matched the status of tragic characters. Larger-than-life figures were conduits for tragedy to penetrate offstage reality, as the tragic world was populated by people beyond the ken of average members of the Roman audience.

Comedy, by contrast, is filled with characters whose behaviors, speech, and concerns are on par with those of the regular people watching from the audience. While tragedy in Aristotle's definition is the domain of σπουδαῖοι, "comedy is an imitation of weaker people" (φαῦλοι), or to put it another way, comedy is populated by the sorts of characters who are equal or inferior to us sitting in the *cavea* and who could just as easily walk unnoticed among us as they walk on the stage.[37] What is more, as we saw earlier, characters in Roman comedy regularly try to join us, breaking the fourth wall to command, confide in, and plead with us. While dramatic genres of every stripe participate in the Roman tendency toward theatricality, slippages between reality and comedy could happen with greater ease and frequency. Indeed, many of our ancient sources comment on the everyday quality of comic speech and how small a gap separates what people say as they go about their lives from what they hear spoken in Roman comedy. In his *Satires*, for instance, Horace derides comedy as artlessly indistinct from normal speech, "except that it differs in having a fixed meter" (*nisi quod pede certo / differt sermoni*, 1.4.47–48).[38] Cicero makes a similar observation, stating that Plato and Democritus are often seen as having a greater claim to poetry "than the work of the comic poets, whose works are not at all different from everyday speech, except they are in some meter."[39] This quality applies to

---

[36] Mercury's point is straightforward, but his broader remarks on genre and *tragicomoedia* (a term he coins here) are complex and have received much attention; see Segal (1975; 1987, 171–91; and 2001, 205–19), Moore (1995 and 1998, 108–25), Manuwald (1999), Lefèvre (1982 and 1999), Slater (1990).

[37] Arist. *Po.* 1449a32 (ἡ δὲ κωμῳδία ἐστὶν ὥσπερ εἴπομεν μίμησις φαυλοτέρων); cf. 1448a2–5 and 16–17, 1448b24–26, and see Janko (1984) and Heath (1989) for fuller discussion.

[38] See Rudd (1955, 152–53).

[39] Cic. *Orat.* 67: *poema putandum quam comicorum poetarum, apud quos, nisi quod versiculi sunt, nihil est aliud cotidiani dissimile sermonis.* This idea of meter as the key factor separating comedy from everyday speech appears frequently. See Plin. *Ep.* 1.16.6, where he says letters written by a friend's

performance as well, as Quintilian remarks that "comic actors deliver their lines not precisely the same way we normally speak, which would be artless, but they're still not far removed from natural speech. If they were, then their impressions would fall flat; instead, they embellish normal everyday speech with a sort of thespian grace."[40] In short, comic characters and comic speech are as much at ease on the stage as they are in the *cavea*, and what Pseudolus and company did and said would seem largely at home in the everyday interactions of the Roman audiences outside the theater.

Like its tragic counterpart, comic theatricality provided a meaningful way for Romans to understand their own characters and those of the people around them, as well as to communicate that understanding. Cicero's depiction of Roscius Jr. as the comic *adulescens rusticus* inhabiting not the theater but the Italian countryside is merely one example, and his other speeches cast the spotlight on multiple other instances of people living theatricalized comic lives. In 69 BCE, for instance, in his defense of Aulus Caecina in a dispute over an inheritance, Cicero represents his opponent Aebutius and his acquaintances as stereotypical parasites from Roman comedy. He calls out one of these men as particularly comic, "the moneylender Sextus Clodius, whose name is Phormio and who is no less black and or audacious than Terence's Phormio."[41] Despite his different profession, Sextus Clodius Phormio necessarily conforms to the *ethos* of the character whose name he shares. Cicero recognized such comic parasites everywhere in Rome, and he refers to one of Marc Antony's friends in a similar way by invoking characters from Terence's *Phormio* and *Eunuchus*, as well as the pimp from Plautus' *Pseudolus*: "Antony hasn't come down here today. Why is that? He's in his garden hosting a birthday party. For whom? I won't name names; suppose that it's for some Phormio or a Gnatho or even a Ballio."[42] In addition to using these characters to label others, Cicero also uses them self-reflexively to delineate his own

---

wife are comparable to Plautus or Terence except in meter, and Ferri (2014, 776–77); cf. similar remarks about Greek comedy at Arist. *Po.* 1449a26, 1459a12, and Mallius Theodorus (*GrL* VI 594 21).

[40] Quint. 2.10.13: *actores comici ... neque ita prorsus ut nos vulgo loquimur pronuntiant, quod esset sine arte, neque procul tamen a natura recedunt, quo vitio periret imitatio, sed morem communis huius sermonis decore quodam scaenico exornant.*

[41] Cic. *Caec.* 27: *argentarius Sex. Clodius cui cognomen est Phormio, nec minus niger nec minus confidens quam ille Terentianus est Phormio.* For Cicero's rhetorical use of the comic *parasitus*, see Damon (1995 and 1997, 195–251).

[42] Cic. *Phil.* 2.15: *hodie non descendit Antonius. cur? dat nataliciam in hortis. cui? neminem nominabo; putate tum Phormioni alicui, tum Gnathoni, tum etiam Ballioni.* See Sussman (1994) on comic characterization in the *Philippics*, as well as Pelling (1988, 35 and 125) on a similar depiction of Antony as *miles gloriosus* attended by parasites in Plutarch's account.

persona: in the *Pro Caelio*, where Cicero represents Clodia as a comic *meretrix* and his client Caelius as an *adulescens amator*, the orator portrays himself as the *servus callidus* whose sharp wit and metatheatrical knowledge help him to develop a rapport with his audience, encouraging them to identify him as the hero of his speech and master of ceremonies for the *ludi Megalenses* that the trial has displaced.[43]

These examples show Romans casting themselves and others as comic stereotypes into whom they merge their own personas, and in many ways this is typical of Roman theatricality: stock types serve as broad character-izations that equate a person with some theatrical counterpart that seems to match their own identities. Deep down, Nero, Pompey, Roscius Jr., Sextus Clodius, and others overlap with their theatrical equivalents and conform to these dramatic roles into which they were born or for which they were destined. None of this is to say, however, that Romans lived their lives in a theatrical fog, believing that everything they did and everyone they saw was a figment of some Divine Playwright and that their reality was somehow "unreal." But they clearly saw that parts of their lives were scripted moments in which their individuality was subsumed to generic roles to which they had to comport themselves. As we will see, Romans often saw their lives in terms of performance: they were how they acted and their sense of individual identity derived from the roles they played in relation to, and often in competition with, other people who were also performing within a social context. Many of these roles were nontheatrical: "elite," "male," "citizen," all parts whose proper performance gave a Roman greater standing relative to others. Failure to perform as such, for whatever reason, was accompanied by a loss of standing. But these roles often also drew on theatrical systems of meaning: the dramatis personae from the Roman stage were available as parts they could put on or take off as necessary or convenient as supplements to the other social roles that they were expected to perform, and Romans such as Cicero and Catullus found comic parts useful for navigating the expectations of elite society.

## Masks of the Self: Persona, Performance, and Exemplarity

Fast-forward twenty-four years after Cicero's success with *Pro Roscio Amerino* to 56 BCE and we find the orator returning to the same play of Caecilius Statius in his defense of M. Caelius Rufus, who had been accused of

---

[43] Karakasis (2014) discusses Cicero's identification with the *servus callidus*; on other stock types in this speech, see Geffcken (1973) and Leigh (2004).

a range of crimes related to *vis*, or violence imperiling public peace and safety. The trial was held during the *ludi Megalenses*, a festival that featured dramatic performances, and Cicero turned the occasion to his advantage. Since the jurors were precluded by their present service from partaking in the shows, he made his entire speech into a piece of theatrical entertainment, in the process blurring the lines between real life and the stage even more fully than he had in the case for Roscius Jr. Katherine Geffcken demonstrated that the *Pro Caelio* draws strongly from Roman comedy, and indeed that Cicero presents the whole cast of this farcical fable as characters ripped from the stage.[44]

One of Cicero's primary challenges was making Caelius likable to the jury in the face of his indefensibly irresponsible behavior and willing association with disreputable people. As with Roscius Jr., comedy presented him with the solution: Caelius was just one in a long line of self-indulgent but lovable *adulescentes amatores*, whose only real flaw was the naiveté that afflicted all young men, whether fictional or not, especially when malevolent and meretricious women like Clodia were there to lead them off the straight and narrow. But this "boys will be boys" defense can take you only so far, and eventually the ridiculous "young lover" has to be held accountable. Cicero turns to the fathers of Roman comedy for inspiration in addressing this issue, trotting out two alternatives to find the best way to deal with Caelius the wayward *adulescens* (37):

> redeo nunc ad te, Caeli, vicissim ac mihi auctoritatem patriam severitatemque suscipio. sed dubito quem patrem potissimum sumam, Caecilianumne aliquem vehementem atque durum:
>
>> "nunc," enim, "demum mi animus ardet, nunc meum cor cumulatur ira."
>
> aut illum:
>
>> "o infelix, o sceleste!"
>
> ferrei sunt isti patres:
>
>> "egone quid dicam, quid velim? quae tu omnia
>> tuis foedis factis facis ut nequiquam velim."
>
> vix ferendi. diceret talis pater: "cur te in istam vicinitatem meretriciam contulisti? cur inlecebris cognitis non refugisti?"
>
>> "cur alienam ullam mulierem nosti? dide ac dissice;
>> per me tibi licet. si egebis, tibi dolebit, non mihi.
>> mihi sat est qui aetatis quod relicuom est oblectem meae."

---

[44] Geffcken (1973); see also Leigh (2004), Goldberg (2005, 92–96), Moretti (2006, 139–64), and Dyck (2013, 11–12 and 59) for theatrical elements Cicero incorporates in this speech.

huic tristi ac derecto seni responderet Caelius se nulla cupiditate inductum
de via decessisse. quid signi? nulli sumptus, nulla iactura, nulla versura. at
fuit fama. quotus quisque istam effugere potest, praesertim in tam maledica
civitate? vicinum eius mulieris miraris male audisse cuius frater germanus
sermones iniquorum effugere non potuit? leni vero et clementi patre cuius
modi ille est:

> "fores ecfregit, restituentur; discidit
> vestem, resarcietur."

Caeli causa est expeditissima. quid enim esset in quo se non facile
defenderet?

Now I come back to you, Caelius, in your turn and I'll take upon myself
fatherly authority and sternness. But I don't know which father I should
most especially play. One of Caecilius' relentlessly harsh ones? For "now,
after all this, my mind rages, now my heart is heaped with anger!" Or
maybe that other one:

> "You hapless wretch!"

Those fathers are iron-hearted:

> "What should I say, what should I want? Everything you do,
> you do disgracefully, so that what I want doesn't matter!"

You could scarcely bear them! That kind of father would say, "Why did you
walk straight into that whore's neighborhood? Why didn't you run away
when you became aware of her snares?"

> "Why did you get to know a woman you had no ties to?
> Scatter and squander! Fine by me. If you're ever in need,
> that'll be your problem, not mine. It's enough for me to take
> care of whatever life I've got left."

To this kind of gloomy and forthright old man, Caelius would respond that
he had strayed from the straight and narrow, but not out of any lust. "Well,
what proof does he have?" He hasn't had any expenses, losses, or loans.
"But there's a rumor." How many people could avoid that kind of talk,
especially in a city so full of badmouthing? Is it any wonder you heard ill of
the neighbor of such a woman whose own brother couldn't escape the
gossip of ill-wishers? But if the father is patient and merciful like the one in
Terence's play who says,

> "He's broken down someone's doors? They'll be replaced.
> He's torn someone's clothing? It'll be repaired,"

then Caelius' case is easily made. For what argument could there be that he
couldn't easily defend himself against?

Up to this point Cicero has been driving home for the jury that Caelius'
behavior is both puerile and yet not unexpected for someone his age,

particularly for a young man who acts just like all the *adulescentes amatores* his listeners know well from the stage.[45] The more significant point of the comic *prosopopoeia*, however, is what it does for Cicero himself: this passage is about the orator's character and, not only that, but about the character of Serious Roman Men and how that dictates how those in the jury should deal with Cicero's foolish young client. His listeners need to decide what to do with a libertine, and here Cicero uses two familiar incarnations of the comic father figure to model how his adult audience should respond to children who have strayed.

On the one hand is the *senex durus*, or "harsh old man," stock type Cicero says was favored by Caecilius Statius, whose natural reaction is to scold the *adulescens* and to write him off as an irredeemable wastrel. The plays that Cicero quotes do not survive, but this type is familiar from his appearance in Terence's *Adelphoe* in the guise of Demea, the grumpy old man who rebukes his gentle brother Micio for parenting that is too indulgent. On the other hand is Micio himself and his stock type, the *senex lenis* (lenient old man), who forgives his adopted son's indiscretions and works to make them right. By wavering between these two exemplars publicly in front of the jury (*dubito quem patrem potissimum sumam*), Cicero implies these are the only real options for responding to a young man like Caelius: he and the jurors must choose to become either the odious grouch or the good-natured mentor. It is clear from his character-ization which is the more reasonable choice in the eyes of Cicero, who subtly leads his audience to prefer the more affable comic father.

As Matthew Leigh observes, Cicero's allusion to Terence's *Adelphoe* does not let Caelius off the hook or give him free rein to continue acting recklessly. Indeed, while the "lenient father" Micio initially seems lacka-daisical about his son Aeschinus' bad behavior in the play, he reveals to the audience his anxiety about the boy and concern that his easygoing approach has caused the problem. By the end of the play, however, Aeschinus has shown that he is growing into the role of an adult male citizen, marrying his beloved Pamphila and achieving one of the prime goals of Roman comedy, namely, the creation and preservation of the family unit.[46] Accordingly, as Leigh argues, Cicero's use of the *senex lenis* Micio as an exemplar is meaningful in this speech "precisely because it forswears the unconditional endorsement of libertinism in favor of a more

---

[45] For the comic *adulescens amator* in Cicero's rhetorical strategy, see Geffcken (1973, 11–14), Craig (1995), and Leigh (2004).

[46] On marriage and the preservation or creation of family as Roman comedy's *telos*, see Braund (2005).

nuanced account of what is to be tolerated and what is not."[47] That is, Micio models how the jurors might best react to Caelius if their ultimate goal is his successful integration into society and transition into his expected role as elite adult male citizen.

This passage has two major implications for our understanding of Roman theatricality in the late Republic. First, it shows that comic figures can represent stable markers of identity, as in the case of Roscius Jr., but more often than not can also serve as temporary roles that can be assumed or discarded at will. Cicero promises that Caelius will stop acting as a foolish *adulescens amator* and graduate into the expected norms of Roman adult male citizens, provided he is encouraged to grow out of this theatrical phase through which young men habitually pass. By submitting to the jurors two different stereotypical comic fathers with whom they might identify – the *senex durus* or *lenis* – Cicero offers a choice of roles they can assume during their deliberations, bringing them as actor-participants into the drama of Caelius' comedic life. Second, it shows that the choice to take up, change, or remove a theatrical persona meaningfully affects one's identity and one's relationship to others in society. Caelius' performance as the comic "young lover" has caused distress for Cicero and other adults. In response to his theatricalized role, the jurors must now decide how they will perform: become the old-fashioned *senex durus* who scolds, blusters, and alienates, or play the part of the *senex lenis*, whose understanding and good will endears him to other characters and the audience. The theatrical roles each Roman performs shape and convey that person's character and serve as a point of ethical reference from which they may be judged.

This kind of modeling of one's behavior on preexisting figures repre-sents a variation on what Matthew Roller identifies as the "discourse of exemplarity," the cultural process by which members of a society select, recall, and purposely imitate prior individuals whose unique actions or character have set them apart as archetypes of a particular set of values deemed worthy by that society of preservation and reenactment. Roller shows convincingly that Romans often turned to historical figures, such as Horatius Cocles and Cloelia, as examples to be followed, condensing a constellation of social and ethical behavior (e.g., *virtus*, *fortitudo*, self-sacrifice, *amicitia*) into an imitable paradigm.[48] He remarks, "Romans had a strong cultural tendency to establish models of social behavior via specific exemplary individuals, who become templates of behavior used by

---

[47] Leigh (2004, 320).
[48] Roller (2004 and 2009); see also Chaplin (2000) and Van der Blom (2010).

Romans to convey particular characteristics with an ethically normative force."[49] Though Roller focuses exclusively on historical individuals, his approach can readily be applied also to literary and theatrical ones, whom we have already seen Cicero and others employ as encapsulations of some set of behaviors and values. Indeed, in many ways characters from Roman comedy were especially handy targets of exemplary discourse, since they needed little intervention to serve as generic models: whatever an *adulescens amator*'s name, he was merely a single instance of a particular stock type with clear ethical borders. The stock characters familiar from comedy came prepackaged as blank exemplars into which later individuals could be fitted. For Cicero, Caelius was easy to construe as a comic "young lover" because all he had to do was to show he displayed the same traits as his theatrical counterpart, such as unconcern for *pietas*, willingness to sacrifice public responsibilities for personal pleasure, and rejection of emotional restraint. The exemplar need not be "real" (i.e., historical) to become a meaningful target of emulation for Romans.

Further, Mira Seo has recently shown that Romans seemed to view literary characters not as written versions of psychologically rounded individuals, as we often do, but rather as complex assemblages of behaviors and traits that become coherent figures only "through our recognition and familiarity with broader cultural modes, referents, and identities."[50] Seo argues that ancient characters can be seen to lack a sense of interiority and to acquire individual personas primarily through their performance of familiar roles and adherence to or rejection of social expectations. In this way, fictional characters and "real" Romans are both theatricalized: they are ultimately the sum of their performances, personas that become recognizable through the parts they play.

Roman notions of identity are intimately wound up in the theater and role-playing, even at the lexical level. The Latin word that denotes a specific person (and indeed, the word from which our word "person" derives) is *persona*. But the meaning "person" is a metaphorical extension of the word's literal meaning, "theatrical mask."[51] According to Gavius Bassus, a contemporary of Cicero who wrote about Latin etymologies, the *persona* is so-called because it is a thing that one "speaks through" (*per + sonare*).[52] Bartsch observes that the emperor Nero took this idea to an

---

[49] Summary of Roller's (2004) main argument by Seo (2013, 9).     [50] Seo (2013, 3–4).
[51] Wiles (1991, 131).
[52] Gellius *NA* 5.7. On Gavius Bassus' work, see *PIR*² IV p. 20 no. 95, Schanz–Hosius I.585–86, and Funaioli s.v. Gavius (11) in *RE* 7.1.866–68. The etymology is not, strictly speaking, accurate –

extreme, performing tragedies in masks depicting his own face; although extraordinary, Nero's decision to play himself playing other people is emblematic of ties Romans saw between the idea of the self and performance.[53] Indeed, Bartsch argues well that "*persona* generally referred to a Roman citizen's behavior in his publicly acknowledged role(s)."[54] That is, Roman notions of selfhood depended not on any kind of Cartesian sense of interiority and personality separate from one's actions, but instead on one's ability to perform successfully one's chosen or expected roles.

In his *De officiis*, Cicero offers a detailed discussion about the nature of the self and how best to understand the role of the *persona*. He explicitly compares the performance of the self to theatrical performance, stating: "Let each person, then, know his own nature and show that he is a keen judge of his own good and bad points, so that actors do not seem to have more wisdom than we do. For they choose not the best plays, but the ones most suitable to themselves."[55] As Bartsch observes, Cicero stresses that we must play parts in the same way as actors and that, if we are wise, in doing so we will choose to perform only the roles that fit our needs and abilities. Cicero goes on to say that these performances need not derive from our own feelings, and indeed that sometimes we must act out emotions that we do not actually have but that are appropriate for our situations. Both here and elsewhere Cicero continually employs the vocabulary of the theater and role-playing to describe how he shapes and conveys his self to others.[56] The persona was not, then, an interior personality, but "a finished artifact which has to be deliberately fashioned out of the uneven raw material of our impulses ... and capacities (*Off*. 1.111)"[57]

The Roman elite taught their children from early on the importance of performance and the need to be able to assume a variety of roles in both public and private. Martin Bloomer demonstrates how school training relied heavily on role-play in a two-step process of *fictio personae* (creation of character) and *sermocinatio* (construction of that character's speech). This activity forced young men to practice speaking in the voice of their ideal future selves – as elite, male, citizen *patres familiarum*.[58] Children

---

*persona* derives from the Etruscan *phersu*, "actor," on which see Wiles (1991, 131) – but it is suggestive of how first-century BCE Romans viewed the role of masks and notions of personhood.

[53] Bartsch (1994, 46–49).     [54] Bartsch (2006, 217).

[55] Cic. *Off*. 1.114: *suum quisque igitur noscat ingenium acremque se et bonorum et vitiorum suorum iudicem praebeat, ne scaenici plus quam nos videamur habere prudentiae. illi enim non optumas, sed sibi accomodatissimas fabulas eligunt.*

[56] Bartsch (2006, 219); see Cic. *Off*. 1.136 for the performance of emotion. For theatrical role-playing and the persona, see Bartsch (2006, 219–24).

[57] Bartsch (2006, 221).     [58] Bloomer (1997).

were thereby socialized from the start as playwrights and actors of their selves, with the ultimate aim of teaching them to adjust their public display to project an identity in comportment with the *mos maiorum* and with the decorum appropriate to their standing. And one of the primary ways they developed these skills was by imitating literary characters, including the stock types of Roman comedy, which offered opportunities to practice domestic roles (e.g., to learn how, as future Roman masters and fathers, they should understand and treat their slaves and their children, as well as how they as children should interact with the fathers who encouraged this educational activity). They thus reproduced idealized social and family order by learning schemata of set themes and expansions on these formulas for behavior. Bloomer summarizes: "Persona writing is a kind of ritualized composition where stereotypes are called out for new service or renewed service in a conflict which itself is a remanifestation of a familiar problem."[59]

Of course, as Bartsch notes, the analogies that Cicero and others draw between persona and acting has led to an incorrect extreme of interpretation, namely, that Romans saw their public selves as feigned performances while they hid their true selves beneath a mask.[60] She counters this potential pitfall cogently, however, arguing that for Romans the persona was "an identity conceived of both as assumed *and* as not-false":[61]

> The *persona* was neither felt to be the whole of the individual . . . nor was it usually felt to be *fake*, a semblance that concealed the truth of who one was. Instead, it seems that in the late Republic the normative usage of the term *persona* outside the literal context of the theater and its actors was to indicate a public role that formed part and parcel of the individual's identity. There is no contrast in our sources from this period between the *persona* and the "real person"; inasmuch as an individual's social and political roles constituted an important part of that real person, the *persona* represented an aspect of being rather than either an exposition or a dissimulation of that person.

In other words, we are the gestalt of all the masks we wear in front of others, not fixed identities, and in constant flux as old masks are taken off and new ones put on. And the theater, as we have already seen and will see in greater detail, offered a ready supply of roles through which Romans such as Cicero and Catullus could become themselves.

---

[59] Bloomer (1997, 59); see Kaster (2001) for how this activity indoctrinated approved values through the repetition of exemplary social roles.
[60] Bartsch (2006, 220).    [61] Bartsch (2006, 217 and 221).

CHAPTER 2

# The Best Medicine
## Comic Cures for Love in the First Century BCE

Built on a malarial swamp and beset by poor sanitation, Rome was no
stranger to illness. But to hear writers of the first century BCE tell it, the
disease that cut the widest and most ruinous swath in Rome was love.
Catullus calls it "a plague and a pestilence that creeps into your marrow
and paralyzes your limbs." Lucretius names it "a festering wound that
flares up and becomes chronic." This erotic hypochondria belonged not to
the poets alone: even Cicero ponders, "After all, what illnesses of the body
can be more serious than the two diseases of anguish and desire?"[1] This
epidemic prompted serious reflection among writers of this period, and as
with other public disasters, they sought guidance in exempla of the past.
But love had never been Romans' strong suit, and the native *mos maiorum*
was ill equipped to address this problem with much more than Puritanical
shunning. Cato the Elder's censorious response on catching a fellow
senator's public display of affection toward his wife, though extreme, is
illustrative:[2]

ἄλλον δὲ βουλῆς ἐξέβαλεν ὑπατεύσειν ἐπίδοξον ὄντα, Μανίλλιον, ὅτι τὴν
αὐτοῦ γυναῖκα μεθ’ ἡμέραν ὁρώσης τῆς θυγατρὸς κατεφίλησεν. αὐτῷ δ’
ἔφη τὴν γυναῖκα μηδέποτε πλὴν βροντῆς μεγάλης γενομένης
περιπλακῆναι, καὶ μετὰ παιδιᾶς εἰπεῖν αὐτὸν ὡς μακάριός ἐστι τοῦ
Διὸς βροντῶντος.

Cato expelled from the senate another man who was thought to have good
prospects for the consulship, namely, Manilius, because he kissed his wife
in broad daylight in front of their daughter. He said that his wife never

---

[1] Catullus 76.20–21: *pestem perniciemque mihi, / quae mihi subrepens imos ut torpor in artus*; Lucretius
4.1068–69: *ulcus enim vivescit et inveterascit,* and see Brown (1987, 208–13) on the medical
significance of these words; Cicero *Tusc.* 3.5: *quibus duobus morbis ... aegritudine et cupiditate, qui
tandem possunt in corpore esse graviores.* On disease metaphors applied to love in Latin literature, see
Fantham (1972, 14–18 and 82–91) and Caston (2012, 21–47). See Scheidel (1994 and 2003) on
malaria in Rome.
[2] Plu. *Cat. Mai.* 17.7; cf. Amm. Marc. 28.4.9. On this anecdote, see Churchill (2001).

70

embraced him unless it thundered loudly and that she playfully said he was
a lucky man whenever Zeus was thunderous.

Aulus Gellius reports an anecdote (19.9) that hints at how scarce home-
grown models for dealing with love were in first-century BCE Rome. One
day, the *rhetor* Antonius Julianus was at a banquet whose after-dinner
entertainment included recitations of Sappho's and Anacreon's poetry.
Once the singers finished, some Greek guests mocked Julianus and
Roman literature broadly, declaring that, except maybe for Catullus and
Calvus, Latin letters "had none of the pleasures or the caress of Venus and
the Muse" (*nullas voluptates nullamque mulcedinem Veneris atque Musae
haberet*, 7). Julianus tried to refute the charge of Rome's "lovelessness"
(ἀναφροδισία), asserting proudly that "we have poets older than those you
named who were amatory and Venereal" (*nostros quoque antiquiores ante
eos, quos nominastis, poetas amasios ac venerios fuisse*, 9). The earliest poems
he can cite, however – four epigrams by the "pre-neoterics" Valerius
Aedituus, Porcius Licinus, and Lutatius Catulus – are the same age as
Cicero, give or take a decade, and only a generation prior to Catullus.[3] And
even these pieces take their lessons on love from non-Romans: all draw
recognizably on Hellenistic sources, and one epigram (Aedituus fr. 1)
explores the symptoms of lovesickness by adapting Sappho's fr. 31 L–P
(φαίνεταί μοι . . .):[4]

> dicere cum conor curam tibi, Pamphila, cordis,
>     quid mi abs te quaeram, verba labris abeunt,
> per pectus manat subito <subido> mihi sudor;
>     sic tacitus, subidus, dum pudeo, pereo.

> Pamphila, whenever I try to tell you my heart's care –
>     what I'm looking for from you – the words leave my lips,
> sweat suddenly drips through my chest as I get hot;
>     so silent, steamy, while I blush, I am lost.

By citing Aedituus to show that Romans were versed in love, the *rhetor*
inadvertently proves his Greek detractors' point. Rome came late to public

---

[3] Ross (1969, 139–60) remains a solid account of the "pre-neoterics," though his dating has been
refuted cogently by Cameron (1993, 51–56); see also Vardi (2000) and Morelli (2007, 531–34). The
likeliest range for the composition of their epigrams seems to be 110–90 BCE.

[4] See Courtney (1993, 72) and Murgia (2002, 67) on *subidus* (otherwise unattested but perhaps
derived from the verb *subare*, used to describe females in heat, or else *subudus*, "wet"). Murgia
proposes *rubido* in place of *subido* at line 3, which would mirror the blushing of *pudeo* in line 4.
Parallels between Aedituus' and Sappho's poems are numerous, particularly in their symptoms: cf.
*verba labris abeunt*, 2, and γλῶσσα ἔαγε, 9; *per pectus*, 3, and ἐν στήθεσιν, 6; *manat . . . sudor*, 3, and
ἴδρως κακχέεται, 13; *subito*, 3, and αὔτικα, 10; *pereo*, 4, and τεθνάκην, 15.

discourse on erotic suffering, and guidance for managing the disease had to come from Greeks – or Romans who spoke as Greeks.[5] For even as they were tentatively ventriloquizing Sappho, Meleager, and other genuinely Greek sources, the "pre-neoterics" also found inspiration closer to home in a ready supply of local role models who had substantial erotic experience but were unconstrained by Rome's sexual conservatism: Greek *adulescentes amatores*, "young men in love," who populated the imaginary world of the *fabula palliata*. Freed by fiction and foreign identity to indulge in affairs that were taboo for upstanding Roman citizens, these stock characters gave their Latin-speaking audiences tried and true models for scrutinizing love.[6] Indeed, Alison Sharrock shows that Aedituus' epigram combines Sappho's erotic subjectivity with the persona of one of Terence's *adulescentes*, even giving to the beloved a name both pointedly Greek (πᾶν + φίλη, "all loving") and evocative of Terence's comedies, three of which feature a beloved name Pamphila and two a lover named Pamphilus.[7]

Although only a handful of their poems are extant, surviving evidence suggests that all the "pre-neoterics" saw the erotic potential that Roman comedy could offer poets who worked outside the drama proper. Porcius Licinus wrote a history of Latin verse containing scandalous gossip about Terence's sexual liaisons with Roman *nobiles*, their abandonment of the playwright, and his eventual death in poverty. And of the two extant epigrams by Lutatius Catulus, one is a homoerotic encomium of the comic actor Roscius (fr. 2), the other an adaptation of Callimachus' *Epigram* 42 that alludes meaningfully to the *adulescens amator* of Plautus' *Bacchides*, through whom he ponders the suffering caused when desire divides a lover's soul in half (fr. 1).[8] Their early attempts to use Roman comedy to explore love's somatic and psychological effects paved the way for writers of the first century BCE not only to consider lovesickness but also

---

[5] On the Greek character and content "pre-neoteric" poetry, see Pascucci (1979), Maltby (1997), Morelli (2007), and Heyworth (2015).

[6] The explicitly Greek identity of Roman comedy's settings and characters gave its playwrights and their audiences critical distance to deal with "un-Roman" topics and behaviors, and Greeks are consistently associated in the genre with sexual and social license; see Segal (1987, 31–35).

[7] Sharrock (2013, 61–63); note that *Hau.* is Terence's only play without a Pamphila/us, but it does feature a beloved named Anti**phila**.

[8] On Roman comedy in the "pre-neoteric" epigrams, see Pascucci (1979), Perutelli (1990), Maltby (1997), Bessone (2013, 46–48), as well as Johnson (2009, 7–11), who discusses the influence comic *adulescentes* had on the "pre-neoterics." Besides Courtney (1993, 87–90), see Welsh (2011) and Davis (2014) on Porcius Licinus and Terence, and for Catulus and Roscius, see Weber (1996) and Duncan (2006, 173–76). For the complex allusion to *Bacchides* in Catulus fr. 1, see Heyworth (2015).

to develop methods to cope with this pernicious disease by turning to the *adulescens amator* for guidance.

### Erotocatharsis, Comic *Adulescentes*, and Terence's *Eunuchus*

In this chapter, I explore how the three contemporary authors mentioned above – Cicero, Lucretius, and Catullus – employ the comic *adulescens* to examine love as a physical and mental disorder. As a broader goal, I aim to show how Romans of the first century BCE conceptualize the roles that exempla drawn from Roman comedy can play in nontheatrical discourse, laying some theoretical groundwork that undergirds subsequent chapters. My more proximate goal in viewing these three side by side is to point out how revolutionary Catullus' adaptation of Roman comedy to personal poetry was. The traditional Roman line held that "*amor* was tolerated, even expected, in a young man, with the understanding, however, that it was but a transient seizure which would not corrupt the responsibility of a Roman citizen (that is, of an aristocrat) toward his republic, his family and his dignity."[9] Even the hyper-Hellenized Catulus, whose fr. 1 represents the earliest experiment in adapting the comic *adulescens* to Latin personal poetry, seems to have viewed his erotic verses as "an occasional diversion from a life still centred on the duties of the citizen."[10] Cicero and Lucretius both toe this line, albeit with different aims, using the comic *adulescens* to drive wayward Roman youths back into the fold to perform according to the conservative norms of their respective communities (for the former, the Roman *optimates*; for the latter, the disciples of Epicurus). For them, the comic lover represents a cautionary example, a readily available and intelligible model against which the behavior and social status of others could be evaluated and, more importantly, with which young Roman men could be brought back to order.

Catullus, by contrast, explores the character from the perspective not of one trying to cure another but of a person going through the experience of the lover and trying to make sense of his complex and contradictory thoughts. In trying to think not *with* the comic *adulescens* but *as* him, Catullus displays something altogether new for a member of the Roman

---

[9] Konstan (1972, 102).

[10] Conte (1994, 137); see also Clausen (1964, 187) and Ross (1969, 152). Catulus' proudest achievement was likely his attainment of the consulship in 102 BCE, on which he wrote a *De consulatu et de rebus gestis suis*; see Courtney (1993, 75) and Cornell (2013, 271–73). Pliny (*Ep.* 5.3) cites Catulus, among others, to defend his practice of writing and reciting erotic poetry as a respite from more serious matters; see Hershkowitz (1995) and Roller (1998).

elite: a sustained interest in the potential subjectivity of individuals from Roman comedy and how their staged experiences might be used to reflect on personal struggles. First-century BCE Romans perceived themselves and those around them as falling into stereotypically dramatic roles – Pompey as Agamemnon, Antony as a "braggart soldier," and so forth – but the fact that they behaved like those characters is where that interest usually ends. When people acted like theatrical characters, it was sufficient to point out that equivalence and to judge them accordingly. This is Cicero's modus operandi in his *Pro Roscio Amerino* and *Pro Caelio*, as we saw in the previous chapter, and as we will see here in his approach to love. Catullus, however, considers not only the bare truth that life can be theatrical, but also what that realization might mean for him personally. It may seem trite to say Catullus found private value in public drama, and other scholars have argued persuasively that in comedy Catullus saw a psychologically useful tool.[11] What has gone underappreciated is how he departs from his contemporaries in this regard, as well as how Roman comedy's *adulescens* serves as a unifying exemplum to which Catullus returns repeatedly and in a variety of different contexts in his poetic corpus. Moreover, his choice to inhabit rather than to reject the "young man in love" is part and parcel of his other countercultural moves: elevation of *otium* over *negotium*, personal pleasure over reputation, and so forth.

Two elements make Roman comedy's *adulescens amator* a useful touchstone for writers of the first century BCE. First, he appears so frequently that allusions to him are practically certain to be recognized. At the same time, while he is recognizable, he is in many ways utterly generic, a blank slate onto which Romans could project their particular preoccupations, assumptions, and stereotypes about love shared by the first-century BCE Roman elite in different ways.[12]

The *adulescens* is one of the commonest characters in Roman comedy, and almost every extant play features at least one young man struggling in his erotic affairs to overcome some set of difficulties, both practical and psychological. His essential challenge remains the same across comedies: a girl he loves is, or is in danger of being, denied to him. While the premise is generic, the particulars vary widely, and each play's distinctive flavor stems from the choice of obstacles it places between the *adulescens* and *puella* (want of money, a disapproving elder's interference, competition from a rival, jealousy prompted by mistaken identity) and from the

---

[11] E.g., Skinner (1971), Connor (1974), and Minarini (1987, 59–79).     [12] Uden (2006).

relationships the *adulescens* develops with other stock characters that help or hinder him along the way.[13] But the lover himself often seems to contribute little to his play beyond the plot's initial motivation, and the *adulescens amator* is arguably the least developed of the genre's main stock characters.[14]

Other stock character types, by contrast, are represented by individual examples so finely delineated as to stand out from their generic category. Ballio, for example, was such a distinctive character from Plautus' *Pseudolus* that he was recognized as an unique incarnation of the comic *leno*, or "pimp." The actor Roscius was famous not for performing *lenones* generally, but Ballio in particular, and Ballio was so distinctive that Cicero alleges one of his opponents is the real-life inspiration for Roscius' interpretation of the fictional character: "See, when Roscius performs as Ballio, that most mischievous and conniving pimp, he's performing as Chaerea. That filthy, foul, detested character is the spitting image of Chaerea in his manners, nature, and life!"[15] And Cicero represents certain comic parasites as unique in their field, particularly the eponymous protagonist of Terence's *Phormio*, who appears repeatedly in his speeches. In his *Pro Caecina*, he rejects the testimony of a banker named Sextus Clodius Phormio on the grounds that "he is no less black and no less brazen than Terence's Phormio."[16] Likewise in *Philippics* 2, when discussing disreputable people to whom Antony turns for advice, he uses pseudonyms taken from the seediest characters of Roman comedy: "I won't name any names. Just imagine one day it's some Phormio, another day it's Gnatho, and yet another it's Ballio."[17] Pimps, parasites, and other comic stock types were

---

[13] Duckworth (1952, 237–42) remains indispensable for the *adulescens'* characterization and the generic mechanics that define his role.

[14] McCarthy (2000, 4) observes that Plautus' *Mostellaria* mostly abandons the young lover after he finishes motivating the plot in act 1; likewise in *Casina*, whose *adulescens* is not even named and is barred from the stage by the prologue speaker: "He ... well, don't wait for him today, he won't return to the city in this comedy; Plautus didn't want him, so he broke the bridge that was along his way" (*is, ne exspectetis, hodie in hac comoedia / in urbem non redibit: Plautus noluit, / pontem interrupit, qui erat ei in itinere,* 64–66).

[15] Cic. *Q. Rosc.* 20: *nam Ballionem illum improbissimum et periurissimum lenonem cum agit, agit Chaeream; persona illa lutulenta, impura, invisa in huius moribus, natura vitaque est expressa.* For Roscius' performances of Ballio, see Garton (1972, 169–88) and Duncan (2006, 173–87).

[16] Cic. *Caec.* 27: *Sex. Clodius, cui nomen est Phormio, nec minus niger nec minus confidens quam ille Terentianus est Phormio.* See Goldberg (2005, 147–54) on Phormio's memorability in the late Republic, as well as Damon (1997, 97–98), who notes that Donatus says Terence put extra effort into his Phormio's characterization.

[17] Cic. *Phil.* 2.15: *neminem nominabo: putate tum Phormioni alicui, tum Gnathoni, tum etiam Ballioni.* Significantly, by recalling individual *parasiti* of Terence's *Phormio* and *Eunuchus*, Cicero implies they are not merely generic stock types.

often drawn by playwrights as memorable individuals even within the highly stereotyped genre.

When later writers recall *adulescentes amatores*, though, they rarely if ever do so by name. Cicero sketches his defendant in the *Pro Caelio* – his most explicitly theatrical speech – as a comic *adulescens* so generic that he cannot decide which father from Roman comedy would be the most apposite to chastise him.[18] Recently, Uden has argued persuasively that Romans in the first century BCE were so well acquainted with the generic figure of the *adulescens*, whether or not they knew or could recognize specific examples from particular comedies, that the character had become little more than a cipher and that "by the late Republic, the stock character of the comedic *adulescens* had acquired a cultural force all its own as the stereotypical expression of the young man who is passionately in love."[19] And Roman comedy's generic "young man in love" had come so fully to define how Romans believed living, breathing young men in love behaved that it is often difficult to say whether depictions of lovers in Latin literature are meant to be comedic or verisimilar. This dilemma has dominated scholarly discussions about Catullus' representation of himself as a lover, especially in poem 8 (*miser Catulle, desinas ineptire*), in which some have seen patent allusions to Roman comedy and others have steadfastly denied any comedic traces.[20]

But certain aspects of the stereotypical lover of first-century BCE Rome are more distinctive than is often appreciated, particularly in the imagery they use to convey their experience of love, and the conception of love as an illness was an especially Terentian contribution to the character of the comic *adulescens*, as Elaine Fantham and John Barsby have shown.[21] Lovesickness, of course, had a long history in Greek literature, and Plautus uses the metaphor occasionally. But the idea of love as a physical and mental disease, so common in Latin literature of the first century BCE, seems to have entered mainstream consciousness through Terence, who uses such imagery more often and more consistently than any of his Greek or Roman predecessors.[22] Indeed, Fantham identifies only a couple examples in Menander and Plautus but dozens in Terence. As Barsby

---

[18] See Geffcken (1973) and Leigh (2004).     [19] Uden (2006, 20–21).

[20] On Roman (and Greek) comedy in poem 8, see Skinner (1971), Connor (1974), McCormick (1981), and Thomas (1984).

[21] Fantham (1972, 14–18) and Barsby (1999b).

[22] Terence otherwise only sparsely employs imagery, particularly when describing the experience of lovers; see Flury (1968, 88–90). On lovesickness in Greek and Latin before Terence, see Fantham (1972, 14–15) and Caston (2012, 29–34).

remarks, "The point here is not that Terence invented these images or was the first to apply them to love, since, even if rare in Greek comedy, they are mostly Greek in origin, but that, by bringing them to prominence in his comedies, he helped to naturalise them and incorporate them into the tradition of educated Latin speech."[23] When late second- and first-century BCE writers looked back to comic *adulescentes* for guidance in dealing with lovesickness, they found its most concentrated form in Terence's "young men in love."

Terence innovated with respect to love in several other ways I think his first-century BCE successors also found particularly appealing. First, although Cicero praises Terence for his skill in adapting Menander faithfully, the Latin poet departs sharply from his Greek predecessor for using distinctly public, political terminology to represent love. Terence employs terms such as *fides* and *mores* far more often than Menander does their Greek equivalents; for example, *fides* appears more than sixty times in Terence, often to describe the (lack of) fidelity of heteroerotic relationships, whereas its Greek equivalent πίστις occurs only four times in Menander's extant corpus. For Terence these terms offered a way to conceive of love in a far more complex way, as an emotion that motivated relationships equally as convoluted and productive of internal turmoil as those between fathers and sons or husbands and wives.[24] And the presence of such public and distinctly Roman values helped later authors, particularly Cicero, contemplate how love and society interacted, as well as the impact that the lover could have on bulwarks of public safety that *fides* and *mores* represented. For Catullus, though, Terence's experiments in appropriating public language to the private sphere remade the vocabulary of public alliance as a tool to explore broader significances of love and to make its stakes clearer, describing not just lust, but deep relationships on par with the most significant ones Latin could describe.

Second, "while Menander represents love as an external divine force . . . Terence treats it as a human condition."[25] Menander consistently ignores personal agency as the principal factor that motivates love or his lovers' responses to the emotion. In the prologue to *Dyskolos*, the god Pan explains, "I made [the young man Sostratos], while under my divine spell, catch hold of love when by chance he came to this here spot" (κατὰ τύχην

---

[23] Barsby (1999b, 11).

[24] On *fides*/πίστις, see Barsby (1999b, 14). For the broader significance of *fides* in relationships more "official" than the typically frivolous sowing of wild oats by the *adulescens*, see Hallett (1973), Hemelrijk (2004, 191–97), and Coffee (2013).

[25] Barsby (1999b, 6–7).

παραβαλόντ' εἰς τὸν τόπον / ἔρωτ' ἔχειν πως ἐνθεαστικῶς ποῶ), and in the prologue to *Eunuchous*, the lover is told, "Don't fight with the divine, and don't stir up other tempests in this business, bear the ones you have to" (μὴ θεομάχει, μηδὲ προσάγου τῷ πράγματι / χειμῶνας ἑτέρους, τοὺς δ' ἀναγκαίους φέρε).[26] Terence's lovers, by contrast, regularly acknowledge their responsibility for falling in love, an idea that is critical for the discussion of lovesickness in the first century BCE. If the disease and its cure lie solely in the hands of the gods, nothing can come of contemplating it, except perhaps pity for the afflicted or relief at being spared. The agency of Terence's lovers lets Cicero, Lucretius, and Catullus use them not merely to pathologize their mental and physical state but also to develop palliative and remedial approaches – even if, in the case of Catullus, such approaches often come up short and leave him to beg the gods to help him help himself.

In short, although the comic *adulescens amator* in general became an important ethical touchstone for first-century BCE writers, Terence's lovers acquired special status in defining how subsequent authors came to understand lovesickness. And of all his comedies, *Eunuchus* held pride of place as a forerunner in the development of Latin's *sermo amatorius*, as David Konstan argues persuasively, as well as the most prominent and frequent exemplar of comic eroticism to which later writers turned.[27] *Eunuchus* was Terence's record-breaking hit, and not only that, but the most successful Roman comedy ever staged. "Indeed," Suetonius reports, "*Eunuchus* was put on twice in one day and earned a price no comedy by anyone before had, namely eight thousand sesterces. This sum is also added to its title tag for this reason."[28] By the mid-first century BCE, the play had lost none of its popularity and cultural cachet: Cicero quotes it liberally in private correspondence, philosophical works, and public legal speeches in ways that suggest Romans of every stripe knew it well;

---

[26] Men. *Dys.* 43–44 and fr. 162K–T. Compare the prologue to *Aspis*, where the goddess Tyche ("Chance") declares she is the manager of all events on stage (πάντων κυρία / τούτων βραβεῦσαι καὶ διοικῆσαι, 147–48), and to the *Perikeiromene*, where the goddess Agnoia ("Ignorance") says, "I drove [the soldier/lover Polemon] to this; he's not like this naturally" (ἐγὼ γὰρ ἦγον οὐ φύσει / τοιοῦτον ὄντα τοῦτον, 164–65). On divine control of events in Menander, see Gutzwiller (2000) with qualifications by Cinaglia (2014, 102–46). Terence's approach to love also stands in stark contrast to that of Plautus, who often ascribes the power of love to Amor/Cupid/Venus; see Anderson (1984) and Zeitlin (2005).

[27] Konstan (1986); see also Barsby (1999b).

[28] Suet. *Poet.* 11 (p. 29 Re): *Eunuchus quidem bis die acta est meruitque pretium quantum nulla antea cuiusquam comoedia, id est octo milia nummorum; propterea summa quoque titulo ascribitur.* Parker (1996, 591–92) observes that Terence's *Eunuchus* stood out as a classic within its genre and the career of the genre's arguably most successful poet.

Lucretius alludes to its opening scene; and Horace after him combines both Terence's play and Lucretius' adaptation to construct a multilayered satirical portrait of the lover, as does Persius, who tosses Horace's version into his mix as well.[29] And Catullus draws on it repeatedly, alluding to precisely the same scene across disparate poems in his corpus to make unified sense out of the chaotic and paradoxical emotions that lovesickness elicits, as we will see. Before that, though, let us see how his more conservative contemporaries, Cicero and Lucretius, bring to bear the *adulescens* of Roman comedy, of Terence, and of the *Eunuchus* in particular on the problem of love in first-century BCE Rome.

## The *Adulescens Amator* as Antidote: Cicero's *Eunuchus* (*Tusc.* 4.65–76)

Cicero was no Casanova, but it is somewhat surprising that, in so voluminous a corpus as his, a theme otherwise as popular in Roman literature as erotic love should find so little foothold. In some speeches Cicero touches on sexual affairs, and in his philosophical works can be found a smattering of remarks on the subject, but these are infrequent.[30] When he finds occasion to opine, he takes a consistently dim view. In his *De senectute*, for instance, he has Cato the Elder cite loss of sexual appetite as old age's greatest gift and articulate the belief – learned while Cato was still an *adulescens* himself – that erotic love is humanity's worst illness (39):[31]

> sequitur tertia vituperatio senectutis, quod eam carere dicunt voluptatibus. o praeclarum munus aetatis, siquidem id aufert a nobis, quod est in adulescentia vitiosissimum! accipite enim, optimi adulescentes, veterem orationem Archytae Tarentini, magni in primis et praeclari viri, quae mihi

[29] Cicero quotes it at, e.g., *Fam.* 1.9.19, *Att.* 7.3.10, *Amic.* 93–94 and 98, *Off.* 1.150, *N.D.* 2.60 and 3.72, *Tusc.* 4.76, and *Phil* 2.15; see Manuwald (2014), who, following Zillinger (1911, 151–55), remarks that Cicero quotes from *Eunuchus* twenty-two times, by far the most of any play of Terence. For the reception of *Eunuchus* in Horace, Persius, and other Latin authors, see Lowe (1983) and Müller (2013).
[30] Scholarship on the topic is also thin; see Brachtendorf (1997), who offers a useful starting point. Caston (2012, 21–47) discusses Cicero briefly to contrast elegiac views of love. See also Geffcken (1973) and Rosivach (1986) on *Pro Caelio*, Cicero's most thorough engagement with erotic love and, not coincidentally, with Roman comedy, as well as scattered remarks in *De amicitia*, where Cicero dismisses "those who relate everything back to pleasure in the manner of livestock" (*qui pecudum ritu ad voluptatem omnia referunt*, 32) and calls sexual pleasure "a thing of the beasts" (*belvarum hoc*, 20).
[31] On this passage's relationship to Greek philosophical traditions and Cicero's other works, see Huffman (2005, 323–37).

tradita est cum essem adulescens Tarenti cum Quinto Maximo. nullam capitaliorem pestem quam voluptatem corporis hominibus dicebat a natura datam, cuius voluptatis avidae libidines temere et ecfrenate ad potiundum incitarentur; hinc patriae proditiones, hinc rerum publicarum eversiones, hinc cum hostibus clandestina colloquia nasci; nullum denique scelus, nullum malum facinus esse, ad quod suscipiendum non libido voluptatis impelleret.

The third criticism leveled at old age is that people say it lacks sexual pleasure. What a splendid benefit of this phase of life, if it takes from us what is the most depraved part of young manhood! Listen up, noble young men, to the old saying by Archytas of Tarentum – a great, outstanding, and splendid man – that I learned when I was a young man living in Tarentum with Quintus Maximus. He said that no disease has been given to humans by nature more lethal than pleasure; that our lusts, eager for this pleasure, spur themselves on recklessly and without restraint in order to possess it. From this are born betrayal of the fatherland, overthrow of the state, secret conversations with the enemy; there exists no crime, in sum, no evil deed that the lust for pleasure does not drive one to undertake.

Though the words are represented as Cato's and the views on erotic love align with those of the historical Censor cited at the start of this chapter, the voice is patently Cicero's, for whom Cato was both an exemplary model and a fictional mouthpiece.[32] Cicero asserts as much at the start of *De senectute*, where he announces, "Cato's words will lay out all of my own thoughts about old age" (*ipsius Catonis sermo explicabit nostram omnem de senectute sententiam, 3*).[33]

For Cato – and thus for Cicero also – love was a plague (*pestem*) to which young men (*adulescentes*) were especially vulnerable. Although he quotes a philosopher, his reaction to this danger goes beyond philosophical contemplation. How he uses Archytas' maxim shows that Cato saw love as a public health crisis threatening the very state (*hinc patriae proditiones, hinc rerum publicarum eversiones*) and curing Rome's newest generation as his duty to the Republic. Adopting a didactic stance (*accipite enim*), he singles out aristocratic youth (*optimi*), offspring and future representatives

---

[32] Van der Blom (2010, 149–83) analyzes Cato's role as an exemplary figure for Cicero. On Cato as a mouthpiece for Cicero, see Astin (1978, 297–99) and van der Blom (2010, 170–71).

[33] This anecdote is probably fictional, constructed by Cicero to lend his work greater weight. Powell (1988, 181–84, 274–75) defends its historical accuracy, but the tradition that Cato spent time in Tarentum under Q. Fabius Maximus is generally seen as fanciful; see Gruen (1992, 66–67) and the bibliography cited by Powell (1988, 274–75). For the likelihood that Cicero invented Cato's knowledge of Greek philosophers, including of Archytas, see Zetzel (1972), Gruen (1992, 58–59), and Huffman (2005, 325–31).

of the *optimates*, the Senate's traditionalist order.[34] He offers an old lesson (*veterem orationem*), passed down to him as a lad (*mihi tradita est cum essem adulescens*) from an elder of the highest esteem in his community (*magni in primis et praeclari viri*). Cato effectively casts himself as a new link in the chain of the *mos maiorum*, the collective received wisdom that defined proper Roman behavior. Through him, the knowledge of past generations is conserved, virtue is instilled in the young, and the Republic proceeds along the straight and narrow – at least as regards sexual mores. By reporting Archytas' instruction via Cato, Cicero takes on the same pose and objectives as his interlocutor: Cato transmits what Archytas taught, and Cicero in turn conveys what Cato taught, each appending himself to his forebear as the latest conduit relaying the *mos maiorum* to his audience.

Of course, Greeks are not usually counted among Rome's *maiores*, so Archytas' position as originating authority on love might seem questionable to Roman readers. As I observed at the start of this chapter, however, Latin writers in the first century BCE regularly turn to Greek rather than Roman models when exploring erotic love, particularly its noxious aspects. Cicero's use of Cato as an intermediary helps to soothe anxieties about the source of this information and offers a safe insertion point for foreign knowledge, properly vetted, into the Roman tradition: yes, this is Greek learning, and from the lips of a Hellenistic philosopher no less, but only the sort that would pass through the sieve of the Censor, who is "*mos maiorum* incarnate."[35] Cicero also uses Cato to define the ideal Roman statesman's duty when it comes to love: he must use knowledge garnered from Greeks, who had more experience in these disreputable matters than Romans did, to warn Rome's vulnerable youth and to inoculate them against its dangers.

Cato's modus operandi here neatly captures Cicero's approach to erotic love elsewhere, including his most extended essay on the topic, at *Tusculan Disputations* 4.65–76. There, too, he laments love's devastating effects on Rome's young men and claims curing them as his personal duty. And like Cato, he turns to a Greek exemplum for help, albeit one more in keeping with his own public persona. While the Censor was the sort to discern and instruct as directly as possible, commanding deference through *auctoritas* alone, the *optimus orator* knows how effective a deft character-sketch can be, and few are more apt

---

[34] For *optimus* as shorthand for conservative Roman elite and senatorial class, see Hellegouarc'h (1963, 495–505) and Lintott (1999, 173–74).

[35] So Baraz (2012, 183–85), who argues the figure of Cato helps Cicero package arguments from the Greek tradition in a wrapper of Roman *auctoritas*. Cato had a reputation for hostility toward Greek philosophers, on which see Gruen (1992, 53–67), as well as Forsythe's (1994) critiques of Gruen's argument.

and relatable to his audience than Cicero's favorite from the theater: Roman comedy's "young man in love."[36] He focuses "on delight and desire" (*de laetitia et de cupiditate*, 65), which he argues are the most toxic disorders of the soul, citing *adulescentes amatores* from multiple comedies as evidence. He begins by contrasting virtuous joy inspired by *pietas*, as displayed by the exemplary Hector in a tragedy of Naevius, with the sordid delights of erotic love and its ill effects on full view in comedies by Trabea and Caecilius Statius (4.67–68):[37]

> aliter enim Naevianus ille gaudet Hector:

> "laetus sum laudari me abs te, pater, a laudato viro,"

> aliter ille apud Trabeam:

> "lena delenita argento nutum observabit meum,
> quid velim, quid studeam: adveniens digito impellam    ianuam,
> fores patebunt: de inproviso Chrysis ubi me aspexerit,
> alacris ob viam mihi veniet complexum exoptans meum,
> mihi se dedet."

> quam haec pulchra putet, ipse iam dicet:

> "fortunam ipsam anteibo fortunis meis."

> haec laetitia quam turpis sit, satis est diligenter attendentem penitus videre. et ut turpes sunt, qui ecferunt se laetitia tum cum fruuntur Veneriis voluptatibus, sic flagitiosi, qui eas inflammato animo concupiscunt. totus vero iste, qui volgo appellatur amor – nec hercule invenio, quo nomine alio possit appellari – tantae levitatis est, ut nihil videam quod putem conferendum. quem Caecilius:

> "deum qui non summum putet,
> aut stultum aut rerum esse imperitum," existumat,
> "cui in manu sit, quem esse dementem velit,
> quem sapere, quem sanari, quem in morbum inici
> . . .
> quem contra amari, quem expeti, quem arcessier."

---

[36] On character sketches in Ciceronian rhetoric, see Wooten (1983, 146–47) and May (1988). Cicero's most well-known use of the comic *adulescens* occurs in his *Pro Caelio*, on which see Geffcken (1973), Leigh (2004), and Goldberg (2005, 92–96); the *adulescens* also appears in his *Pro Roscio Amerino*, *Pro Quinctio*, *In Pisonem*, and elsewhere; see Vasaly (1985 and 1993, 157–62), Hughes (1997), and Harries (2007).

[37] On Hector as an exemplum of Roman virtue, see Goldschmidt (2013, 149–50). Byrne (2000, 24–25) and Higbie (2011, 379) note passages where Cicero uses Hector as an exemplum for his own behavior; this line by Naevius seems to have been a favorite, as he quotes it twice in his letters to cast himself as Hector and Cato the Younger and L. Lucceius as Priam (*Fam.* 15.6.1 and 15.12.7, respectively). On the significance of the distinction Cicero makes between Hector's positive *gaudium* and the lover's negative *laetitia*, see Brachtendorf (1997), Graver (2002, 178), and Potkay (2007, 6), as well as *Tusc.* 4.66.

o praeclaram emendatricem vitae poeticam! quae amorem, flagitii et levitatis auctorem, in concilio deorum collocandum putet. de comoedia loquor, quae, si haec flagitia non probaremus, nulla esset omnino.

You see, it's one thing to rejoice like Hector in Naevius' tragedy:

> "I am glad, father, to be praised by you, a man of praise."

It's another thing to rejoice like that lover in Trabea's comedy:

> "The madame mitigated by money will look for my nod,
> to see what I want, what I'm eager for; when I come to her,
> I'll push the door with my finger and the way will open.
> When Chrysis unexpectedly sees me, in a flash she'll come
> to me and, aching for my embrace, give herself to me!"

Then he says how fine he thinks these words are:

> "I'll outstrip Fortuna herself with in my fortunes!"

To see with perfect clarity how degrading this kind of delight is, all you need is to pay careful attention. And just as those people are degraded who get carried away with delight when they revel in Venus' pleasures, so too are they criminals who long for them in their inflamed soul. In fact the whole feeling that is commonly known as "love" – and Hercules help me, I can't find any other term for it – is of such exceeding capriciousness that I see nothing that I think compares with it. Of Caecilius makes the following judgment:

> "Whoever thinks Love is not the greatest god,
> is either a fool or someone with no experience in life;
> Love holds the power to madden whomever he will,
> to make him wise or drive him out of his mind, to disease,
> to make beloved, sought for, and beckoned."

What a splendid reformer of life this poetry is! It thinks love, creator of disrepute and capriciousness, should find a place in the council of gods. I'm speaking of comedy, which wouldn't even exist if we didn't approve of these disreputable things.

These comic lovers are not isolated cases, and soon after Cicero quotes Turpilius' *Leucadia* (72–73) for further proof that love is a mental illness and "lust is the reason the lover does and says such disreputable things" (*propter libidinem tanta flagitia et faciat et dicat*, 73).

Coming from a man who knew comedy intimately, quoted from it liberally, and extolled its playwrights and performers from the start of his career to its bitter end, his scornful quip that the genre "wouldn't even exist if we didn't approve of these disreputable things" (*si haec flagitia non probaremus, nulla esset omnino*) is startling at first glance.[38] But the target of his criticism is less comedy itself and more its audience, at least those who approve of such behavior (*flagitia . . . probaremus*) in their own lives, whose own moral turpitude is the root cause of everything base on stage. To Cicero, after all, comedy was "an imitation of life, a mirror of custom, an image of truth" (*imitationem vitae, speculum consuetidinis, imaginem veritatis*).[39] If comedy had a fault, it lay in the living people whose negative traits were reflected back to its audience. Paradoxically, this reflective quality was also the genre's saving grace, for while comedy contained much that Cicero deemed *infra dignitatem*, including the ideas and behaviors of *adulescentes* he criticizes here, what mattered was not so much the plays' content as how it was put to use. Cicero makes this very point in his famous discussion of humor in *De oratore*, where he has Crassus explain that shameful acts can be made to benefit others if handled carefully by an orator (2.236): "But the seat and region, so to speak, of humor lies in a certain disgrace and ugliness; the only, or at any rate the best, way to cause laughter is to point out and mark something as disgraceful without doing so disgracefully" (*locus autem et regio quasi ridicule . . . turpitudine et deformitate quadam continetur; haec enim ridentur vel sola, vel maxime, quae notant et designant turpitudinem aliquam non turpiter*). This sort of ridicule that exposes unbecoming conduct to the disinfectant of public scorn was one of the ideal orator's most powerful tools.

Cicero employs precisely this rhetorical gesture when he explicitly identifies comedy's young lovers as negative *exempla*, remarking that "to see with perfect clarity how degrading this kind of delight is, all you need is to pay careful attention" (*haec laetitia quam turpis sit satis est diligenter attendentem penitus videre*). Significantly, Cicero repeatedly describes the *adulescens'* crimes as *flagitia*, that is, behavior worthy of *flagitatio* or corrective public abuse, naming love the *flagitii auctor* and those enthralled by it *flagitiosi*.[40] He wants his audience to observe and to be repelled by

---

[38] Cicero's earliest speech, *Pro Quinctio* (delivered 81 BCE), includes an allusion to Caecilius Statius' comedies and was motivated by his close friendship with the great comic actor Roscius, the defendant's brother-in-law; see Harries (2007, 133–34); Cicero uses comedic stereotypes to lambast Antony in *Philippics* 2, one of his final works (likely published in December of 44 BCE, less than a year before his death, Ramsey [2003, 158–59] shows); see Sussman (1994).

[39] Evanthius, *Excerpta de Comoedia* 5.1; see discussion of this idea above in Chapter 1. On mirrors as correctives, see Bartsch (2006, 32–33 and 183–90) and Taylor (2008, 6–9).

[40] Walters (1998, 360–62) discusses *flagitium* and its ties to *flagitatio*. On the real and literary use of *flagitationes* to regulate Roman behavior, see Usener (1901) and Fraenkel (1961). The practice had strong connections to comedy; see LeFèvre (1997, 53–54). Cicero knew the power of *flagitatio* well, having experienced it himself after his return from exile; see Walters (2017, 92–93).

comic *adulescentes* and, what is more, to be repelled by their own and their peers' behavior if it matches what they see. His ultimate goal in abusively showcasing these shameful characters is rehabilitation. Cicero's exclamation that comedy is a "splendid reformer of life" (*praeclaram emendatricem vitae*), sarcastic on its face, serves as both a personal challenge and a statement of methodology. On its own, comedy does a poor job of signaling that audiences ought not emulate the young men on stage, and naive spectators might expect nothing more than some entertaining diversion. In the hands of someone like Cicero, however, who knows that objects in the mirror of comedy are closer than they appear and can be deployed to remedy Romans' ethical shortcomings, it becomes an honest-to-goodness *emendatrix vitae*. As Graver observes, Cicero opens his discussion of emotions generally in *Tusculans* 3 with an implied claim that "while the uncritical reading of literature is indeed a cause of moral error, this pernicious influence can be neutralized by thoughtful and selective use of the same material, and that teaching such critical reading is an important task of philosophers."[41] The skilled orator knows how to turn lemons into lemonade – or, a metaphor better fitting this situation, to turn a virus into a vaccine.[42]

Besides offering the clearest diagnostic tool for the disease of love, comedy's *adulescens* also offers Cicero its surest cure. Directly after sketching its symptoms through the *adulescentes* of Trabea, Caecilius, and Turpilius, he articulates his remedy for Rome's lovesick youth through the famous opening scene of Terence's *Eunuchus* (74–76):

> sic igitur adfecto haec adhibenda curatio est, ut et illud quod cupiat, ostendatur quam leve, quam contemnendum, quam nihili sit omnino, quam facile vel aliunde vel alio modo perfici vel omnino neglegi possit.... maxume autem admonendus est, quantus sit furor amoris. omnibus enim ex animi perturbationibus est profecto nulla vehementior, ut, si iam ipsa illa accusare nolis, stupra dico et corruptelas et adulteria, incesta denique, quorum omnium accusabilis est turpitudo, sed ut haec omittas, perturbatio ipsa mentis in amore foeda per se est. nam ut illa praeteream, quae sunt

---

[41] Graver (2002, 76). In the preface to *Tusculans* 3, Cicero stresses that humans must rely on their own analytic ability (*ratio*) and proper guidance (*doctrina*) to discern correct from corrupt in the lessons of their teachers, including "the poets, who are heard, read, learned by heart and cleave deeply in our minds, since they hold forth the great prospect of teaching and wisdom" (*poetae, qui cum magnam speciem doctrinae sapientiaeque prae se tulerunt, audiuntur, leguntur, ediscuntur et inhaerescunt penitus in mentibus*, 3.3).

[42] Knowledge of vaccination postdates classical antiquity, but acquired immunity through exposure was known since at least the Athenian plague of 430 BCE (see Thuc. 2.51.6), and in Cicero's day Mithridates VI was famous for inuring himself to poison by ingesting toxins; see Silverstein and Bialasiewicz (1980), Cilliers and Retief (2000), and Mayor (2014).

furoris, haec ipsa per sese quam habent levitatem, quae videntur esse mediocria:

> "iniuriae, suspiciones, inimicitiae, indutiae,
> bellum, pax rursum: incerta haec si tu postules
> ratione certa facere, nihilo plus agas,
> quam si des operam, ut cum ratione insanias."

haec inconstantia mutabilitasque mentis quem non ipsa pravitate deterreat? est etiam illud, quod in omni perturbatione dicitur, demonstrandum, nullam esse nisi opinabilem, nisi iudicio susceptam, nisi voluntariam. etenim si naturalis amor esset, et amarent omnes et semper amarent et idem amarent, neque alium pudor, alium cogitatio, alium satietas deterreret.

For a man afflicted in this way, this is the regimen that must be administered: show how trivial, how despicable, how entirely worthless the object of his desire is, how easily it can either be gained from somewhere else or in some other way or be entirely disregarded.... But most importantly, you must warn him how great is the frenzy of love. For out of all disturbances of the soul, absolutely none is more violent, so that even if you are not willing to reprimand its actual effects – I mean the illicit sex and seductions and adulteries, even incest, all acts whose degradation is reprehensible – but to skip these, the disorder of the mind in love is in and of itself detestable. For to pass over those effects that belong to its frenzy, how innately trivial are those properties that seem ordinary:

> "outrages, suspicions, enmities, reconciliations,
> war, back to peace. If you propose to make what's uncertain
> certain by means of reason, you'll accomplish nothing more
> than if you worked to be mad with reason."

Whom would this inconsistency and fickleness of the mind not scare away by its very depravity? You also have to show the following aspect that is said to be part of all its disorder, namely, that there is no example of love that is not a matter of belief, not begun without judgment, not a voluntary choice. For, if love were in fact merely a force of nature, everyone would be in love and would always be in love and be in love with the same thing, and one lover wouldn't be deterred by shame, another by contemplation, another by getting their fill.

At last Cicero appears to move from describing love's symptoms to actually addressing them, and he frames his approach here explicitly in medical terms that correspond to his portrayal of love as an illness: "this is the regimen that must be administered to the afflicted" (*adfecto haec adhibenda curatio est*). Step one is to show the lovesick that the object of their affection is trivial, despicable, or easy to replace (*ostendatur quam leve, quam contemnendum, quam nihili sit omnino, quam facile vel aliunde vel alio modo perfici*). Step two is to rebuke them until they perceive that their feelings are merely a powerful form of madness (*maxume autem admonendus est, quantus sit furor amoris*). The ultimate goal, and inevitable outcome, of Cicero's remedy is deterrence from love's corrupting influence (*haec inconstantia mutabilitasque mentis quem non ipsa pravitate deterreat*).

This prescription should feel familiar, because Cicero has subtly been playing doctor on us this whole time, using comedy's "young men in love" as his delivery mechanism to administer the very same treatment to his readers. Cicero's parade of *adulescentes amatores* is designed to put the lover's mental and social defects on full display (*ostendatur*). The verb he employs to describe his therapeutic method is also significant, as *ostendere* has semi-technical meaning. Rhetoricians use it to describe the presentation of exempla to be examined closely, especially when the object of study is meant to be visualized.[43] Quintilian considered Cicero especially skillful in employing *ostentatio* (6.2.29–32) to provoke strong emotional reactions:

> quas φαντασίας Graeci vocant (nos sane visiones appellemus), per quas imagines rerum absentium ita repraesentantur animo ut eas cernere oculis ac praesentes habere videamur, has quisquis bene ceperit is erit in adfectibus potentissimus. quidam dicunt εὐφαντασίωτον qui sibi res voces actus secundum verum optime finget: quod quidem nobis volentibus facile continget; nisi vero inter otia animorum et spes inanes et velut somnia quaedam vigilantium ita nos hae de quibus loquor imagines prosecuntur.... insequetur ἐνάργεια, quae a Cicerone inlustratio et evidentia nominatur, quae non tam dicere videtur quam ostendere, et adfectus non aliter quam si rebus ipsis intersimus sequentur.

> The person with the greatest power in effecting emotions will be the one who has mastered what the Greeks call *phantasms* (but let's call them "visions"), by which the images of things that are absent are presented to the mind in such a way that we seem to see them with our eyes and to have them physically present before us. Some call a person who creates impressions of things, voices, and behaviors that are exceptionally true to life most *euphantastic*. In fact, this happens easily when we will it to, except when the images that I am discussing steal upon us when our minds are at rest or idly hoping or daydreaming about something.... From this comes *vividness*, which Cicero terms "illustration" or "portrayal," by which he seems to

---

[43] At *Inst.* 8.3.64, Quintilian remarks, "Cicero is especially outstanding in this area" (*plurimum in hoc genere sicut ceteris eminet Cicero*); cf. *Inst.* 8.3.66, where Quintilian says Cicero is sufficient in himself for showing off this practice. On the role of imagistic realism in Ciceronian exempla, see Innocenti (1994, 375–76) and Penwill (1994, 70), and cf. *Rep.* 2.1.3, where Cicero has Cato assert that showing the image of something tangible is more effective than something made ad hoc, contrasting *ostendero* with *finxero*. See also Quint. *Inst.* 4.2.11, where he says that auditors are most moved when Cicero "does not so much narrate as illustrate" (*non tam narraret quam ostenderet*). For *ostendere* and its use in corrective mirror metaphors, see Sen. *Cl.* 1.1.1 (*scribere de clementia, Nero Caesar, institui, ut quodam modo speculi vice fungerer et te tibi ostenderem*).

present not so much with words as with visual display, and the emotions
that follow are no different from if we were actually present at the events.

Significantly, what Quintilian describes is similar to the phenomenon
Lucretius attributes to the theater, namely, its ability to create waking
visions, and directly after this remark he connects the emotional power of
*ostentatio* with the work of actors, both tragic and comic (*histriones atque
comoedos*, 35). Quintilian generally finds little use in Roman comedy, but
he does recommend it for one particular thing: *ethopoeia*, or drawing
character sketches.[44] These comic *adulescentes* that Cicero brings out over
the course of this passage serve as forceful negative exempla, each chosen to
highlight vividly how trivial and contemptible is the target of his desire
(*quod cupiat, ostendatur quam leve, quam contemnendum ... sit*). Notably,
Cicero's approach to the lover here corresponds to the primary method
Cicero outlines earlier in the *Tusculans* for banishing destructive emotions,
namely, revealing how worthless and easily replaced is the object of the
lover's affection.[45]

The comic *adulescens* is particularly well suited to Cicero's goal of
devaluing the lovers' experience. As I noted at the start of this chapter,
he is an utter stereotype, the most indistinct of comedy's stock characters.
By trotting out one comic lover after another, Cicero overwhelms the
reader with sheer numbers, revealing how perfectly monotonous love is.
No matter how unique a young Roman may think his emotions and
beloved are, it turns out they are nothing special after all. Cicero's decision
to close this section by quoting from Terence's *Eunuchus* delivers the
knockout blow. The *adulescens amator* was comedy's most banal stock
character, and the *Eunuchus'* lover Phaedria was its Platonic form in the
minds of first-century BCE Romans. He may have gained this status at
least in part because the *Eunuchus'* prologue sets us up to view him that
way. Cicero does not recite the relevant section, but he clearly takes his cue
here from Terence himself, who asserts fewer than twenty lines before the
passage quoted by Cicero that, when it comes to "love, hatred, and
suspicion, nothing's said now that hasn't been said before" (*amare odisse
suspicari? denique | nullumst iam dictum quod non dictum sit prius*, 40–41).
The lover is always already a cliché, and anyone in love who thinks himself
otherwise is absorbed in self-deception.

---

[44] Lucr. 4.973–83. Goldberg (1987) and Fantham (2002) discuss Quintilian's views on the fraught
relationship between oratory and acting. On the utility of comic characters in Cicero's production
of vivid character sketches, see Hughes (1997, 193–96).

[45] See Graver (2002, 171–73) on *Tusc.* 4.58–62.

There is one major difference between how Cicero uses the other comic *adulescentes* as negative exempla and his invocation of Terence's *Eunuchus* at the close of his discourse on love: whereas he quotes the words spoken by Trabea's, Caecilius', and Turpilius' lovers themselves to highlight their disordered thinking, here he reports those of the *servus* Parmeno, who is responding to the self-centered lament of the *adulescens* Phaedria. The change in perspective fits the change in Cicero's focus at *Tusc.* 74, when he ends his parade of lovers and transitions to his prescription for curing lovesickness. In the first section, Cicero uses the *adulescentes* themselves to show off their own words and deeds, making clear that they must be taken as models whose shameful behavior is to be avoided. When he gets to the actual treatment of love, however, he is not interested in getting into the heads of *adulescentes amatores*, since subjective introspection plays no role in his therapy, and so takes on the role of an outsider who can judge and critique the lover. His approach precisely mirrors his use of comedy in the *Pro Caelio*, where he avoids empathizing with the *adulescens* and puts on the masks of comic *senes duri* and *lenes*, who are invoked to chastise Caelius-as-lover. His invocation of Parmeno's critique performs a similar function: he adopts the perspective of someone who sees the lover for what he is and attempts to shame him into changing his behavior, giving his audience an exemplary guise for how to treat emotionally disturbed young men. In Cicero's mind, the only cure for erotic love is the tough love of clear-eyed outsiders – the *servus* Parmeno, Cato, Cicero, and others – whose shaming of the young man can get him to see his own ridiculous state.

Cicero disagrees with the comic *servus* in one respect, though. Parmeno advises Phaedria to stop fighting love, because it is an unreasonable disorder and you cannot reason your way out of it. Cicero, by contrast, closes this section by asserting precisely the opposite: when it comes to lovesickness, "it must be made clear that love is nothing but a matter of belief, nothing but an act of judgment, nothing but a voluntary choice" (*demonstrandum nullam esse nisi opinabilem, nisi iudicio susceptam, nisi voluntariam,* 76). Indeed, while lovesickness' symptoms may manifest in the body and the consequences are largely external and behavioral, the root of the disorder is in the mind (*perturbatio ipsa mentis in amore foeda per se est,* 75). In other words, it can be cured by proper *voluntas, iudicium,* and *opinio* – that is, by *ratio*, the working of a rational mind, if only the lover can be made to see and correct his error. Indeed, *ratio* stands behind all of Cicero's advice on avoiding destructive emotion in the *Tusculans*, since he claims that mental disturbances are wholly within our own power to avoid or heal, as he asserts immediately before he begins his diatribe on love (*Tusc.* 4.65):

> mihi quidem in tota ratione ea, quae pertinet ad animi perturbationem, una res videtur causam continere, omnis eas esse in nostra potestate, omnis iudicio susceptas, omnis voluntarias.

> As far as I'm concerned, everything to do with the disorder of the mind seems to center on one issue, namely, that all emotions are in our power, all are subject to judgment, all are voluntary choices.

This overarching statement closely mirrors Cicero's specific prescription for love at the end of his diatribe ten sections later, where he claims the key to curing lovesickness is to make clear to a lover that his desire is *opiniabilis, suscepta iudicio,* and *voluntaria* (76). Notably, Cicero believed even the comic *adulescens* – and therefore the Roman youth who acts like him – had this mental power. Around the same time he wrote this passage of the *Tusculans,* he expressed this very idea in his *De natura deorum,* again with specific reference to Phaedria, the comic *adulescens* of Terence's *Eunuchus* (3.72):

> levitates comicae parumne semper in ratione versantur? parumne subtiliter disputat ille in "Eunucho":
> "quid igitur faciam?... exclusit, revocat; redeam? non si me obsecret."

> Do you think the trivialities of comedy never deal much in reason? Does that guy in Terence's *Eunuch* argue with any less nuance, saying [46–49]:
> "Well, what should I do?... She shut me out, she calls me back. Should I go? Not even if she begs!"

He goes on to quote the *adulescentes* of Caecilius' *Synephebi* and Terence's *Phormio* to show that young men in love often employ logic and judgment in managing their affairs, exclaiming, "How, then, could their plots, devices, deceptions, and tricks exist without reason?" (*quid ergo isti doli, quid machinae, quid fallaciae praestigiaeque num sine ratione esse potuerunt?,* 3.73).

In Cicero's view, both fictive and living lovers are susceptible to change, and the power to do so lay in their own minds. What the comic *adulescens* lacks, but which fortunately Cicero's Roman youth has, is the benefit of distance and perspective that cautionary exempla can provide. Phaedria does not get to watch a comedy that shows another fool, and indeed despite inhabiting a genre that is deeply metatheatrical, *adulescentes* are consistently unaware of their own status as characters. Cicero's audience, though, has the benefit of Cicero's guidance to see how ridiculous and shameful the *adulescens* is and can use that experience to help themselves. Cicero holds up the mirror of comedy so that his target can see himself more clearly in the sufferings of the stage and be scared away. Notably, Cicero closes his diatribe against love by asserting that there are many qualities that can correct lovers if given the chance: "shame deters one, reflection another, satiety yet another (*alium pudor, alium cogitatio, alium satietas deterreret*, 76). *Pudor, cogitatio*, and *satietas* are all part of Cicero's method here: filling his audience with so many examples of *adulescentes* that they cannot bear to let themselves be yet another victim of the disease, Cicero employs corrective shame and forces his readers to use their own mental capacity to reflect on the state of the lover, both comic and "real." With this comic regimen, Dr. Cicero helps Rome's men cure themselves as they pass through one of the inevitable diseases of youth. If all goes well, they will be protected against any future threats of lovesickness and ready to pass on the same immunity to future generations through the exemplary lessons of Cicero, Cato, and the comic playwrights.

## The *Adulescens Amator* as Gateway Drug: Lucretius' *Eunuchus* (*DRN* 4)

Cicero held little common ground with Epicurus, and on the topic of pleasure, he often painted contemporary Epicureans as hedonists who were selfishly withdrawn from the affairs of the Republic.[46] When it came to erotic love, though, they were of similar minds. In the midst of his diatribe against lovers in the *Tusculan Disputations*, Cicero uncharacteristically turns against Plato and the Stoics to commend Epicurus on the topic: "Let's come now to those philosophers, the teachers of virtue, who quarrel with Epicurus (who isn't far from the truth, in my opinion) by denying that love is a crime." From its start, Epicureanism denounced emotional attachment in sexual relations, and Epicurus' Roman disciple Lucretius zealously advocated his prohibition.[47]

Cicero would certainly have found much to praise in the portrayal of the lover in Lucretius' *De rerum natura* (*DRN*) (4.1037–191), which offers an

---

[46] The bibliography on Cicero's attitude toward Epicureanism is enormous. Stokes (1995), Striker (1996, 196–208), Nicgorski (2002), and Hanchey (2013) offer good overviews, especially with reference to pleasure and public duty.

[47] *Tusc.* 4.70: *ad magistros virtutis, philosophos, veniamus, qui amorem negant stupri esse et in eo litigant cum Epicuro non multum, ut opinio mea fert, mentiente.* I disagree with Graver (2002, 174–75) that Cicero's endorsement of Epicurus here "is sheer hyperbole, meant to point up the extreme unfitness of the Platonic and Stoic stance," both because his praise is still quite muted and because Lucretius' and Cicero's views on lovesickness and the necessity and method of its treatment via Roman comedy overlap so well. For the sources on Epicurus' erotic opinions, see Graver (2002, 179).

even more forceful vituperation of *amor* than Cicero's. Indeed, it was Lucretius' vehement attack on erotic love that likely inspired his sole surviving *testimonium vitae*: Jerome reports that Lucretius, "driven to madness by a love potion, committed suicide at the age of forty-five, after he had written – between gaps of insanity – a number of books, which Cicero later published." The tale is clearly apocryphal, but while it is of little value as biography, it suggests how strong an impression *DRN*'s anti-erotic tirade left on its ancient audience.[48]

Like Cicero, Lucretius uses metaphors of illness to describe love in this passage of *DRN* 4. He begins by claiming that arousal occurs when "the body seeks that which has wounded the mind with love" (*idque petit corpus, mens unde est saucia amore*, 1048), and he compares the psychological effects of love to a physical wound (*vulnus*, 1049). His images become grotesque as he explains that early treatment is the only way a lover can save himself (1063–72):

> sed fugitare decet simulacra et pabula amoris
> absterrere sibi atque alio convertere mentem
> 1065 et iacere umorem collectum in corpora quaeque
> nec retinere, semel conversum unius amore,
> et servare sibi curam certumque dolorem.
> ulcus enim vivescit et inveterascit alendo
> inque dies gliscit furor atque aerumna gravescit,
> 1070 si non prima novis conturbes vulnera plagis
> vulgivagaque vagus Venere ante recentia cures
> aut alio possis animi traducere motus.

> But you should flee from mental images of your beloved and
> scare off what sustains your love, turning your mind elsewhere
> and casting off your built-up fluid into any body you can find
> rather than retaining it, once and for all turned by love for one person,
> and tending worry and guaranteed pain for yourself.
> For the festering wound flares up and becomes chronic when
> you nourish it, and each day madness flares up and the affliction
> gets worse, unless you disrupt your previous wounds with fresh lancing
> and care for them while fresh by promiscuously pursuing promiscuous love,
> or if you're able to transfer your mental disturbance somewhere else.

---

[48] Jerome *Chr.* s.v. 94 BCE: *postea, amatorio poculo in furorem versus, cum aliquot libros per intervalla insaniae conscripsisset, quos postea Cicero emendavit, propria se manu interfecit anno aetatis XLIIII.* Betensky (1980, 291), Fitzgerald (1984, 73), Brown (1987, 70–71), and Nussbaum (1994, 140–45) discuss how Lucr. 4 likely inspired the anecdote; see also Ziegler (1936) and Holford-Strevens (2002) on reasons to doubt the story's accuracy.

To Lucretius, love is a festering wound (*ulcus*) that flares up and becomes chronic (*vivescit et inveterascit*, 1068), triggering anguish both mental and physical (*furor ... aerumna*, 1069).[49] But the problem with love is not merely that it engenders pain. Lucretius implies that its real danger lies in its root cause: perfectly natural, healthy sexual desire becomes tangled up in ardor for a single person (*conversum unius amore*, 1066), which forces a man in love to hold onto his care (*servare sibi curam*, 1067). The lover's behavior represents the opposite of the Epicurean sage's primary goal, *ataraxia*, which is translated into Latin by Lucretius and other Roman authors as *securitas* (*se-*, "without" + *cura*, "care").[50] Rather than separating himself from care, the lover saves it up inside himself. Love, then, is fundamentally incompatible with what Epicureanism views as the basis for the good life, and those who want to be as carefree as the Epicurean sage must also banish love and the *cura* it provokes.

Luckily for those suffering from an onset of lovesickness, Epicureanism is a remarkably "practical" philosophy, for all Cicero's critiques of its detachment. "Empty," Epicurus remarks, "is the philosopher's word that does not heal a person's suffering. For just as medical treatment is pointless when it does not eradicate sickness from the body, so too is philosophy if it does not eradicate suffering from the soul." As Martha Nussbaum has argued persuasively, Epicureanism is essentially therapeutic, aiming to alleviate the pain of the human condition by curing people of misapprehensions, and the good Epicurean must help others escape from care.[51] Lucretius brings the same seriousness to his duty as a doctor as Cicero does, and their prescriptions also overlap to a remarkable extent. Like Cicero, Lucretius sees fear and disgust as the surest cure, using images of the bodily grotesque to help lovers shun and scare off deceptive mental visions that feed love (*fugitare decet ... et pabula amoris / absterrere*, 1063–64), and both emphasize that getting the lover to see his beloved as cheap and replaceable is a first step in their treatment.[52]

Unlike Cicero, however, whose goal is to promote abstinence from love, Lucretius urges promiscuity to treat erotic attachment, advising the afflicted lover to displace one amatory wound with another continually (*prima novis conturbes vulnera plagis*, 1070). Nevertheless, although he

---

[49] Fitzgerald (1984) and Brown (1987) discuss the medical significance of these terms, as well as for the distinction between *aerumna* and *furor*.

[50] See *OLD* s.v. *se-* and Sklenář (1999, 287) and Gellar-Goad (2018, 8).

[51] Epicurus fr. 221 Usener; see Nussbaum (1994, 102–91).

[52] See Graver (2002, 121–23 and 171–73) for vilification as an approach to consoling grief and treating love in Cicero; for this approach in Epicureanism, see Nussbaum (1994, 104–15).

suggests sexual activity is natural and necessary for a man to stay sane, Lucretius observes it does not represent a cure for lovesickness per se. Sex keeps a lover's wounds fresh and clean and his cares constant (*recentia cures*, 1071), at best allowing him to redirect his mental disturbances (*alio possis animi traducere motus*, 1072) so that he does not perish from the disease, but it never cures him of his illness. Shortly after this passage, he sketches the shortcomings of the orgasm as a treatment for lovesickness (4.1113–20):

> usque adeo cupide in Veneris compagibus haerent,
> membra voluptatis dum vi labefacta liquescunt.
> 1115   tandem ubi se erupit nervis collecta cupido,
> parva fit ardoris violenti pausa parumper.
> inde redit rabies eadem et furor ille revisit,
> cum sibi quid cupiant ipsi contingere quaerunt,
> nec reperire malum id possunt quae machina vincat:
> 1120   usque adeo incerti tabescunt vulnere caeco.

> In such utter desire they are caught in Venus' nets,
> while their limbs, loosened by pleasure's force, become jelly.
> At last when their desire, built up in their loins, bursts forth,
> there briefly occurs a small pause in their passion's violence.
> And then the same madness returns and that fury comes back,
> when they seek to attain what they crave for themselves,
> but they can't find the equipment to overcome that evil frenzy.
> In such utter uncertainty they waste away from their unseen wound.

Sexual release provides relief to the lover's burning sensation (*fit ardoris violenti pausa*), but it is brief and temporary (*parva ... parumper*, 1116). The mental symptoms return (*redit rabies eadem et furor ille revisit*, 1117) because love's unseen wound (*vulnere caeco*, 1120) remains untreated. Orgasms can do only so much. Lovers need more to obtain long-term health, and at the close of this passage Lucretius hints at the source of a more permanent treatment he has in mind. Notably, he describes the true means to cure love as *machina* (1119), a Latinization of μηχανή. As Sedley and others have shown, Lucretius does not employ Greek loan words willy-nilly, and never does he use *machina* to mean merely *modus*.[53] Indeed, 200 lines before this passage it occurs in a perfectly literal sense, as an example of how a crane turns small force into substantial power: "and

---

[53] Sedley (1999). The word *machina* appears only here, at 4.905–6, and at 5.96 (*machina mundi*), where Lucretius uses it as a metaphor for the physical workings of the universe. Brown (1987, 247) notes *machina*'s predominantly technical meaning in Latin, though he argues that it should be understood here as a "siege-engine."

through its pulleys and wheels, a crane moves and lifts up many things of great weight with a light effort" (*multaque per trocleas et tympana pondere magno / commovet atque levi sustollit machina nisu*, 4.905–6). Having seen Lucretius turn to theatrical metaphors and images again and again in *DRN* 4 – awnings over the theater (72–86), an actor's mask (292–301), dancers and musicians performing on stage (973–83) – a perceptive reader is primed to take *machina* here as the most famous type of crane in antiquity: the one by which actors were hoisted over the *scaena* in dramatic performances.[54] In this capacity it serves as yet another metapoetic marker that cues the reader to theatrical allusions in the coming lines, where he administers his treatment of love. To find the "equipment that overcomes this evil" (*malum ... quae machina vincat*, 1119), the lover must turn to where *machinae* are found – namely, the theater – and to the closest theatrical model for this illness, the *adulescens amator* of Roman comedy.

In the passage that immediately follows this one, Lucretius sketches a portrait of lovers in the worst light possible, and as Rosivach, Brown, and others have shown, his primary inspiration for this disgusting characterization is Roman comedy's "young man in love."[55] Remarkably, the poet uses the *adulescens* in much the same way as Cicero employs the mirror of comedy to show off the lover's flaws, making love's "unseen wound" (*vulnere caeco*, 1120) visible to his readers. Here he is following the same approach that he takes with other theatrical metaphors throughout *DRN* 4: the colors of the awnings reveal the invisible workings of atoms, the actor's mask shows the process by which transparent mirrors reflect images, and so forth. The *adulescens*, however, offers Lucretius something extra, namely, the means to entice resistant readers into an Epicurean understanding of love. The "young man in love" is familiar, entertaining, and, most importantly, a direct conduit into his Roman readers' everyday anxieties, which he highlights by outlining the high costs of the lover's lifestyle (4.1121–32):

> adde quod absumunt viris pereuntque labore,
> adde quod alterius sub nutu degitur aetas.
> languent officia atque aegrotat fama vacillans.                                1124
> labitur interea res et Babylonia fiunt                                           1123
> unguenta et pulchra in pedibus Sicyonia rident,                                  1125

---

[54] On *machina*, see Mastronarde (1990). The *machina* is associated with tragedy, but Greek comedy mentions it occasionally (e.g., Ar. *Nu.*, Men. *Theophoroumene* fr. 227 K). Christenson (2000, 315) makes a persuasive argument for its deployment in Pl. *Ps.* 1131–43.

[55] Rosivach (1980) and Brown (1987, 135–36 and 248–307); see also, e.g., Kenney (1970, 384–87), Gale (2007), and Taylor (2016, 141–43).

scilicet et grandes viridi cum luce zmaragdi
auro includuntur teriturque thalassina vestis
adsidue et Veneris sudorem exercita potat.
et bene parta patrum fiunt anademata, mitrae,
1130   interdum in pallam atque Alidensia Ciaque vertunt.
eximia veste et victu convivia, ludi,
pocula crebra, unguenta, coronae, serta parantur . . .

Add the fact they use up their strength and succumb to the effort,
add the fact their prime of life is spent at another's beck and call,
their obligations decline and their lurching reputation falls ill.
Meanwhile their estate dissipates and turns into Babylonian
perfume, and beautiful shoes from Sicyon twinkle on her feet,
and emeralds – huge ones, of course – with their green luster
are set in gold, and sea-dark clothing is worn out with constant
fondling and, worked over, it soaks up the moisture of Venus.
And their fathers' hard-won earnings become tiaras, headbands,
now and then they turn into cloaks of Alidensian wool and Cian silk.
They put together banquets with choice linens and victuals, games,
plentiful cups, perfumes, wreaths, garlands . . .

Clothing and gold – *vestis/palla et aurum* – are the traditional gifts that
*adulescentes* give to their *puellae* in Roman comedy, and the way they pay
for these is invariably by spending their fathers' hard-won fortunes (*bene
parta partum*, 1129), as Rosivach documents. Indeed, Hanses further
shows that Lucretius' *palla* here acts as a metapoetic marker of the *fabula
palliata*, much as I suggest the *machina* does above.[56] And like comic
lovers, Lucretius' dissolute youths waste time and money on partying,
gambling, drinking, perfume, crowns, and garlands (*convivia, ludi, / pocula
crebra, unguenta, coronae, serta*, 1131–32).[57] Indeed, the whole passage is
shot through with the most stereotypical tropes and attributes of the
generic *adulescens amator* from Roman comedy, and Lucretius' heavy
and atypical heaping of Latinized Greek vocabulary transports his reader
to the *fabula palliata*'s semi-Greek, semi-Roman setting.[58]
   Significantly, Lucretius' focus here is not the mental disturbance that
looms so large over his initial discussions of love's dangers (e.g., *furor*,

---

[56] Hanses (2015, 96–97).
[57] Rosivach (1980). Cf. Pl. *Cist.* 487 (*instruxi illi aurum atque vestem*); *Men.* 739 (*pallam atque aurum*);
   *MG* 1099 (*aurum atque vestem muliebrem*); *Truc.* 52 (*aurum . . . pallula*).
[58] Rosivach (1980); see also Brown (1987, 135–36 and 248–64) for further parallels to Roman
   comedy. Bailey (1947, 138–39) notes Lucretius' erotic section is "the most remarkable passage in
   the poem in its use of Greek words," documenting more than twenty usages, including sixteen in
   the short space of 4.1160–69; cf. Sedley (1999, 238–41), who argues that the Greek highlights
   foreign luxury and exotic locales, to which the settings of Roman comedy belong.

1069; *animi ... motus,* 1072; *rabies eadem et furor,* 1117), nor the bodily harm that the lover endures (e.g., *aerumna,* 1069; *membra labefacta,* 1114). Lucretius here is concerned with love's social costs and the negative effect the *adulescens amator* has on society and those around him. When the lover squanders his vigor and prime of life (*viris ... aetas,* 1121–22), what suffers is his *officia* ("obligations," 1123), *fama* ("reputation," 1124), and *res* ("estate," 1123) – that is, what he owes to others, what others think of him, and what others in his family worked to create and preserve for their heirs (*bene parta partum,* 1129). And after all, "to a Roman anything destructive of *res, officia,* and *fama* must have seemed dangerous indeed."[59] Lucretius thus uses the stereotypical *adulescens* to call attention to the dangers lovesickness poses to Roman society and its traditional values rather than to the lover himself. Like Cicero in the *Tusculan Disputations,* Lucretius ignores the subjective experiences of the *amator* and takes the stance of a conservative critic looking on with disgust.

But Lucretius' concern for these traditional Roman ideals of *officia, fama,* and *res* strikes a discordant tone within the *DRN,* because none of these would represent a particularly important loss to a proper Epicurean. Quite the opposite, in fact: "The essence of Epicurus' position is well known, and easily summed up: do not take part in politics, live unknown."[60] Reputation is never something Lucretius or his Epicurean predecessors were eager to preserve, and Myrto Garani has shown cogently that Lucretius rejects *fama* as a viable source of happiness, contrasting its empty external validation with true internal contentment: "they [sc. ambitious politicians] learn wisdom from others' lips and seek truth from what they hear rather than their own senses" (*sapiunt alieno ex ore petuntque / res ex auditis potius quam sensibus ipsis,* 5.1133–34).[61] Likewise with *officia,* which Konstan argues was virtually anathema to Lucretius and the Epicureans: "Lucretius rarely uses the word *officium ...* only five times does the word occur in *De rerum natura,* and in three of these it just means 'natural function.' In fact, Cicero attacked Epicureanism on just this point and because it afforded no *officii praecepta,* denied it was a philosophy at all."[62] Last, concern for wealth was right out when it came to Epicurean happiness: Epicurus rejected the pursuit of money, and while Philodemus and the Roman Epicureans seem to have moderated their views on

---

[59] Frank (1968, 235).     [60] Fowler (2007, 400).
[61] Garani (2016), who also outlines evidence for Epicurean attitudes toward reputation.
[62] Konstan (1972, 3), who also notes that Lucretius' use of *officium* at 4.1124 represents the only instance in *DRN* where the word carries its common sense of everyday obligations to others. For Cicero's criticism of Epicureanism's lack of *officii praecepta,* see *Off.* 1.2.5–6.

economics for their aristocratic audience, Lucretius asserts that the invention of *res* represented the first violation of nature and the beginning of society's degradation, a kind of fall from grace: "later wealth was introduced and gold discovered, which easily stripped both the strong and the beautiful of their honor" (*posterius res inventast aurumque repertum, / quod facile et validis et pulchris dempsit honorem*, 5.1113–14).[63] To an Epicurean, the lover might represent a sort of unknowing savant, a person who, unaware of what he was doing, nevertheless managed to shed the societal concerns that stood in the way of *ataraxia* – if only he weren't afflicted with love's inherent mental disturbance.

For a Roman youth still uninitiated into Epicureanism, though, all three concerns would have been familiar anxieties that their *patres* had cultivated in them throughout their whole lives, and therefore pre-tied to emotional strings taut for the plucking. By showing off how the familiar *adulescens amator* of Roman comedy threatened these entrenched values, Lucretius deploys the harm that this exemplary stock character represents to the *mos maiorum* to deter his readers from acting in the same way. This approach largely parallels Cicero's own use of the *adulescens* as a deterrent in the *Tusculan Disputations*, but it also constitutes only part of what Lucretius aims to achieve. What remains is the inner turmoil, which Cicero's approach does not address but whose removal is crucial for achieving *ataraxia*. At the end of this passage he changes tack, moving away from the effects that love has on others to different types of internal *cura* that disturb the lover's mind (4.1133–44):

> nequiquam, quoniam medio de fonte leporum
> surgit amari aliquid, quod in ipsis floribus angat,
> 1135 aut cum conscius ipse animus se forte remordet
> desidiose agere aetatem lustrisque perire,
> aut quod in ambiguo verbum iaculata reliquit,
> quod cupido adfixum cordi vivescit ut ignis,
> aut nimium iactare oculos aliumve tueri
> 1140 quod putat in vultuque videt vestigia risus.
> atque in amore mala haec proprio summeque secondo
> inveniuntur: in adverso vero atque inopi sunt,
> prendere quae possis oculorum lumine operto,
> innumerabilia . . .

> . . . but it's all for nothing, since there gushes from the midst of this
> fountain of delights a bitter liquid that chokes them among the flowers:

---

[63] See Asmis (2004) and Schiesaro (2007) on Epicureanism's negative attitude toward money.

either a guilty conscience gnaws at him, when he happens to realize
that he's living his life in sloth and wasting away in dens of iniquity,
or else his beloved has shot out a word that she's left ambiguous
and it sticks in his passionate heart and proliferates like a fire,
or she shoots too many glances and gazes too much at another man,
and he sees what he thinks is the trace of a smile on her face.
And these evils are found in a love that is stable and perfectly
fortunate; but in love that's hostile and helpless, there are
countless evils you can catch even with your eyes shut!

The comic *adulescens* continues to stand in the background of Lucretius'
character sketch of the lover, though he subtly moves from the generic
stock character to a more specific allusive target, as Brown observes: "the
closest equivalent in comedy to Lucretius' psychological interpretation of
erotic misery is the opening scene of Terence's *Eunuch*, in which Phaedria
bemoans the fickle behavior of the *meretrix* Thais and is counseled by the
slave Parmeno" and where the playwright draws attention to love's "intrin-
sic irrationality and planlessness." Lucretius' lover "exhibits a similar
mixture of desire, anger, irresolution, and self-reproach" to what
Phaedria displays and Parmeno rebukes in his master.[64] This affinity was
noted even in antiquity: Horace's adaptation of the same Terentian scene
in *Satires* 2.3.246–80 also alludes repeatedly to this passage of *DRN*, while
Persius combines all three in his send-up of the lover at *Satires* 5.161–74.[65]
The dialogue between the *adulescens* Phaedria and his *servus* Parmeno in
the opening of *Eunuchus* is mirrored by Lucretius' description of the lover's
internal struggles (46–63):

PHAED: quid igitur faciam? non eam ne nunc quidem
cum accersor ultro? an potius ita me comparem
non perpeti meretricum contumelias?
exclusit, revocat: redeam? non si me obsecret.
siquidem hercle possis, nil prius neque fortius.                    50
verum si incipies neque pertendes gnaviter
atque ubi pati non poteris, cum nemo expetet,

[64] Brown (1987, 136). Saylor (1975) argues that planlessness as a quasi-philosophical theme is unique among Roman comedy to Terence's *Eunuchus* and notes the relationship between this passage and Lucretius.
[65] On Horace, Brown (1987, 136); on Horace and Persius, Lowe (1983), who notes a scholiast claims that "Persius took this passage over from Menander's *Eunuchus*" (*hunc locum de Menandri Eunucho traxit*). While not an ancient reader, Machiavelli also considered Lucretius and the *Eunuchus* a pair. MS Ross. Lat. 884 (XI.37), copied by Machiavelli ca. 1497, contains only the text of Lucretius and Terence's *Eunuchus* alone; see Finch (1960) and Palmer (2014, 87), who says Machiavelli saw *Eunuchus* as a "remarkable companion for Lucretius" as both challenged "Petrarch's concept of a virtuous antiquity."

infecta pace ultro ad eam venies, indicans
te amare et ferre non posse, actumst, ilicet,
55 peristi; eludet ubi te victum senserit.
proin tu, dumst tempus, etiam atque etiam cogita.
PARM: ere, quae res in se neque consilium neque modum
habet ullum, eam consilio regere non potes.
in amore haec omnia insunt vitia: iniuriae,
60 suspiciones, inimicitiae, indutiae,
bellum, pax rursum. incerta haec si tu postules
ratione certa facere, nihilo plus agas
quam si des operam ut cum ratione insanias.

PHAED: "Well, what should I do? Should I not go,
not even now, when she summons me herself? Or should I
get ahold of myself and not put up with prostitutes' insults?
She shut me out, she calls me back. Should I go? Not even if she begs!
Oh, Hercules, if only you could, nothing would be better or braver.
But if you start and don't carry it through to the end
and, when you can't put up with it, when no one asks for you,
you go to her on your own without making peace first, showing
that you love her and can't endure – then it's all over, it's finished,
you're dead. She'll toy with you when she realizes you're beaten.
So while you've got time, you better think again and again."
PARM: "Master, you can't use planning to rule
what doesn't have any planning or moderation to it.
All these vices are inherent to love: outrages,
suspicions, enmities, reconciliations,
war, back to peace. If you propose to make what's uncertain
certain by means of reason, you'll accomplish nothing more
than if you worked to be mad with reason."

Lucretius and Parmeno list the dangers that hide in love (*atque in amore mala haec*, Lucr. 1141; *in amore haec omnia insunt vitia, Eun.* 59), focusing particularly on suspicion, passion, and loss of restraint and logic. The poet similarly airs the same sorts of jealousy and indecision that Phaedria voices in his opening lament. By allusively drawing on both sides of the dialogue, the lover and the critic, Lucretius makes visible to his audience the internal struggle and self-recrimination that lay invisibly beneath the surface of his torment.

Lucretius' initial focus on the external concerns of *officia, fama,* and *res* is designed to elicit horror at the lover's behavior and its effects on those around him. Once he has caught the interest of his reader and demonstrated that his actions are detrimental, he then shifts attention to the negative effects of love on the lover's mental state. Remarkably, though,

Lucretius is not that interested in diagnosing the precise cause of the lover's disturbance. The tricolon list of possible sources for his anxiety (*aut cum ... aut quod ... aut nimium*, 1135–40) diminishes the importance of identifying the origin of his *cura*, as does Lucretius' appropriation of Parmeno's generalizing quips about all the sorts of *vitia* produced by love, which downplay Phaedria as no more special than any other generic victim of lovesickness. Indeed, Parmeno's flippant responses throughout this passage are world-weary, and one of his final pieces of advice is just to get through the whole experience as quickly as possible (74–78):

PARM: quid agas? nisi ut te redimas captum quam queas
minumo; si nequeas paullulo, at quanti queas.
et ne te afflictes. PHAED: itane suades? PARM: si sapis,
neque praeterquam quas ipse amor molestias
habet addas, et illas quas habet recte feras.

PARM: "What should you do? Why, nothing but ransom yourself
for as little as you can; if you can't for a bit, pay whatever you have to.
And don't worry yourself." PHAED: "That's your advice?"
PARM: "If you're smart. And don't add troubles besides what
love already has in store, and properly put up with what it has got.

As Hankinson demonstrates, the therapeutics of Epicureanism, which famously promoted multiple explanations as the best way to understand phenomena, are not concerned to identify precisely the mechanisms by which human suffering is enacted. What matters for the Epicurean trying to cure a person's lovesickness is merely achieving the ultimate therapeutic effect of removing the lover's irrational *cura* by whatever means.[66] Neither Parmeno nor Lucretius cares about the particulars of their deluded lover's situation: in the end, both merely want to help the lover obtain happiness – the comic *servus* by helping him come together with his *meretrix*, the philosopher by producing the deterrent emotions that can overcome *cura amoris*.

At the close of his anti-erotic tirade, Lucretius outlines this goal more explicitly, revealing that once Roman comedy's *adulescens* has served his purpose as an easy-to-grasp and forceful exemplum of why love inhibits *ataraxia*, the final cure lay in peeking behind the curtain to see the ugly truth behind the comic lover's obsession (4.1177–89):

[66] Hankinson (2013); on Epicurean epistemology and the cultivation of multiple explanations, see also Allen (2001, 194–241).

at lacrimans exclusus amator limina saepe
floribus et sertis operit postisque superbos
unguit amaracino et foribus miser oscula figit;
1180   quem si, iam admissum, venientem offenderit aura
una modo, causas abeundi quaerat honestas,
et meditata diu cadat alte sumpta querella,
stultitiaque ibi se damnet, tribuisse quod illi
plus videat quam mortali concedere par est.
1185   nec Veneres nostras hoc fallit; quo magis ipsae
omnia summo opere hos vitae poscaenia celant
quos retinere volunt adstrictosque esse in amore,
nequiquam, quoniam tu animo tamen omnia possis
protrahere in lucem atque omnis inquirere risus ...

But weeping, the lover shut out by his beloved often
darkens her doorstep with flowers and garlands and
smears her disdainful doorposts with marjoram-scented
perfume and wretchedly plants kisses on her door;
but if he's been received and let in and just a single
unpleasant whiff strikes his nose, he hunts for polite
excuses to leave, and his lamentations, long rehearsed and
deeply felt, would stop short, and right then and there he'd
scold himself for his stupidity, when he sees he's attributed to her
more than is right to grant a mortal woman.
Our Venuses know this well, so they work even harder to
hide what goes on behind the scenes of their lives from
the men they want to hold onto bound up in love –
but in vain, since you can still use your mind to drag all this
out into the light and seek the cause of all their laughter ...

In this famous satirical sketch of the *exclusus amator* ("shut-out lover"), Lucretius again draws on the stock character of the comic *adulescens*.[67] His approach becomes more complex than the basic use of the figure as a negative *exemplum*, however, as he turns from theater to metatheater. Lucretius says that the lover will be cured of his infatuation if his senses can perceive just how disgusting his falsely divinized beloved really is. In order to do this, he has to learn "everything behind the scenes of their lives that women conceal from men" (*omnia summo opere hos vitae poscaenia celant*, 1186). Lucretius' *postscaenia* calls attention to the fact that the beloveds are putting on their own little performance, mortals playing the role of Venus

---

[67] On the *exclusus amator* and *paraclausithyra* (speeches outside the closed door) in Roman comedy, see Copley (1956, 28–42), McKeown (1979, 82), and Brown (1987, 135 and 297–303), who remarks that "the scene featuring the *exclusus amator* has the character of a small drama."

in this theatricalized reality. What is more, the women are producing a comedy at which they themselves are players and spectators alike, filling the scene with an abundance of laughter (*omnis . . . risus*, 1189) that recalls their knowing giggles (*vestigia risus*, 1140) at the lover's earlier bewilderment. It is also significant that Lucretius' prescription extends beyond merely recognizing that there are hidden *postscaenia* and *risus*: deception of the lover is bad, but he already fully knows that the woman is misleading him, since he has perceived her ambiguous words and telling smiles (1137–40), none of which has diminished his lovesickness.[68] As Lucretius notes at the start of his discussion, if he is to cure the lover's illness, he needs something that can put to flight and scare away positive mental *simulacra* of his beloved (*fugitare decet . . . et pabula amoris / absterrere*, 1063–64), and what is more powerful than the repulsive innuendo in the *aura* of her *postscaenia*, which he calls "revolting scents" (*taetris . . . odoribus*, 1175)? What precisely he smells is unclear, and scholars have proposed a range of possibilities from vaginal fumigants and perfumes to the "naturally" foul odor Greeks and Romans associated with female genitalia. I think, however, that the ambiguity is part of the point, and Lucretius intends his reader to wrack his brain for the most grotesque bodily activity he can imagine that will activate his disgust.[69]

As soon as he catches a whiff of what goes on behind the theatrical curtain, the lover will cease to act like an *adulescens amator*, quite literally. All the complaints of the *exclusus amator* that he has "long rehearsed" (*meditata diu*, 1182) end abruptly. Lucretius' choice of participle is not accidental: *meditari* also occurs in Roman comedy to denote rehearsals of their performances by metatheatrically aware characters. The *servus* Sosia in Plautus' *Amphitruo*, for instance, says, "But I want to practice by myself first in what way and with what words I should put on my act" (*sed quo modo et verbis quibus me deceat fabularier, / prius ipse mecum etiam volo hic meditari*, 201–2), before he runs into his mistress so that he can put on his own little *fabula intra fabulam palliatam*. Perceiving his beloved's *postscaenia* is too much for the lover: if Lucretius can shatter his theatrical illusions

---

[68] Taylor (2016) argues that Lucretius uses this scene to get his readers to respond to love with Epicurean rationalism by rejecting the beloved for "being denied access to good evidence about her true nature"; I agree that this is a component of the passage, and that the theater represents to Lucretius generally an important touchstone for considering ethics and epistemology, but I think that disgust is the dominant factor in his treatment of lovesickness through Roman comedy.

[69] See Brown (1987, 296–97 and 2017) and bibliography there for these and other possibilities, including flatulence, defecation, and menstruation, as well as Nugent (1994), Nussbaum (1994, 179–81), Bradley (2015), and Butler (2015). For ancient associations of female genitalia with foul odors, see Richlin (1984).

about the woman, he will no longer want to play the part of the *adulescens* and will give up his *cura*.

For Lucretius, then, the *adulescens amator* offers a concrete exemplum that shows off the costs of being in love, in terms of both external social effects and internal psychological effects. Seeing this character and his little dramatic vignette paraded before his eyes, the reader gains a measure of metatheatrical awareness about his situation, and no longer will he be forced by his ignorance to perform as the comic stock type or be duped by a woman's deceptions into seeing love as anything other than an empty performance. When this tirade begins, the lover can laugh at the *adulescens amator* as a hopeless wretch, just as Lucretius says that "some men mock others and prod them to propitiate their Venus, since they are afflicted by foul love – but those poor fools don't look back at their own, often exceptional miseries" (*atque alios alii irrident Veneremque suadent | ut placent, quoniam foedo adflictentur amore, | nec sua respiciunt miseri mala maxima saepe*, 1157–59). But Lucretius soon shows him that he has been performing the same way, and what is more, that acting as a stock character is detrimental to *ataraxia*. Given this distance, the former lover now grasps the utility of looking at comedy from the outside rather than playing it inside the drama. In fact, once his former role-playing is revealed, Lucretius stresses the value to the lover of keeping his memory of the comic *adulescens amator* fresh: the beloved's theatrical deceptions "are in vain, since you can still use your mind to drag all this into the light and seek the cause of their laughter" (*nequiquam, quoniam tu animo tamen omnia possis | protrahere in lucem atque omnis inquirere risus*, 1188–89). And it is no coincidence that Lucretius chose the theater to equip the former lover in this fashion. Soon before he begins denouncing love, while illustrating how memory works, he uses a theatrical example to show that sensations recur long after we experience them, explaining that images from *ludi* "can return, and for many days these same things appear before our eyes, and even while awake they seem to see them" (*possint . . . simulacra venire. | per multos itaque illa dies eadem obversantur | ante oculos, etiam vigilantes ut videantur | cernere*, 977–80). So too will the ridiculous, terrifying, and disgusting images that Lucretius draws from Roman comedy return to deter the ex-lover from falling for these theatrical deceptions again.

Unlike Cicero, who uses the mirror of comedy to reveal truths, Lucretius uses comedy as a tool to dispel lies, to pull his reader through the looking glass so he can observe the play of life and reject it in favor of reality. In this way, pulling away the curtain of comedy and seeing life's *postscaenia* parallels what Lucretius in his opening proem says Epicurus himself did, namely, "to break first the tightly closed doors of nature" and so let "the lively power of his mind prevail" by rejecting false beliefs (*effringere ut arta / naturae primus portarum claustra cupiret. / ergo vivida vis animi pervicit*, 1.70–72). But not everyone is Epicurus, and his doctrine is hard to swallow for anyone unused to it. Lucretius therefore explains in the proem to *DRN* 4 how to achieve this feat, subtly laying the foundation for his approach to love and the *adulescens amator* a thousand lines later. He begins by describing his own state of being as Epicurean poet (4.1–9):

> avia Pieridum peragro loca nullius ante
> trita solo. iuvat integros accedere fontis
> atque haurire, iuvatque novos decerpere flores
> insignemque meo capiti petere inde coronam
> unde prius nulli velarint tempora Musae;
> primum quod magnis doceo de rebus et artis
> religionum animum nodis exsolvere pergo,
> deinde quod obscura de re tam lucida pango
> carmina, musaeo contingens cuncta lepore.
> id quoque enim non ab nulla ratione videtur.

> I wander the pathless places of Pieria never before
> trod by another's foot. I enjoy approaching pure springs
> and gulping them down, and I enjoy plucking fresh flowers,
> making from them – from which the Muses have covered
> no other's temples before – an illustrious crown for my head.
> First, because I teach about great things and proceed to free
> the mind from the close-tied knots of superstition;
> next, because I lay out in the open shadowy material in
> shining songs, touching everything with the Muses' charm.
> For this too seems not to be without reason.

Significantly, Lucretius' description of himself in the proem to *DRN* 4 shares multiple points of contact with his description of the deluded lover later in the same book: both are surrounded by springs (*fontis*, 2; *fonte*, 1133) and flowers (*flores*, 3; *floribus*, 1134) and wear crowns (*coronam*, 4; *coronae*, 1132). But Lucretius' springs are pure (*integros*, 2) while the lover's gush forth bitter liquid (*surgit amari aliquid*, 1134), and the poet delights in gulping down water and plucking the flowers (*iuvat ... haurire, iuvatque ... decerpere*, 2–3) while the lover chokes on his poison among the plants (*in ipsis floribus angat*, 1134). Lucretius' crown is "distinguished" (*insignem*, 4), while the lover's is "all for nothing" (*nequiquam*, 1133). These are effectively before-and-after shots of Epicurean indoctrination, a picture of someone afflicted with *amor* and *cura* and of another who enjoys complete *ataraxia* and has the power to share it with others through *ratio*. He proceeds by identifying himself explicitly as a doctor and his teachings as medicine (4.11–25):

> nam veluti pueris absinthia taetra medentes
> cum dare conantur, prius oras pocula circum
> contingunt mellis dulci flavoque liquore,
> ut puerorum aetas improvida ludificetur
> labrorum tenus, interea perpotet amarum
> absinthi laticem deceptaque non capiatur,
> sed potius tali pacto recreata valescat,
> sic ego nunc, quoniam haec ratio plerumque videtur
> tristior esse quibus non est tractata, retroque
> vulgus abhorret ab hac, volui tibi suaviloquenti
> carmine Pierio rationem exponere nostram
> et quasi musaeo dulci contingere melle,
> si tibi forte animum tali ratione tenere
> versibus in nostris possem, dum percipis omnem
> naturam rerum ac persentis utilitatem.

> For just like when doctors try to give foul-tasting
> wormwood to little boys, first they apply sweet and
> golden syrup of honey around the rims of the cup,
> so that the boys in their naive youth are tricked
> as far as the lips; before they know it, they drink
> down the bitter juice of wormwood, and they are deceived
> but not betrayed, as they grow strong and are cured this way –
> so now do I act. Since this doctrine seems quite unpleasant to
> those who have not yet experienced it, and common people
> shrink back from it, I want to lay out my doctrine to you
> with the smooth-speaking song of Pieria and
> to apply to you the Muses' sweet honey, as it were,
> to see if I can happen to keep your mind by this method
> on my verses, while you take in fully the whole nature
> of things and absolutely perceive its usefulness.

This prologue, I believe, represents a road map for everything that Lucretius does in prescribing treatment for lovesickness. Knowledge that love is delusional and therefore a hindrance, rather than a path, to peace and happiness is Lucretius' wormwood draught. The *adulescens amator* is the honey: familiar, palatable, even pleasant to recall from the times his readers would have seen his antics on stage or read them on the page. The patient resistant to being cured may need to be tricked (*ludificetur*, 4.14) indirectly with such enticing characters from the *ludi scaenici*, but the deception is well intentioned. When the medicine hits, his eyes are cleared, he sees the beloved's *postscaenia*, and he realizes that he has been living his life inside a Roman comedy. It may be unpleasant, even disgusting, but the treatment of the *fabula palliata* runs its course and cures the lover of his *cura*.

## The *Adulescens Amator* as Restorative Therapy: Catullus' *Eunuchus* (Poems 5, 7, 6, 8, 51, 85, 75, 72, and 109)

Ever the iconoclast, Catullus did not think highly of Cicero's and Lucretius' approaches to erotic criticism, and in poem 5 he flatly rejects Rome's conservative *maiores* and the censure of their contemporary torchbearers:

> vivamus, mea Lesbia, atque amemus,
> rumoresque senum severiorum
> omnes unius aestimemus assis!
> soles occidere et redire possunt;
> nobis, cum semel occidit brevis lux,                                    5
> nox est perpetua una dormienda.
> da mi basia mille, deinde centum,
> dein mille altera, dein secunda centum,
> deinde usque altera mille, deinde centum;
> dein, cum milia multa fecerimus,                                       10
> conturbabimus, illa ne sciamus,
> aut ne quis malus invidere possit
> cum tantum sciat esse basiorum.

> Let us live, my Lesbia, and let us love
> and assess all the grumblings of grave
> old men as worth a single penny!
> Suns can set and rise, but for us,
> when our brief light has set one time,
> we must sleep for an unending night.
> Give me a thousand kisses, then an hundred,
> then another thousand, then a second hundred,
> then yet another thousand, and an hundred,
> then, when we've counted up many thousands,
> let's jumble our accounts so that we don't know,
> or so that no malevolent person can cast their evil eye
> on us when he knows the sum total of our kisses.

A young man in love dismisses the patronizing rebukes of harsh old men to pursue time with a beloved: this is the essential plot of Roman comedy, with a cast of character stock types pulled straight from the stage. Charles Segal and Matthew Dickie have suggested that Catullus' *senes severiores* are drawn from the stereotypical *senex durus*, comedy's "stern older man, censorious of youthful follies."[70] Indeed, the two main cares of the comic *senex* feature prominently in poem 5, namely, *fama* and *res*, "reputation" and "wealth," and are handled flippantly by Catullus as the *adulescens amator*.[71] Maynes notes that Roman comedies "are premised upon the idea that young men cannot be trusted with the family's reputation without sober, paternal supervision. While out of sight of their fathers, the young men … fall in love with inappropriate partners and … threaten the family's financial welfare."[72] By not only dismissing the *rumoresque senum severiorum* (2), but also taking steps to escape their watchful eye (*invidere*, 12 – properly "to cast the evil eye," but also *in* + *videre*, "to look upon"), Catullus declares the concerns of the *senes* for his *fama* worthless and aligns himself with Roman comedy's *adulescentes amatores*, who spend their entire plays concealing their indecorous erotic affairs from their elders.[73]

What is more, the terminology he uses to dismiss their care for reputation wryly satirizes the related care for wealth: Catullus "assesses as worth a single penny" (*unius aestimemus assis*, 3) the old men's grumblings, appropriating the vocabulary of financial accounting here to mock the *senes*' focus on the sphere of public business and repute. He carries on with this language of bookkeeping when he counts up his kisses, as if on an abacus, which he then shakes abruptly to throw onlookers off the trail of his erotic accounts.[74] As Fordyce points out, *conturbare* (11) "is a technical term for fraudulent bankruptcy with concealment of assets," an act unthinkable for the upright *senes duri* of Roman comedy but utterly normal for the *adulescentes amatores*, for whom driving their family into virtual bankruptcy was merely the cost of doing erotic business. By applying financial vocabulary to his otiose kisses, Catullus exchanges the traditional Roman form of valuation – that is, in monetary or social terms – with a new one based on amatory pleasure, substituting the priorities of comic *adulescentes*

---

[70] Dickie (1993, 21); see also Ramminger (1937, 29–34), Segal (1968, 289), Fredericksmeyer (1970, 437–43), Syndikus (1986, 143–44), Nappa (2001, 54–57), and Hanses (2015, 122–23).

[71] Rosivach (1986, 181) remarks that "in comedy concern for reputation is usually joined with and subordinate to a concern for money," attributing these anxieties to *senes*' inability to control *adulescentes*, who endanger both.

[72] Maynes (2016, 307) touches on several issues in Catull. 67 related to my reading of poem 5.

[73] See Kroll (1959, 12) and Segal (1968, 289) on the implications of sight in *invidere*.

[74] For financial metaphors and abacus, see Levy (1941), Pratt (1956), Grimm (1963), along with notes on the accounting significance of *aestimemus assis* (3), *fecerimus* (10), and *conturbabimus* (11) by Fordyce (1961, 106–8) and Thomson (1998, 219–21). On accounting in Catullus, see Syndikus (1984, 96 n. 19) and Leigh (2013, 81–82), as well as Wiseman (1985, 101–7) for a different interpretation of Catullus' valuation of personal relationships. Cairns (1973) notes Pl. *Truc.* 373 features kiss-counting but attributes it to Greek New Comedy rather than Roman.

*amatores* for those of the genre's *senes duri*. This mirrors Catullus' transvaluation of the napkins of poem 12 and other ostensibly frivolous objects I examined in the Introduction, which calls attention to their typical value "at the same time as it rejects this form of valuation."[75] Indeed, I think it is not coincidental that poems 5 and 12 are the only places in which the words *aestimatio* (12.12) or *aestimare* (5.3) appear in his corpus and that both prioritize idiosyncratic, personalized worth over what society thinks ought to be the measure of worth. What matters for Catullus is not what value can be assigned by the public at large, but only the value derived from the intimate relationships between him and his peers. By contrasting himself with the old grouches and adopting the utter lack of fiscal interest displayed by the spendthrift comic lover, he sets up a contrast with those moralizers who try to stop the *adulescens amator* or, as Cicero and Lucretius, try to use the stock character to stop others.[76] For Catullus, comic love in poem 5 represents a preferred state of alternative values and valuation rather than a transient state to be escaped.

Two poems later, Catullus returns to the same theme of uncountable kisses, reinforcing its comic affiliation by alluding, as William Batstone argues, to "the secret nocturnal affairs of comic drama" (7.7–12):[77]

> aut quam sidera multa, cum tacet nox,
> furtivos hominum vident amores;
> tam te basia multa basiare
> vesano satis et super Catullo est,
> quae nec pernumerare curiosi
> possint nec mala fascinare lingua.

> As many as the stars that look on people's
> stolen loves when the night grows quiet:
> that's how many kisses are enough and more
> for mad Catullus to kiss you with –
> so many that the busybodies can't count
> or bewitch them with their evil tongues.

---

[75] Young (2015, 61).

[76] On elegiac praise of *paupertas* and comedy's promotion of the prodigality of the *adulescens amator*, see Rosivach (1986).

[77] Batstone (2007, 246). Rosivach (2012, 36) discusses links between nighttime and sexual license in Roman comedy, citing Pl. *Bac.* 87–88 ("For a young man, nothing can be more seductive than this: night, a woman, and wine," *istoc illecebrosius / fieri nil potest, nox, mulier, vinum, homini adulescentulo*) and Cic. *Leg.* 2.36 ("But comic poets give evidence as to what I don't like about nighttime rituals," *quid autem mihi displiceat in nocturnis, poetae indicant comici*).

Again he rejects not only their complaints, but even their basic approach to valuation: no more counting dollars, Catullus and Lesbia will be counting stars. Still, although Catullus dismisses the *senes* and *curiosi*, they loom large in the background of Roman social noise, and his keen awareness that he is being watched (*invidere*, 5.12; *vident*, 7.8) and that scolds and busybodies could turn his kisses against him reveals anxieties that he may have to deal with consequences of his erotic affairs if he is not careful to conceal from the *senes* what he has been up to.

This equation of *malitia*, *invidia*, and *curiositas* is not original to Catullus, and as Leigh and Schlam point out, it finds its earliest appearance in Latin literature in Roman comedy.[78] The parasite Gelasimus from Plautus' *Stichus* complains about the malevolence of *curiosi* (198–200):

> sed curiosi sunt hic complures mali,
> alienas res qui curant studio maxumo,
> quibus ipsis nulla est res quam procurent sua.

> But there are a whole lot of bad busybodies here,
> who meddle in other people's business with the greatest zeal
> and don't have anything of their own to meddle with.

Soon after he makes a sweeping statement that "no one's a busybody who isn't also malevolent" (*nam curiosus nemo est quin sit malevolus*, 208). This same apprehension about being observed by others dogs the comic *adulescens* as well, and soon after Chaerea, one of the "young lovers" of Terence's *Eunuchus*, rapes the *puella* Pamphila, he comes on stage and expresses worry – not at his own deeds, but at the possibility that *curiosi* might be watching him (549–56):

> numquis hic est? nemost. numquis hinc me sequitur? nemo homost.
> iamne erumpere hoc licet mi gaudium? pro Iuppiter,
> nunc est profecto interfici quom perpeti me possum,
> ne hoc gaudium contaminet vita aegritudine aliqua.
> sed neminemne curiosum intervenire nunc mihi,
> qui me sequatur quoquo eam, rogitando obtundat, enicet
> quid gestiam aut quid laetus sim, quo pergam, unde emergam, ubi siem
> vestitum hunc nanctus, quid mi quaeram, sanus sim anne insaniam!

> Is anyone here? No one's around. Is anyone following me from here? Not a soul. Now may this joy of mine burst forth? By Jupiter,

---

[78] See Schlam (1968, 121) and Leigh (2013, 61–63), the latter of whom notes that anxieties over *curiositas* appear as early as Livius Andronicus, whom Festus (384L) says coined *sollicuria* to mean "curious in every matter" (*in omni curiosa*); Barton (1993, 88) briefly compares Catullus 7 with the passage at Pl. *St.* 198–208.

now truly is when I can endure being killed,
before life ruins my joy with some sickness.
But no busybody now gets in my way, following me
wherever I go, pounding me with questions, torturing me to death by asking
what I'm up to or why I'm happy, where I'm off to, where I'm coming from,
where'd I get this clothing, what I'm looking for, whether I'm healthy or insane!

Significantly, Chaerea uses disease imagery throughout this passage, preferring sudden death in the midst of erotic mania to the possibility that life
will ruin his joy with some mental illness (*contaminet vita aegritudine
aliqua*, 552).[79] Nevertheless, he recognizes that his current state is akin
to sickness, since he is certain that someone running into him on the street
at this moment would not be able to tell whether he was healthy or not
(*sanus sim anne insaniam*, 556). Even if he does not want some other ill to
displace his joy, neither does he hope for a clean bill of health, preferring
the *insania* that currently holds him.

Chaerea fears meeting some busybody (*curiosum*, 553), but after deliv-
ering his soliloquy he runs into Antipho, another *adulescens* in the play.
And indeed, Antipho asks exactly the sorts of questions that the rapist did
not want to answer: "Chaerea, how come you're carrying on like this? How
come you're dressed like this? How come you're so happy? What are you
up to? Are you healthy?" (*Chaerea, quid est quod sic gestis? quid sibi hic
vestitus quaerit? / quid est quod laetus es? quid tibi vis? satine sanu's?*,
558–59). Chaerea's response is entirely unexpected: "Oh happy day!
Greetings, friend! There's no one on earth I'd rather see right now than
you!" (*o festus dies! amice, salve. hominum omnium / nemost quem ego
nunciam magis cuperem videre quam / te*, 560–62). Although Chaerea
claimed to want to shun all *curiosi*, it turns out it is only judgmental *senes*
he wishes to avoid; he's more than eager to converse about his sexual
escapades with another *adulescens* like himself, which he proceeds to do.
Leigh notes that "the very interrogation that in a *curiosus* would seem the
height of impertinence, when launched by a trusted friend, prompts the
long and gloating narrative of the rape that many readers find so
distasteful."[80]

Catullus takes this same tack in poem 6, where he interrogates Flavius, a
friend who has been trying to hide his liaisons in a way similar to Chaerea,
and like Antipho Catullus wants to talk him into sharing his story:

---

[79] On *aegritudo* as a term for erotic illness, see Preston (1916, 6–8); Barsby (1999a, 189) notes that
*aegritudo* always refers to mental distress in Terence, though Fantham (1972, 18) connects its
cognates *aegrotus* and *aegrotare* to related vocabulary of lovesickness that Terence deploys.
[80] Leigh (2013, 63).

Flavi, delicias tuas Catullo,
ni sint illepidae atque inelegantes,
velles dicere nec tacere posses.
verum nescioquid febriculosi
5        scorti diligis: hoc pudet fateri.
nam te non viduas iacere noctes
nequiquam tacitum cubile clamat
sertis ac Syrio fragrans olivo,
pulvinusque peraeque et hic et ille
10        attritus, tremulique quassa lecti
argutatio inambulatioque.
nam nil stupra valet, nihil, tacere.
cur? non tam latera effututa pandas,
ni tu quid facias ineptiarum.
15        quare, quidquid habes boni malique,
dic nobis. volo te ac tuos amores
ad caelum lepido vocare versu.

Flavius, you'd want to talk to Catullus about
your sweetheart and you couldn't keep quiet,
unless she were uncharming and inelegant.
No, you revere some unknown fever-ridden
slut, but you're ashamed to admit it.
It's useless for your bed to be quiet, since it
reeks of garlands and Syrian olive oil, shouting
that you aren't lying without a mate at night;
so does your pillow, compressed evenly
on this side and on that side, and the shaken
creaking and ambling of your wobbly bed.
You see, it's no good keeping your illicit affairs quiet.
Why? You wouldn't be exhibiting such fucked-out sides
if you weren't doing something gauche.
So tell me whatever you've got, the good and
the bad. I want to sing you and your love
all the way to heaven in my charming verse.

Between his *latera effututa* (13), *ineptia* (14; cf. *inepta crura* of the collapsing bridge in 17.2–3), and his febrile girlfriend (*febriculosi*, 4), Flavius is not faring well, at least in Catullus' telling.[81] Notably, the poet's description of his friend shares points of contact not only with the desperate lover of Lucretius but also with the comic allusions behind him. Flavius' bed

---

[81] Stevens (2013, 19–46) notes, however, that Catullus' telling is tendentious and spins his own imaginative tale without autopsy or any input from Flavius himself; see also Uden (2005) on the speaker's one-sided portrayal.

"smells of Syrian olive oil" (*Syrio fragrans olivo*, 8; cf. *Babylonia ...
unguenta* at Lucr. 4.1124–25), and his "pillow is worn" (*pulvinusque ...
attritus*, 9–10; cf. *teriturque ... vestis* at Lucr. 4.1127), he has garlands at
hand (*sertis*, 8; cf. *serta* at Lucr. 4.1132), and results of his affair are
ambiguous (*boni malique*, 15; cf. *in amore mala haec proprio summeque
secundo / inveniuntur* at Lucr. 4.1141–42). What is more, as Morgan
notes, *febriculosus* has a special comic connotation, as it appears only one
time before Catullus, namely, in Plautus' *Cistellaria* as an insult to comic
*meretrices*, "wretched, fever-ridden girlfriends" (*febricul<osae m>iserae
amicae*, 406).[82] Flavius thus shares many of the same traits as the comic
*adulescens*, whose interaction with his febrile *deliciae* has exposed him to
injury and disease.

In contrast to the portrayals of the *adulescens amator* in Cicero and
Lucretius, however, Flavius' lovesickness is not a source of anxiety or
shame. Like Antipho in *Eunuchus*, Catullus wants to know everything
about the lover's strange behavior, not to criticize or convert him but to
elevate it to the skies in song (*volo te ac tuos amores / ad caelum lepido vocare
versu*, 16–17). Flavius' ailments become an object of veneration, and
Catullus' eagerness to publicize them to heaven mirrors his own desire to
extend his kisses past the reach of the *curiosi* and to the stars, who are
always already keeping lookout on mortal love affairs (*sidera multa, cum
tacet nox, / furtivos hominum vident amores*, 7.7–8).[83] Poem 6 offers the
idea that lovesickness ought not to be hidden, but experienced fully and
shared with others, as the *adulescens* Chaerea does on stage for his
friend Antipho.

Such performance, of course, does not necessarily imply erotic suffering
is pleasant for the lover to experience, and indeed throughout the corpus
Catullus shifts his position repeatedly on what should be done to deal with
lovesickness, often by alluding to the generic *adulescens amator*, as well as
specific incarnations of the stock character. Rand calls *Eunuchus'* Chaerea
"a Catullus in action," though I think we could just as easily flip and
complicate this identification: Catullus himself plays Chaerea in action in
poems 5 and 7, but in poem 6 he takes the role of his friend Antipho, the
well-wishing *curiosus*.[84] Indeed, one element of Catullus' approach to the
*adulescens amator* that has been well documented is that he seems to divide

---

[82] Morgan (1977).
[83] See Tesoriero (2006); Fitzgerald (1995, 54) observes that "these stars, watching the lovers in the
silent night, are the audience listening with bated breath to Catullus telling of his erotic life."
[84] Rand (1932, 58).

himself in allusive directions simultaneously, splitting his psyche into multiple comic characters as he tries to come to grips with the complex and competing emotions of being in love. In particular, Marilyn Skinner argues that in poem 8 – the piece in the Catullan corpus that has longest been noted for alluding to Roman comedy – Catullus takes on two distinct perspectives, one of the speaker who acts as an *adulescens amator* and the other of the poet, who patiently but firmly rebukes his speaker for his irrational behavior:[85]

> miser Catulle, desinas ineptire,
> et quod vides perisse perditum ducas.
> fulsere quondam candidi tibi soles,
> cum ventitabas quo puella ducebat
> 5   amata nobis quantum amabitur nulla.
> ibi illa multa cum iocosa fiebant,
> quae tu volebas nec puella nolebat,
> fulsere vere candidi tibi soles.
> nunc iam illa non vult; tu quoque inpote<ns noli>,
> 10   nec quae fugit sectare, nec miser vive,
> sed obstinata mente perfer, obdura.
> vale, puella. iam Catullus obdurat,
> nec te requiret nec rogabit invitam.
> at tu dolebis, cum rogaberis nulla.
> 15   scelesta, vae te! quae tibi manet vita?
> quis nunc te adibit? cui videberis bella?
> quem nunc amabis? cuius esse diceris?
> quem basiabis? cui labella mordebis?
> at tu, Catulle, destinatus obdura.

> Wretched Catullus, stop being a fool
> and consider lost what you see has been lost.
> Once bright days shone for you,
> when you used to go wherever your girl led,
> a girl loved as much by us as no one will ever be loved.
> Then when you had many laughs,
> which you wanted and your girl did not not want,
> truly bright days shone for you.
> Now she does not want: so you, too, don't want helplessly,
> or follow one who flees, or be wretched,
> but endure with a steadfast mind, stay strong.
> Goodbye girl, now Catullus stays strong,
> and he will neither seek nor ask for you unwilling.

---

[85] Skinner (1971); see also McCormick (1981) on the divided personalities in Catul. 8.

> But you will grieve, when you are called by no one.
> Wretch, woe to you! What life is left for you?
> Who will approach you now? To whom will you seem beautiful?
> Whom will you love? Whose will you be said to be?
> Whom will you kiss? Whose lips will you bite?
> But you, Catullus, endure and stay strong.

E. P. Morris first observed the presence of the *adulescens amator* from Roman comedy in the background of poem 8 and suggested that Catullus adapts the generic figure from drama to the new context of personal lyric. He summarizes the correspondences thus:

> The essential element is the humorous portrayal, through a soliloquy, of a lover trying to win back the favor of the girl by the threat – which he both hopes and fears that he may not carry out – of leaving her forever. With this, as secondary elements, go usually some reference to the happiness of the past and some prediction of the misery that will ensue, if he is allowed actually to go.[86]

As parallels, he cites the soliloquies of the *adulescens* in Plautus's *Asinaria* (127–52), *Bacchides* (500–525), and *Truculentus* (758–69), and the opening of Terence's *Eunuchus* (lines 46–80), which share the same basic outline.[87] Morris concludes that the point of the comic allusion is to provide ironic distance between the biographical poet Catullus and his foolish speaker: "Catullus the lover in this little dramatic lyric tries to touch the heart of the girl, but Catullus the poet trusted to the acuteness of his readers – and of Lesbia – to see that this is only a scene in a pretty comedy."[88] Skinner follows this same basic approach, refining Morris' argument by moving beyond the simplistic dichotomy of ridiculous versus sympathetic that has dominated scholarly debate on the poem and suggesting that the dissonance between these two apparently irreconcilable aspects of the poem is embedded in the poem itself and that the two voices are "attempts to present both sides of a paradoxical situation, to reflect the fragmented, chaotic nature of human experience" (298). She concludes that "the comic *persona* projects the discrepancy between the idealized and the real nature of Catullus' relationship with his mistress . . . Whatever the

---

[86] Morris (1909).

[87] The *Eunuchus* scene, as Morris (1909) points out, is not a soliloquy proper, since the *amator* is accompanied on stage by a slave during the speech, but he notes correctly that the lover is not actually addressing the slave, but only dissertating on his predicament as the slave takes the role of an audience member.

[88] Morris (1909, 147).

real nature of the affair, this *persona* as *persona* becomes a distancing device, a means of artistic control over feelings of frustration and self-pity."[89]

While we can certainly understand the two voices here as the generic *adulescens amator* and the poet, I think there is good reason to take the latter out of the equation and instead see two voices that are themselves both fictive personas drawn from Roman comedy. Although she does not engage directly with Skinner's interpretation, Dyson provides compelling reasons to be skeptical of seeing the biographical poet as omniscient character here.[90] Further, Selden argues that one of the definitive markers of Catullus' poetry is its consistent creation of readings that are internally contradictory, arguing that his corpus is "principally a site for the inter-section of two irreconcilable systems of meaning . . . In each case, Catullus' text not only generates two equally plausible, yet contradictory under-standings of the poet's circumstances, heart, and mind . . . the piece is so constructed as to make it effectively impossible for the reader to decide between them." In his reading of poem 8, the tragic and comic, the resolute and indecisive, "are not just polysemically opposed, but mutually parasitic in a way that enables one construction of the poem always to denounce the other."[91] For this reason and others, I think we can fruitfully read poem 8 not as a display merely of the generic *adulescens* but of the particular opposing characters in the opening of Terence's *Eunuchus*, the *adulescens* Phaedria and the *servus* Parmeno, who mutually reinforce the sense of psychological division inherent in giving and receiving advice for dealing with love.[92]

Skinner says that "the most extensive dramatic development of the irresolute *amator* situation is the opening scene of Terence's *Eunuchus*," noting that this scene stands apart from the rest for its dialogue form: the lover turns to someone else – here, his *servus* – for advice and receives "a frank, unflattering description of his complete subjection" to his beloved.[93] I would argue a step further, that for Romans in the first century BCE –

---

[89] Skinner (1971, 298 and 305). Dyson (1973), Adler (1981), and Janan (1994) parallel this idea of fragmented experience in their analyses of the Catullan corpus. See also Gaisser (2009, 60) on how the mixture in poem 8 of elements from elsewhere in Catullus and Roman comedy enables these dual readings.

[90] Dyson (1973).     [91] Selden (1992, 475 and 471).

[92] Thomas (1984) argues instead for Menander's *Samia* as a specific target of Catullus' poem 8; some of his parallels are persuasive, and Catullus may be combining the formal elements of the Greek source with the allusions to the Latin play, much as he does with Callimachus and Plautus in poem 70.

[93] Skinner (1971); Goldberg (2005, 100) also says that "Phaedria's complaint at the beginning of *Eunuchus* is the most famous example of the type" before dismissing it as a specific allusion in poem 8 as "hardly unique" as a representative of the comic lover's soliloquy. Barsby (1999b, 19) calls

for whom *Eunuchus* had become the textbook definition of the lover's experience and was handled so pervasively by Catullus' contemporaries when discussing lovesickness – this scene would have been front and center in their minds while reading Catullus. Moreover, the way Catullus describes himself as a lover recalls details unique to Terence's *Eunuchus*. The opening command to "stop being a fool" (*desinas ineptire*, 1) stands out as significant, because, as Goldberg and others remark, "*ineptus* is the condition of Terence's Phaedria," and soon after the opening scene his *servus* Parmeno laments the connection between the *adulescens'* lovesickness and his resulting *ineptia* (225–27):[94]

> di boni, quid hoc morbist? adeon homines immutarier          225
> ex amore ut non cognoscas eundem esse! hoc nemo fuit
> minus ineptus, magis severus quisquam nec magis continens.

> Good gods, what is this illness? People can be so changed by love
> that you wouldn't recognize them as the same person! No one was less
> tactless than this guy, nor was anyone more grave or more self-possessed.

This is Parmeno's response immediately after discussing Phaedria's waffling behavior, where we see many of the same sentiments and even words that Catullus uses in poem 8 (216–25):

> PHAED: censen posse me offirmare et
> perpeti ne redeam interea?
> PARM: tene? non hercle arbitror;
> nam aut iam revortere aut mox noctu te adiget horsum insomnia.
> PHAED: opus faciam, ut defetiger usque, ingratiis ut dormiam.          220
> PARM: vigilabis lassus: hoc plus facies.
> PHAED: abi, nil dicis, Parmeno.
> eicienda hercle haec est mollities animi. nimis me indulgeo.
> tandem non ego illam caream, si sit opus, vel totum triduom?
> PARM: hui! universum triduom? vide quid agas.          225

> PHAED: "Do you think I can stay firm and
> endure without returning to her in the meantime?"
> PARM: "You? Hercules, I don't. Either you'll return
> right away or soon when night comes insomnia will drive you here."
> PHAED: "I'll work so hard I'm so exhausted that I'll sleep against my will."
> PARM: "You'll just lie awake tired; that's all you'll manage."
> PHAED: "Come on, Parmeno, you're saying nonsense.
> By Hercules, I need to cast out this softness of heart. I'm indulging

---

Phaedria "the most penetrating portrayal in comedy of a young man in love with an established *meretrix*."

[94] Goldberg (2005, 100); Skinner (1971, 302–3) also picks up on the centrality of *ineptia* here.

myself too much. Couldn't I at least be without her, if I have to, for
three whole days?"
PARM: "Ha! Three whole days? Just watch yourself."

Sharrock points out that Phaedria's "need to cast out this softness of heart"
(*eicienda hercle haec est mollities animi*, 223) and question about whether he
can "stay firm and endure" (*offirmare et / perpeti*, 217–18) is picked up by
Catullus' language and thought in *sed obstinata mente perfer, obdura*
(8.11).[95] Likewise, the focus on departing and returning in *redeam* (218)
and *revortere* (220) are mirrored in *requiret* (8.13) and *adibit* (8.16). In
poems 5–7, Catullus revels in the back-and-forth of erotic gossip, but in
poem 8 he shifts quite abruptly into new characters, ditching mutual
admiration by Chaerea and Antipho for Parmeno's clearsightedness and
the introspective suffering of another *adulescens* in the *Eunuchus*, Phaedria.
Indeed, the opening scenes between *servus* and *adulescens* are touchstones
for exploring lovesickness to which Catullus repeatedly returns throughout
the corpus to consider the range of amatory emotions and experiences: love
and hatred, suspicion and determination. Not only that, it serves as a
unifying target of allusion, I argue, that provides Catullus with a measure
of psychological stability: after rapid shifts between various comic characters, he merges with Phaedria, whom he echoes in multiple other poems in
the corpus. Phaedria, I will show, offers a kind of restorative therapeutic for
Catullus, an exemplary figure that anchors his erotic experience across the
gaps between poems.

Phaedria's *ineptia* goes hand in hand with another quality Catullus
highlights in poem 8, namely, *miseria* (*miser Catulle*, 1). Terence's *adulescens*
exclaims "*me miserum*" (71) in response to Parmeno's rebuke, and the slave
attributes the lover's exclusion by his beloved Thais to his "miserable love"
(*misera prae amore exclusti hunc foras*, 98). Hinds remarks that the phrase *me
miserum* was "a common piece of verbal furniture" in a wide variety of Latin
literature but also points out that it and other uses of *miser* hold wide sway in
Roman comedy.[96] Moreover, Catullus' other self-appellations of *miser* frequently occur alongside allusions to the suffering of the comic *adulescens*.
Take poem 51, for example, where Catullus describes the physiological
breakdown that simply looking at Lesbia provokes in him (5–12):

> . . . misero quod omnis
> eripit sensus mihi: nam simul te,
> Lesbia, aspexi, nihil est super mi

---

[95] Sharrock (2009, 230–31).     [96] Hinds (1998, 29–31).

lingua sed torpet, tenuis sub artus
flamma demanat, sonitu suopte
tintinant aures, gemina teguntur
   lumina nocte.

. . . which snatches from wretched me
all my senses: for as soon as I have
seen you, Lesbia, there remains
<no voice in my mouth>,
but my tongue goes numb, a thin flame
trickles beneath my limbs, my ears ring
with their own sound, my eyes are covered
   by a twin night.

The poem is primarily an adaptation of Sappho's famous fr. 31, but there is much more going on than a word-for-word translation, including multiple allusions to Roman comedy. Baker argues that *misero* at 51.5, "itself an importation into the poem by Catullus with no counterpart in Sappho, has already suggested that this poem lies in the literary tradition of the *miser amator*, with a code of conduct well outside the framework of traditional Roman values."[97] Likewise, I argued in the Introduction that poem 51's final stanza on *otium* finds a parallel in the speech of Lesbonicus at Plautus' *Mostellaria* (655–58), and Sharrock observes that in *Eunuchus* Phaedria's *nimis me indulgeo* (223) is picked up by this same stanza's phrase *otio exsultas nimiumque gestis* (51.14). She further argues that there is a complex allusive chain at work through which Catullus adapts Sappho: the laments of Terence's Phaedria are themselves allusive reworkings of fr. 31.[98] If we compare Phaedria's fearful statement to Parmeno about interacting with his beloved, we can see these clearly. He describes the effects the sight of his beloved has on him: "Parmeno, I started trembling all over and shuddering as soon as I saw this girl" (*totus, Parmeno / tremo horreoque, postquam aspexi hanc*, 83–84), which picks up Sappho's "for when I see you a little" (ὡς γὰρ ἔς σ᾽ ἴδω βρόχε᾽, 7) and "trembling catches hold of me all over" (τρόμος δὲ / παῖσαν ἄγρει, 13–14).

    Terence's phrasing here makes clear that Catullus has both in mind, as his reference to the sight of Lesbia (*nam simul te, / Lesbia, aspexi*, 6–7) mirrors Phaedria's more closely than Sappho's. *Eunuchus'* Phaedria thus acts as a "window reference" for Catullus: Terence alludes to Sappho, and

---

[97] Baker (1981, 319) and Hinds (1998, 29–34); cf. Commager (1965, 88).
[98] Sharrock (2009, 226–32).

Catullus reads Sappho both by herself and through the lens of Terence's *adulescens*, in much the same way we saw Valerius Aedituus do at the start of this chapter.[99] In the process, he once again turns to the *Eunuchus* as a unifying way to understand the symptoms of his lovesickness.

The physicality of poem 51's erotic disease is also mirrored by the emotional illness of 76, where Catullus most explicitly and fully explores the idea of *amor* as *morbus* (10–26):[100]

10      quare cur tete iam amplius excrucies?
        quin tu animo offirmas atque istinc te ipse reducis
            et dis invitis desinis esse miser?
        difficile est longum subito deponere amorem,
            difficile est, verum hoc qua lubet efficias;
15      una salus haec est, hoc est tibi pervincendum,
            hoc facias, sive id non pote sive pote.
        o di, si vestrum est misereri, aut si quibus umquam
            extremam iam ipsa in morte tulistis opem,
        me miserum aspicite et, si vitam puriter egi,
20          eripite hanc pestem perniciemque mihi,
        quae mihi subrepens imos ut torpor in artus
            expulit ex omni pectore laetitias.
        non iam illud quaero, contra ut me diligat illa,
            aut, quod non potis est, esse pudica velit:
25      ipse valere opto et taetrum hunc deponere morbum.
            o di, reddite mi hoc pro pietate mea.

> Why are you torturing yourself still further?
> Why don't you firm up your heart and take yourself back,
>     and stop being wretched, since the gods are unwilling.
> It's difficult to put off a long-standing love quickly;
>     it's difficult, but you should go through with it anyway.
> This is your one chance of health. This is what you've got to beat.
>     Do this, whether it's possible or not possible.
> Gods, if it's in you to show pity, or if you've ever given
>     last-ditch help to people on the verge of death itself,
> look at miserable me and, if I've led a pure life,
>     snatch this plague and pestilence from me,
> which creeps deep into my limbs like a numbess and
>     has driven out happiness from my whole breast.
> I'm not asking for this: that she love me back,
>     or – what can't be – that she be willing to be chaste.

---

[99] For "window reference," see Thomas (1984).

[100] On disease imagery in this poem, see Skinner (1987) and Booth (1997). See also Dyson (1973) for connections between Catull. 76 and 8.

I want myself to be well and to put off this foul disease.
Gods, grant me this in exchange for my observance.

Catullus' lament that "numbness creeps deep into my limbs" (*subrepens imos ut torpor in artus*, 21) picks up similar ailments in poem 51 (*lingua sed torpet, tenuis sub artus / flamma demanat*, 51.9–10), and his exclamation "*me miserum*" (19) and self-exhortation to "stop being miserable" (*desinis esse miser*, 12) are callbacks to *misero* at 51.5 and *miser Catulle, desinas* at 8.1. Poem 76 essentially explicates and amplifies the sense of physical and mental illness the other poems introduce through their allusions to comic *adulescentes*. Additionally, many of the thoughts and phrases in poem 76 are repeated elsewhere in his epigrams, especially in poems that also allude to the opening of Terence's *Eunuchus*. Catullus' question, "Why are you torturing yourself still further?" (*quare cur tete iam amplius excrucies?*, 76.10), finds a close parallel in his most famous epigram, the pithy poem 85:

> odi et amo. quare id faciam, fortasse requiris.
>   nescio, sed sentio et excrucior.

> I hate and I love. You ask, perhaps, how I do this.
>   I don't know, but I feel it and am tortured.

Uden observes that this poem shares a striking similarity to Terence's complaint in the prologue to *Eunuchus*, where the playwright condenses the experience of love in Roman comedy as "loving, hating, being suspicious" (*amare, odisse, suspicari*, 40).[101] And soon after, Terence introduces the idea of amatory torture in the opening scene of the play. When she sees him, Phaedria's beloved Thais begs the *adulescens*, "Please, don't torture yourself, my soul, my Phaedria" (*ne crucia te, obsecro, anime mi, mi Phaedria*, 95), and a few scenes later Phaedria's friend Chaerea calls women "those tortures, who hold us and our youth in contempt and who torture us always and in every way" (*illis crucibus, quae nos nostramque adulescentiam / habent despicatam et quae nos semper omnibus cruciant modis*, 383–84). Minarini points out some additional points of contact between Phaedria's laments before meeting Thais and poem 85: *odi et amo* parallels Terence's balanced doublet *et taedet et amore ardeo* (72), *excrucior* plays off of *pereo* (73), and *nescio* is a contraction of *nec . . . scio* (73).

Catullus elaborates this conflict between love and hate and the resulting schizophrenia of the lover in poem 75, which Uden shows shares a number

---

[101] Uden (2006, 19).

of thematic parallels with both poem 85 and Phaedria's dialogue, including the idea that love has destroyed (*perdidit*, 75.2; cf. *pereo, Eunuchus* 73) the lover:[102]

> huc est mens deducta tua, mea Lesbia, culpa
> >atque ita se officio perdidit ipsa suo,
> ut iam nec bene velle queat tibi, si optima fias,
> >nec desistere amare, omnia si facias.

> My mind has been led up to this point, Lesbia, through your fault,
> >and so has ruined itself by its own devotion,
> so that now it cannot wish you well, if you should become very good,
> >or stop loving you, if you should do everything.

But what about the third theme in Terence's prologue to *Eunuchus*, suspicion (*suspicari*, 40)? Catullus' poem 72 displays it prominently, joining Phaedria's paradoxical experience and the themes of poems 75 and 85 with Plautine elements of deception from poem 70 that I discuss in the Introduction:

> dicebas quondam solum te nosse Catullum,
> >Lesbia, nec prae me velle tenere Iovem.
> dilexi tum te non tantum ut vulgus amicam,
> >sed pater ut gnatos diligit et generos.
> nunc te cognovi; quare, etsi impensius uror,
> >multo mi tamen es vilior et levior.
> qui potis est, inquis? quod amantem iniuria talis
> >cogit amare magis, sed bene velle minus.

> You said once that you knew Catullus alone,
> >Lesbia, and would not want to hold Jove before me.
> I cherished you then not so much as the crowd loves its girlfriend,
> >but as a father cherishes his sons and sons-in-law.
> Now I know you: so even if I burn more fiercely,
> >still you are much cheaper and lighter to me.
> How is this possible, you ask? Because such harm
> >forces a lover to love more, but to wish well less.

The suspicions of infidelity hinted at by the Hellenistic and Plautine elements in poem 70 recur in line 2 of poem 72 (*nec prae me velle tenere Iovem*; cf. *nulli se dicit mulier mea nubere malle / quam mihi, non si se Iuppiter ipse petat*, 70.1–2), combined at lines 5–6 and 7–8 with the love-and-hate contrast in poems 85 and 75, respectively (5–6: **quare** etsi *impensius uror, / multo mi tamen es uilior et leuior. / qui potis est,* **inquis?**;

---

[102] Minarini (1987, 64); see also Barsby (1999b, 7–8) and Uden (2006).

cf. *odi et amo.* **quare** *id faciam, fortasse* **requiris**. | *nescio, sed sentio et excrucior,* 85.1–2; 7–8: *quod amantem iniuria talis* | *cogit* **amare** *magis, sed* **bene uelle** *minus*; cf. *ut iam nec* **bene uelle** *queat tibi, si optima fias,* | *nec desistere* **amare**, *omnia si facias,* 75.3–4). And these elements of the poem are tied back to the Terentian scene by the phrase *nunc te cognovi* (5), which Minarini connects back to Phaedria's *nunc ego ... sentio* (*Eunuchus* 70).[103]

Allusions to Phaedria's lament in the *Eunuchus* bind all these poems together, informing their relation to one another and providing a sense of continuity and unity from Catullus' disjointed and conflicted emotions. Catullus divides his references to Phaedria's emotions between multiple poems, but his decision repeatedly to invoke this same intertextual target connects the individual epigrammatic voices into a sustained elegy.[104] Moreover, these allusions do double duty, because while they create a sense of coherence to the speaker and elaborate aspects of his point of view, they also reveal ambiguous aspects of the speaker's self-presentation. The *Eunuchus* also stands behind poem 109, the last poem about Lesbia in the collection, which holds out a reconciliation between the lovers. As with the other Catullan poems just discussed, this epigram also alludes to elements of Phaedria's erotic conflict, but here gives greater voice to the *meretrix* Thais:

> iucundum, mea vita, mihi proponis: amorem
> hunc nostrum inter nos perpetuum usque fore.
> di magni, facite ut **vere** promittere possit,
> atque id **sincere dicat** et **ex animo**,
> ut liceat nobis tota perducere uita
> aeternum hoc sanctae foedus amicitiae.

> My life, you propose something pleasant to me: that this love
> of ours between us will last from now until the end of time.
> Great gods, make it so she can promise truly,
> and say it sincerely and from her heart,
> so we can maintain through our whole life
> this eternal bond of sacred friendship.

Barsby argues that this poem invokes the scene in Terence's *Eunuchus* that follows the opening dialogue between Parmeno and Phaedria, in which the *adulescens* accuses Thais of infidelity and the *meretrix* defends her actions (175–77):[105]

---

[103] Minarini (1987, 64).
[104] Wills (1998) discusses "divided allusions" in Vergil and their unifying qualities, which offer fruitful comparanda for Catullus' technique here.
[105] Barsby (1999b).

utinam istuc verbum **ex animo** ac **vere** diceres:
"potius quam te inimicum habeam"! si istuc crederem
**sincere dici**, quidvis possem perpeti.

Would that you were saying from the heart and truthfully,
"rather than have you as an enemy"! If I believed that was
said sincerely, I could put up with anything.

That both share three adverbial phrases (*ex animo*, *vere*, and *sincere*) is clear,
and yet again the poet uses Phaedria's unified voice to make sense of the
fragmentary experience spread across multiple poems.[106] Here, though, we
hear both Thais and Lesbia – or at least what Catullus wants us to think
Lesbia has said. Victoria Pedrick points out that Lesbia's speech in these
epigrams is reported indirectly through the filter of the Catullan speaker,
and therefore we should question the degree to which the epigrams can be
read as a fair representation of the relationship in the poems between the
speaker and Lesbia.[107] But the intertexts between Catullus' epigrams and
the *Eunuchus* I have just discussed, particularly this final one, hint that the
Catullan speaker is less sympathetic than has generally been assumed.[108]
By casting his lament in terms of Phaedria's internal conflicts and suspicions, Catullus can also be seen indirectly to import Thais as a parallel for
the silent Lesbia. In the process, he also casts doubt on the speaker's
representation of Lesbia, because Thais is the most sympathetic character
in Terence's play.[109] While it is true that she has mercantile interests and
manipulates both Phaedria and the *miles* Thraso, her direct address to the
audience (which we expect to be an unfiltered representation of her true
thoughts, since there is no one on stage for whom she must dissemble)
reveals she is more sympathetic and concerned for Phaedria than the
*adulescens* suggests in his opening rant. This allusion in poem 109 colors
the other allusive links between the Catullan speaker of the epigrams and
*Eunuchus*'s Phaedria, since it casts Lesbia in the role of the good-hearted
and long-suffering *bona meretrix*. In so doing, it modifies the way suspicion
can be read in the epigrams. Instead of accepting Catullus' assertions of
fidelity at face value, the reader aware of the Terentian intertext can see

---

[106] So Ellis (1889, 489), Konstan (1986, 391), and Barsby (1999b, 7–8).
[107] Pedrick (1986). See also Fitzgerald (1995, 134–39), who discusses the confessional rhetoric the
speaker uses and the doubt this approach casts on his own presentation of Lesbia's words.
[108] See discussions and bibliography in Pedrick (1986); Fitzgerald (1992); Janan (1994, 81–88).
[109] See Moore (2013), Caston (2014), and James (2016) on Thais' abuse at the hands of the men in
this play, her lack of control over the plot, and her character as an unexpectedly *bona meretrix* in
contrast to the "wicked woman" (*scelestam*, 71) Phaedria portrays her as, which even Donatus
observes is exceptional.

there are two sides in this argument. Lesbia is not altogether devoid of self-interest, but neither is the speaker entirely objective or honest in his self-presentation. We might even understand this as a consequence of his lovesickness: when the *morbus* takes hold, he represents himself as the victim, but when it abates – as it seems in poem 109 – and *ratio* reasserts itself, Catullus becomes gentle again. In the process, he inadvertently proves, but also actively dismisses, Cicero's and Lucretius' point: lovesickness has harmful effects on those around the *adulescens* and the lover that neither can see. To confront and reject it are acts of both self-preservation and self-sacrifice for others. But to revel in it, to focus on the subjective personal experience at the expense of exterior judgment or concerns, is to heighten your understanding of emotions without any hope of changing them.

# CHAPTER 3

# Heroic Badness and Catullus' Plautine Plots

One of the most distinctive features of Catullus' poetry is the way he employs intratextual echoes to bind disparate poems across his corpus, encouraging readers to view a poem about one topic or situation alongside another with which it seems, at first glance, to share little in common but on closer inspection reveals striking parallels of thought or theme. Take poem 3, on the death of Lesbia's sparrow, which is described as "hopping around now here, now there" (*circumsiliens modo huc modo illuc*, 9). We find almost exactly the same phrasing in poem 50, on an afternoon spent writing poetry with Licinius Calvus, with whom Catullus recalls composing verses "now in this meter, now in that one" (*numero modo hoc modo illoc*, 5). This is a puzzling collocation: the former a hyperbolic eulogy for a dead pet, the latter a memory of a pleasant poetic jam session.

Catullus seems to be asking, "Why is a raven like a writing desk?" – or in this case, a *passer* like a poet. Viewed side by side, though, points of contact come into focus: the joy of playtime when the sparrow was alive (*ludere*, 2.2 and 2.9) and Catullus' delight at playing with Calvus (*lusimus*, 50.2; *ludebat*, 50.5) yield to the anxiety of loss when both bird and friend go their separate ways (*it . . . illuc*, 3.11–12; *illinc abii*, 50.7), which troubles the eyes of those they leave behind (*rubent ocelli*, 3.18; *nec somnus tegeret quiete ocellos*, 50.10) and evokes chthonic imprecations (*malae tenebrae / Orci*, 3.13–14; *poenas Nemesis reposcat te*, 50.20). Over the course of each poem, we get the sense that the relationship between Lesbia and *passer* and Catullus and Calvus is more than friendship, and the joking (*iocari*, 2.6; *iocum*, 50.6) and play reveal a sexual aspect to these scenes: sparrow and poet are eroticized (*deliciae*, 2.1; *delicatos*, 50.3) by their admirers, as well as symbols of the fragility of Catullus' emotional state, which depends so much on relationships and time spent with others.[1] Catullus' intratextual

---

[1] Segal (1970, 26–27) discusses additional correspondences between Catull. 2, 3, and 50; see also Van Sickle (1981) and Batstone (2007, 244). For erotic connotations of *ludere*, see Stroup (2010,

echo helps to strengthen and complicate the individual poems, juxtaposing surface differences to get at the core of the relationships and of their shared emotional experience.

This is only one example of the poetic phenomenon, and scholars have unpacked many of these self-reflexive allusions throughout Catullus' work.[2] But one notable set of intracorpus echoes has gone largely unexamined, presumably because it unites three poems that appear to be so utterly mismatched as to seem that they cannot comment on one another, namely, the openings of poem 21 (a rebuke of Aurelius, the poet's sometimes-friend, sometimes-enemy, for his lusty designs on Catullus' *puer*), poem 24 (a financial warning to Juventius, Catullus' male beloved), and poem 49 (a panegyric of Cicero, who makes his single cameo appearance in Catullus' work here, for his patronage). Viewing them one after another brings their similarities, both lexical and syntactic, into sharp focus:

> Aureli, pater esuritionum,
> non harum modo, sed quot aut fuerunt
> aut sunt aut aliis erunt in annis

> Aurelius, father of hungers,
> not of these only, but all who either were
> or are or will be in other years

> o qui flosculus es Iuventiorum,
> non horum modo, sed quot aut fuerunt
> aut posthac aliis erunt in annis

> O you who are the little flower of the Juventii,
> not of these only, but all who either were
> or afterward will be in other years

> disertissime Romuli nepotum,
> quot sunt quotque fuere, Marce Tulli,
> quotque post aliis erunt in annis

> Most learned of Romulus's grandsons,
> all who are and all who were, Marcus Tullius,
> and all afterward who will be in other years

230–31). On *deliciae* and *delicatus* as markers of Catullan aesthetics and eroticism, see Fitzgerald (1995, 35–37).
[2] Recent discussions of Catullan intratextuality can be found in Farrell (2009) and chapters in Harrison, Frangoulidis, and Papanghelis (2018).

The correspondences are striking. Each features a second-person invocation in the opening line's first position (*Aureli, o, disertissime*). Each dubs its addressee with an extreme modifier, either superlative (*pater, dissertissime*) or diminutive (*flosculus*), and qualifies this descriptor with a plural genitive of a class to which they belong (*esuritionum, Iuventiorum, nepotum*).[3] Each then compares its addressee with all who were, are, or will be in that class (lines 2–3), ending with an identical four-word coda (*aliis erunt in annis*, 3). And the sequence of thought in each is the same: a self-contained vocative address highlights some quality of the addressee and amplifies it to a superlative pitch over the course of three lines.

Scholars have generally assumed the similarities here are purely coincidental, the result of Catullus's borrowing of an idiomatic rhetorical construction from everyday Latin speech and nebulous Greco-Roman cultural patrimony.[4] But this phrasing is far from common, and the parallels regularly cited derive from contexts that do not suggest this construction was a standard feature of *sermo cotidianus* before Catullus' day.[5] Even if it were, Catullus goes out of his way to link these poems through this collocation. Why should he so forcefully encourage readers to understand them together? One answer lies in a particular model to which I argue Catullus can be seen to allude here, a stock routine from Roman comedy that Plautus uses in which the *servus callidus*, or "clever slave," celebrates his successful manipulation and entrapment of the play's primary antagonist.[6] In this chapter, I show that this familiar routine can be seen to bind these three poems together and to illustrate how Catullus engages in social competition with his peers and rivals among the Roman elite. The "clever slave" provides Catullus a model for displaying what William Anderson has dubbed "Heroic Badness," a distinctly Plautine virtue by which the underdogs of Roman comedy gain the upper hand over blocking figures who hinder them from achieving their goals, despite the fact that they suffer from social and situational impairments. I will also outline why a member of the elite, like Catullus, would have found value in identifying with Roman comedy's *servus callidus* and implications this affinity has for Catullus' depiction of himself and others in his poetry.

[3] For *pater* as functionally a superlative, see Ellis (1889, 69) and Quinn (1970, 154).
[4] See Ellis (1889, 69), Kroll (1959, 39), Quinn (1970, 154–55), and Agnesini (2004, 75–76).
[5] Ellis (1889, 69) and Agnesini (2004, 76 n. 93) provide comprehensive lists. Notably, Cicero uses it twice, at *Fam.* 11.21.1 (*homini nequissimo omnium qui sunt, qui fuerunt, qui futuri sunt*) and *Red. Pop.* 16 (*Cn. Pompeius, vir omnium qui sunt, fuerunt, erunt, virtute sapientia gloria princeps*); Catullus may simultaneously be parodying Cicero's style at the same time that he invokes the comic allusions I argue for here.
[6] For Plautus' exaggerated comparisons, see Fraenkel (2008 [1922], 5–16). Ellis (1889, 69) and Fordyce (1961, 234) note parallels I discuss but leave their significance unexamined.

Nothing about the situations of poems 21, 24, or 49 explicitly announces the presence of Roman comedy, but the connection becomes obvious when they are viewed alongside examples of the schtick to which they allude. In Plautus' *Bacchides*, the *adulescens* Mnesilochus has fallen in love with a *meretrix* named Bacchis, who to his misfortune has already been hired for the year by someone else. To have her released from this contract, Mnesilochus asks the *servus callidus* Chrysalus for help in defrauding his father, the *senex* Nicobulus, of the money he needs to buy off the other man. Chrysalus manages to trick Nicobulus three times before the old man realizes what has happened and flies into a frustrated rage, comparing himself to all the buffoons that are, were, and ever will be (1087–1089):

> quiquomque ubi sunt, qui fuerunt quique futuri sunt posthac
> stulti, stolidi, fatui, fungi, bardi, blenni, buccones,
> solus ego omnis longe antideo stultitia et moribus indoctis.

> Whoever anywhere are, who were, and who will be later
> foolish, hardheaded, ignorant, lumps, dolts, fatheads,
> I alone outdo them all in stupidity and ignorant manners.

More or less the same scene also appears in Plautus' *Persa*, a play whose plot and characters are radically different from those of the *Bacchides*. Despite the disparate circumstances, the situation and phrasing of the scene in which this parallel occurs are nearly identical to Nicobulus' lament. In the *Persa*, the *servus callidus* Toxilus must find money to buy his beloved, a *meretrix* owned by the *leno* Dordalus. He borrows money from his fellow slave Sagaristio, whom he promises to repay by tricking the pimp through an elaborate scheme. Once he secures his beloved, he gets the parasite Saturio to dress up his daughter, a freeborn Athenian woman, as a Persian slave, whom Sagaristio (disguised as a foreign slave-dealer) claims to sell to Dordalus. After Sagaristio takes the money and runs off, Saturio rushes in to reclaim his daughter and drags the pimp to court for dealing in free women. Toxilus thus bilks Dordalus out of both the girl and the money he has to repay the original loan from Sagaristio. Later, Dordalus discovers the deception and returns on stage to complain he is more miserable than any who live, have lived, or ever will live (777–78):

> qui sunt, qui erunt quique fuerunt quique futuri sunt posthac,
> solus ego omnibus antideo facile, miserrumus hominum ut vivam.

> Those who are, who will be and who will have been and who will later be,
> I outdo them all easily, as most wretched of men as I am.

It is not surprising that these two self-shaming monologues are so similar; Roman comedy, and Plautus in particular, revels in repetition, whether it be of character types, of joke routines, or of plot structures. But Plautus does not recycle haphazardly, and such schticks share commonalities that belie their differences.

The basic routine that underlies these two scenes runs as follows: an individual, once confident in his unassailable position and superiority over others (the *senex* and *leno*), has just learned that he has been duped by another individual in an initially inferior position (the *servi callidi*). Realizing the deceit, the target of the slave's clever ruse announces to the audience that he belongs to a certain class of people (*Bacchides*: *stulti, stolidi, fatui, fungi, bardi, blenni, buccones*, 1088; *Persa*: *omnibus . . . hominum*, 778). Then he compares himself to all who are, were, or ever will be in that class, using polyptoton to repeat the verb "to be" (*Bacchides*: *quiquomque ubi sunt, qui fuerunt quique futuri sunt posthac*, 1087; *Persa*: *qui sunt, qui erunt quique fuerunt quique futuri sunt posthac*, 777). He closes by marking himself as a superlative example (*Bacchides*: *longe antideo*, 1089; *Persa*: *antideo facile*, 778). In other words, this is a self-consistent stock routine that shares the same basic elements as the three poems of Catullus that we saw above.

It is also significant that in both plays the person who ultimately deceives the antagonist puts on a guise of mock humility beforehand, as a way to ingratiate himself with his prospective victim. In *Persa*, Toxilus gives Dordalus a letter supposedly from his master that lures the pimp into buying the daughter of Saturio. Toxilus wrote the letter himself but claims ignorance and subservience in the face of Dordalus (492–502):

> TOX: ita me di ament ut ob istanc rem tibi multa bona instant a me.
> nam est res quaedam quam occultabam tibi dicere: nunc eam narrabo,
> und' tu pergrande lucrum facias: faciam ut mei memineris, dum vitam
> vivas. DORD: bene dictis tuis bene facta aures meae auxilium exposcunt.
> TOXILUS: tuom promeritum est merito ut faciam. et ut me scias esse ita facturum,
> tabellas tene has, pellege. DORD: istae quid ad me? TOX: immo ad te attinent et tua refert:
> nam ex Persia sunt haec allatae mi a meo ero. DORD: quando? TOX: hau dudum.
> DORD: quid istae narrant? TOX: percontare ex ipsis: ipsae tibi narrabunt.
> DORD: cedo sane [mihi]. TOX: at clare recitato. DORD: tace, dum pellego.
>  TOX: [recita,] haud verbum faciam.

> TOX: "So help me gods, since because of this many good things are coming from me
> to you. See, there's a certain matter that I was hesitant to tell you about: now I'll tell you

how you can make a ton of profit. I'll make you remember me, as long as I live."

DORD: "My ears ask for kind deeds to help your kind words."

TOX: "You deserve what I do deservedly. And so you know that I'll do it, take these tablets, read them through." DORD: "What do these have to do with me?" TOX: "Really, they concern you and matter to your matters. See, they've been brought to me from Persia by my master." DORD: "When?" TOX: "Just a bit ago."

DORD: "What do they say?" TOX: "Ask them. They'll tell you themselves." DORD: "Fine, give them to me." TOX: "But read them clearly."

DORD: "Shut up while I read."

TOX: "Read on. I won't make a peep."

*Bacchides* features a nearly identical letter exchange. The *servus* Chrysalus helps the *adulescens* Mnesilochus write a letter to trick his father, the *senex* Nicobulus, but then feigns ignorance as he presents it to the old man (786–93):

> CHRYS: nosces tu illum actutum qualis sit.
> nunc hasc' tabellas ferre me iussit tibi.
> orabat, quod istic esset scriptum ut fieret.
> NIC: cedo. CHRYS: nosce signum. NIC: novi. ubi ipse est?
> CHRYS: nescio.
> nil iam me oportet scire. oblitus sum omnia.
> scio me esse servom. nescio etiam id quod scio.
> nunc ab transenna hic turdus lumbricum petit;
> pendebit hodie pulchre, ita intendi tenus.

> CHRYS: "You'll know what sort he is soon.
> Now he's ordered me to bring these tablets to you.
> He asked that you do what has been written there."
> NIC: "Fine." CHRYS: "See his seal?"
> NIC: "I see. But where is he?" CHRYS: "I don't know.
> It's not right for me to know. I'm ignorant of everything.
> I know that I'm a slave. I don't even know what I know.
> <aside> Now this thrush here is looking for a worm from my trap;
> today he'll hang beautifully, just as I've set him up."

In the *Bacchides* example, Chrysalus pushes his humility to the extreme, claiming he recognizes that he is a lowly slave (*scio me esse servom*, 791) and therefore he does not even know what he knows (*nescio etiam id quod scio*, 791). It is appropriate, after all, for someone so inferior to the *paterfamilias* to be ignorant (*nil iam me oportet scire*, 790) and incapable of guile. This pose is one of the clever slave's most useful tools. While he has access to the most intimate secrets of the household, his very status as a slave requires that he be inconspicuous and harmless to his superiors, practically trained to be unaware.[7] Consequently, no one suspects him either to know enough to subvert dominant individuals or to have the wherewithal to use that knowledge to his own ends. As we will see, Catullus also takes the same approach, wheedling his target to gain his trust only to execute a trick fueled by Plautine *malitia* to gain the upper hand.

## Entrapping Aurelius (Poems 15 and 21)

Few of the characters in Catullus' poetry are as baffling as Aurelius: now a sympathetic friend (poem 11), a boorish critic (poem 16), and a refined hedonist (poem 81), his relationship to the speaker is constantly in flux. In poems that mention him, Aurelius' status relative to the speaker is a constant source of anxiety.[8] These paradoxes are particularly apparent in poems 15 and 21, a complementary pair addressed to Aurelius in which Catullus sets up a Plautine trap to tempt the man into becoming a rival for a *puer*'s affections and before threatening violence as soon as he takes the bait. In poem 15 Catullus offers to entrust his beloved to Aurelius:

> commendo tibi me ac meos amores,
> Aureli. veniam peto pudenter,
> ut, si quicquam animo tuo cupisti,
> quod castum expeteres et integellum,
> conserves puerum mihi pudice,
> non dico a populo – nihil veremur
> istos, qui in platea modo huc modo illuc
> in re praetereunt sua occupati –
> verum a te metuo tuoque pene
> infesto pueris bonis malisque.
> quem tu qua lubet, ut lubet, moveto
> quantum vis, ubi erit foris paratum;
> hunc unum excipio, ut puto, pudenter.
> quod si te mala mens furorque vecors
> in tantam impulerit, sceleste, culpam,
> ut nostrum insidiis caput lacessas,
> a tum te miserum malique fati!
> quem attractis pedibus patente porta
> percurrent raphanique mugilesque.

---

[7] Fitzgerald (2000, 13–31) discusses this paradoxical relationship between master and slave and the training for ignorance required to maintain it.

[8] See Fitzgerald (1995, 44–55) for a metapoetic reading of his anxieties of publication and Nappa (2001, 45–58) for anxieties of social standing and reputation.

I entrust to you me and my love,
Aurelius. I seek a modest favor,
that, if you have desired anything in your heart
that you would ask be chaste and untouched,
protect my boy chastely,
not, I say, from the people – I'm not afraid
of those, who pass in the street now here, now there,
busied in their own affairs –
In truth, I fear you and your penis,
hostile to boys good and bad.
Let it go wherever it likes, as it likes,
as much as you wish, when it's got a chance to be out:
I exclude this boy alone, and modestly, I think.
But if your malicious mind and raving madness
drive you into such an offense, you criminal,
that you wound my life with your tricks,
how wretched and ill-fated you'll be!
With your feet pulled apart and your hole opened,
radishes and mullets will run you through!

Catullus' initial request seems genuine, asking Aurelius to guard the boy's chastity and treat him just as he would want his own *puer delicatus* to be treated (3–4). But we soon learn that Aurelius is an odd choice for guardian. Catullus reveals that his main concern is not the common crowd, but Aurelius himself, whose penis threatens all boys alike (*non dico a populo ... verum a te metuo tuoque pene / infesto pueris bonis malisque*, 6–10). The remainder of the poem acknowledges Aurelius's propensity for lust (*mala mens furorque vecors*, 14) and his sexual license, which the speaker allows for (*quem tu qua lubet, ut lubet, moveto / quantum vis, ubi erit foris paratum*, 11–12), provided it does not touch on his own interests (*hunc unum excipio*, 13). It concludes with a vivid threat: if Aurelius touches Catullus' boy with his lecherous traps (*insidiis*, 16), he will suffer public humiliation and sexual penetration with radishes and mullets (18–19), a punishment associated with adulterers.[9]

A known philanderer in the habit of seducing boys is the last person to whom Catullus should entrust his *puer delicatus*. His safeguarding from rivals, whose number surely includes Aurelius, cannot be the point of this interaction here, and indeed close reading suggests Catullus has ulterior motives that have little to do with the boy's best interests or with his feelings toward the *puer*. MacLeod argues that poem 15 is a parody of the

---

[9] O'Bryhim (2017) discusses the literary, cultural, and legal connotations of Catullus' *raphani mugilesque*; see also Thomson (1998, 249).

traditional *commendatio* letter and "a monstrous travesty of such a request" offering a "comic presentation of the lover's feelings." Such letters are often as much about the relationship between the writer and recipient as between the writer and recommendee, and here Catullus takes this function even further than usual.[10] For while poem 15 revolves *around* the *puer*, it isn't really *about* him: the boy appears only three times and always as an object, never by name (*meos amores*, 1; *puerum*, 5; *hunc unum*, 13). By contrast, the speaker refers to himself five times (*commendo ... me ac meos*, 1; *conserves ... mihi*, 5; *veremur*, 6; *metuo*, 9; *nostrum ... caput*, 16) and to Aurelius nine times (*tibi*, 1; *Aureli*, 2; *animo tuo*, 3; *a te ... tuoque pene*, 9; *tu*, 11; *quantum vis*, 12; *te*, 14; *te miserum*, 17; *quem* [sc. *te*], 18). The opening line encapsulates the thrust of the poem: this situation involves Aurelius (*tibi*), the speaker (*me*), and the boy (*meos amores*), but the *puer* is merely a possession, a symbolic object of a social transaction between the other two individuals, the "I" and the "you" (*commendo tibi*, 1).[11] Catullus deploys the *puer* as an object of contention through which he attemps to display his superiority and embarrass his rival, sketching and redefining his relationship with Aurelius so that he comes out on top.

But the boy is not a neutral object of social exchange; he is bait. Catullus knows Aurelius, unlike those busy with their own affairs (*in re ... sua occupati*, 8), is constantly occupied with his lust to such a degree that he and his penis are known as ravenous predators of any and all boys. And Catullus not only understands this perfectly, but even encourages Aurelius to go hunting as often as he likes and to take advantage whenever the opportunity arises (11–12). Throughout the first half of poem 15, Catullus effectively represents himself as Aurelius' trustworthy confidante, mirroring attempts by Plautus' *servus callidus* to get close to his victim. When Catullus finally gets to his request in line 13 and threat in lines 17–19, he has spent considerable effort titillating Aurelius with the possibilities of seduction and working him into a frenzy of sexual temptation (*furorque vecors*, 14). When he does make his threat, he is confident Aurelius will give Catullus an opening to assert his dominance over his rival, publicly and graphically.[12]

Poem 15's sequel, poem 21, presents the foreseeable outcome of the speaker's deceptive assignation of his *puer* to Aurelius:

[10] MacLeod (1973, 298). On *commendationes* and how they use the recommendee to define and modify the relationship between writer and recipient, see Cotton (1986) and Hall (2009, 30–34).
[11] Peek (2002) rightly observes that the point of the poem is Aurelius' ridicule, not the *puer*.
[12] See Fitzgerald (1995, 44–58) for a reading of these rhetorical mechanics.

Aureli, pater esuritionum,
non harum modo, sed quot aut fuerunt
aut sunt aut aliis erunt in annis,
pedicare cupis meos amores.
nec clam: nam simul es, iocaris una,
haerens ad latus omnia experiris.
frustra: nam insidias mihi instruentem
tangam te prior irrumatione.
atque id si faceres satur, tacerem;
nunc ipsum id doleo, quod esurire
a te mi puer et sitire discet.
quare desine, dum licet pudico,
ne finem facias, sed irrumatus.

Aurelius, father of hungers,
not of these only, but all who either were
or are or will be in other years,
you desire to fuck my love.
And not secretly: for as soon as you are with him, you joke
together and clinging to his side you try everything.
Futile! For I will hit you with mouthfucking first
when you are laying traps against me.
And if you did that when you were full, I'd be quiet.
Now I grieve, because my boy will learn
from you to thirst and to hunger.
Therefore stop, while you can decently,
or else you'll end – but end up mouthfucked.

Unlike poem 15, poem 21 begins brusquely with a rebuke of Aurelius as
father of all appetites (*pater esuritionum*, 1). A character trait that Catullus
acknowledged and accepted in Aurelius in poem 15 (9–12) suddenly
becomes scandalous. As MacLeod and others have argued, "the point of
mocking someone's hunger is commonly to stigmatize him as a parasite,"
and by using this trait to criticize him, Catullus degrades him to the level
of the comic *parasitus*, "a shocking offence against the class-distinctions
which obtain in ancient poetry, as in ancient life."[13] Still, despite the
harsher tone, the terms of the social transaction are the same as before.
Poem 21 is as little concerned with the boy's own interests as poem 15:
again he appears only three times and always as an objectified possession

---

[13] MacLeod (1973, 299); see also Richardson (1963, 103), Ferguson (1985, 65–66), and Dettmer
(1997, 43). Cf. Peek (2002), who argues that Catullus' focus on Aurelius' hunger is about lack of
sexual control rather than parasitical social status; while I agree this is a component of the poem,
I think the elements of Roman comedy that run throughout also lend the interpretation of Aurelius
as *parasitus* what Hinds (1998, 17–34) calls "collective security."

(*meos amores*, 4; *ad latus*, 6; *mi puer*, 11), in contrast to six references to the speaker (*meos*, 4; *mihi*, 7; *tangam*, 8; *tacerem*, 9; *doleo*, 10; *mi*, 11) and nine to Aurelius (*Aureli*, 1; *cupis*, 4; *es*, 5; *iocaris*, 5; *experiris*, 6; *te*, 8; *faceres*, 9; *a te*, 11; *finem facias*, 13). The *puer* remains merely an object whose control is the main issue, and Catullus knows his prey well enough to be certain Aurelius will have taken the bait, just as the clever slaves in *Persa* and *Bacchides* are that their victims could not resist the temptations they offer their antagonists. Aurelius' attempt to seduce the boy puts him in a position of weakness, which Catullus promptly exploits. He threatens Aurelius with oral rape (*tangam te ... irrumatione*, 8; *finem facias, sed irrumatus*, 13) if he does not learn his place as second to Catullus. Indeed, while *irrumatio* has a strong sexual sense, Baehrens, Quinn, and others have suggested it also contains the sense of "cheating," that is, publicly making someone look like a fool by taking what belongs to him, a synonym for *ludificatio*.[14]

In explicitly documenting Aurelius' subordination, Catullus also marks Aurelius as the victim of his scheme by applying to him the same superlative formula that both the *leno* and the *senex* in Plautus use to describe themselves after their subversion at the hands of slaves. Just as Nicobulus in *Bacchides* suffers loss of status because he excelled in his stupidity and foolishness (*stultitia et moribus indoctis*, 1089) all who are, were, or ever have been, Aurelius too suffers for outstripping in his lust all who are, were, or ever have been. Catullus, acting like an ostensibly subservient and ignorant *servus callidus*, has turned the tables on Aurelius by using a carefully devised trap that played on his target's own weaknesses and active attempts to control another. Catullus thus asserts dominance meant to train his potentially unruly rival to steer clear of what he claims as his own property, reserving the *puer* for himself. This is not the only time he uses this trick, and indeed the second allusion to this Plautine schtick turns it against Catullus' *puer delicatus* himself.

## Boy for Sale (Poems 48, 99, 24, 81, 23, and 106)

In Catullus's poetry, Juventius is less a love interest, or even a sexual diversion, than a living symbol of control and dominance in the speaker's

---

[14] For *irrumare* as "to cheat," see Baehrens (1876) and Quinn (1970, 155); cf. Richlin (1992) and Adams (1982, 125–30), who documents instances of the word's weakened meanings. At Catull. 10.12–13, *irrumator praetor* clearly describes Memmius' cheating Catullus and his peers out of opportunities to enrich themselves, and Adams cites an inscription at Ostia that uses the verb in a similar way: *amice fugit te proverbium bene caca et irrima medicos* ("Friend, have you forgotten the saying? 'Shit well and screw the doctors!'").

social contests. Two poems focus on amatory themes (48 and 99) and involve the speaker and boy to the exclusion of all others, but more than twice that many poems (15, 21, 24, 81, and 106) present the *puer* as an object up for bid – sometimes metaphorically, sometimes literally – and focus on the speaker's anxieties over possession and competition with rivals.[15] While in poems 15 and 21 the speaker fully objectifies the boy, in other poems it becomes clear that the speaker's *puer delicatus* has a mind of his own and, what is more, that his devotion to Catullus is more tenuous than we are led to believe in the kiss poem (48). Even here, the status of their relationship is questionable:

> mellitos oculos tuos, Iuventi,
> si quis me sinat usque basiare,
> usque ad milia basiem trecenta;
> nec mi umquam videar satur futurus,
> non si densior aridis aristis                5
> sit nostrae seges osculationis.

> If someone should let me, Juventius,
> keep kissing your honey-sweet eyes,
> I'd kiss them three hundred thousand times
> and I'd never seem to be going to be sated,
> not if the crop of our kissifications
> should be denser than dry wheat.

This poem is more tentative than the other poems on kisses. Poem 5 rushes with urgent jussives, imperatives, and verbs in the future tense (*vivamus, amemus*, 1; *aestimemus*, 3; *da*, 7; *fecerimus*, 10; *conturbabimus*, 11), each conveying Catullus' confidence. In poem 48, however, the speaker is tentative, waiting for permission (*si quis me sinat*, 2) from some unnamed outsider and relying entirely on subjunctives (*sinat . . . basiem . . . videar . . . sit*). His relationship with Juventius is defined by future-less-vivid possibility rather than avowed certitude. Catullus' hesitation here gains new significance in poem 99, where the speaker laments Juventius' reaction when he fails to wait for the permission he implicitly seeks in poem 48 and oversteps:

> surripui tibi, dum ludis, mellite Iuventi,
> saviolum dulci dulcius ambrosia.
> verum id non impune tuli: namque amplius horam
> suffixum in summa me memini esse cruce,

---

[15] See Wray (2001, 71–75) on love objects in Catullus "whether woman or boy, whose function in the text is primarily as a contested property and a coin of invective exchange."

5       dum tibi me purgo nec possum fletibus ullis
            tantillum vestrae demere saevitiae.
        nam simul id factum est, multis diluta labella
            guttis abstersti mollibus articulis,
        ne quicquam nostro contractum ex ore maneret,
10          tamquam commictae spurca saliua lupae.
        praeterea infesto miserum me tradere amori
            non cessasti omnique excruciare modo,
        ut mi ex ambrosia mutatum iam foret illud
            saviolum tristi tristius elleboro.
15      quam quoniam poenam misero proponis amori,
            numquam iam posthac basia surripiam.

        I stole from you while you played, honey-sweet Juventius,
            a little kiss sweeter than sweet ambrosia.
        But I did not take it unpunished: for more than an hour
            I remember that I was fixed on the top of a cross
        while I apologized to you, and I could not with any tears
            remove the smallest bit of your savage hostility.
        For as soon as it happened, you wiped your lips
            washed with many teardrops using your soft fingers,
        so that nothing from my mouth would stay on yours,
            as if it were the filthy spit of a pissed-on whore.
        Then you did not stop handing me over to hostile love
            in my misery and torturing me in every way possible,
        until that little kiss of mine, changed from ambrosia,
            was more bitter than bitter hellebore.
        Since you demand this penalty for my miserable love,
            never from now on will I steal kisses.

In contrast to the unnumbered kisses he yearns for in poem 48, Catullus
steals only one little peck (*saviolum*, 2). But even this is too much, and
Juventius responds vehemently, subjecting him to emotional punishment
reminiscent of the physical sort experienced by slaves in Roman comedy
(*suffixum in summa me ... cruce*, 4; *excruciare*, 12), which serves as a
symbol of their subjugation to the power of another and lack of personal
agency.[16] This relationship is not based on equality. Indeed, Nappa has
recently argued that it is not an erotic relationship at all, except in Catullus'
own head.[17] There is no reason in either of these poems to think Juventius
saw himself as Catullus' *puer*, and his reaction in poem 99 suggests that

[16] For links between control, clever slaves, and torture in Roman comedy, see Parker (1989) and
Richlin (2017, 28–34).
[17] In a not-yet-published paper delivered in 2018 at the 114th annual meeting of the Classical
Association of the Middle West and South, in which Nappa argues for a resistant approach to

Catullus' love for him is unrequited and that his courtship has not
gone well.

The other poems where Juventius appears make clear that the relationship between *puer* and Catullus is at best tenuous and in need of reaffirma-
tion, and more probably one in which the boy is actively evading Catullus
and the speaker is trying to change his mind. Poem 24 certainly suggests
that Juventius is on the market:

> o qui flosculus es Iuventiorum,
> non horum modo, sed quot aut fuerunt
> aut posthac aliis erunt in annis,
> mallem divitias Midae dedisses
> isti, cui neque servus est neque arca,                   5
> quam sic te sineres ab illo amari.
> "quid? non est homo bellus?" inquies. est:
> sed bello huic neque servus est neque arca.
> hoc tu quam lubet abice elevaque:
> nec servum tamen ille habet neque arcam.                 10

> O you who are the little flower of the Juventii,
> not of these only, but all who either were
> or afterward will be in other years,
> I would rather you had given the wealth of Midas
> to that man, who has neither a slave nor a strongbox,
> than allow yourself to be loved so by that man.
> "What? Isn't he a fine man?" you say. He is:
> but he's a fine man who has neither a slave nor a strongbox.
> Toss this away and throw it out however you like:
> still, he doesn't have a slave or a strongbox.

As with Aurelius, Catullus finds use for the Plautine *servus callidus*, wearing
a comic mask to subvert Juventius and exploit his subservient pose as a
means to overcome the boy's resistance. Juventius seems to be interested in
another lover, whom he calls a "pretty man" (*homo bellus*, 7), but the
speaker tries to convince the boy that any reciprocation would be a bad
idea. He may be pretty (*est*, 7), but he is also poor and does not have even a
slave or a strongbox (*neque servus est neque arca*, 5, 8; *nec servum tamen ille
habet neque arcam*, 10).

Who could this undesirable man be and why would the speaker have
such strong feelings about Juventius's affairs with him? Answers can be
found in two intratextual references that point elsewhere. First, the phrase

Catullus' presentation of the relationship with Juventius in the vein of Pedrick's (1986 and 1993)
reading of his speaker's representation of his relationship with Lesbia.

*homo bellus* appears one other time in poems about Juventius, at poem 81. As in poem 24, Catullus warns him away from a man in whom he shows interest:[18]

> nemone in tanto potuit populo esse, Iuventi,
>     bellus homo, quem tu diligere inciperes,
> praeterquam iste tuus moribunda ab sede Pisauri
>     hospes inaurata pallidior statua,
> qui tibi nunc cordi est, quem tu praeponere nobis
>     audes, et nescis quod facinus facias?

> Can no one in so great a populace, Juventius, seem
>     a fine man whom you would begin to cherish,
> besides that diseased fellow from the seat of Pisaurum,
>     a stranger paler than a gilt statue,
> who now is in your heart, whom you dare to prefer
>     to me, and you do not know what crime you commit?

Poem 81's *bellus homo* is unnamed, but Catullus' dubbing him the "host paler than a gilt statue" (*hospes inaurata pallidior statua*, 4) contains a punning allusion to **Aur**elius, which is reinforced also by his reference to Midas's wealth and its implicit connection to gold in poem 24 (*divitias Midae*, 4).[19] But a second intratextual reference in the poem complicates this identification, as it points instead to Aurelius' friend, Furius. The two appear as peas in a pod at two other moments in the corpus (*Furi et Aureli, comites Catulli*, 11.1; *Aureli pathice et cinaede Furi*, 16.2), and in poem 23 he begins his address by mocking Furius' poverty: "Furius, who has neither a slave nor a strongbox" (*Furi, cui neque servus est neque arca*, 1). This prominently positioned opening line picks up three different instances in poem 24 where the unnamed *homo bellus* is said to lack the same possessions (*cui neque servus est neque arca*, 5; *huic neque servus est neque arca*, 8; *nec servum tamen ille habet neque arcam*, 10).[20]

So which man is the *bellus homo*? Scholars generally assume that the proximity of poems 23 and 24 confirms that he is Furius, but nothing precludes either possibility.[21] But this ambiguity is not problematic – in

---

[18] Krostenko (2001a, 274–76) notes that *audes ... facinus facias* in Catull. 24.6 might represent another allusion to Roman comedy, since this collocation "suggests the nexus of *audacia* and *facinus (facere)*, common for 'outrageous' acts in comedy," citing close parallels at Pl. *Aul.* 460, *Bac.* 682, *Capt.* 753, *Ps.* 541–42, Ter. *An.* 401, and *Eu.* 644 and 958–59.
[19] Thomson (1998, 82) and Marsilio and Podlesney (2006).
[20] See Syndikus (1984, 165–66), Dettmer (1997, 48), and Wray (2001, 73).
[21] See, e.g., Richardson (1963), Wray (2001, 73), and Marsilio and Podlesney (2006). Green (1940) and Thomson (1998, 265) allow that poem 24's *homo bellus* may be Aurelius.

fact, I think, it is purposeful and pointed. By simultaneously inscribing both men as his rivals for Juventius' attention in poem 24, he undermines their relevance as individual people, in much the same way as he diminishes Juventius' identity by objectifying him in poems 15 and 21. The focus in this poem is on the struggle for power in the erotic relationship between the speaker and the boy. The particular identities are largely irrelevant, including that of the *puer* himself: Catullus calls him the *flosculus Iuventiorum*, "little flower of the Juventii," and although this appellation may suggest the boy's descent from the illustrious Tuscan family of the Juventii, as Fordyce argues, it was also standard practice when naming a beloved to use a pseudonym.[22] The same holds true for Juventius, which is surely just as fictive and etymologically significant a name as Lesbia ("the woman from Lesbos").[23] Juventius may be taken as merely a nominalized form of *iuvenis*, "young man," and thus *flosculus Juventiorum* as something like "a particularly delicate example of the many young men being pursued in Rome." His name genericizes the boy, diminishing the importance of his identity as anything other than a target for control just as the ambiguity of Furius and Aurelius in poem 24 marks them as nothing more significant than generic rivals to be overcome.

Notably, at the opening of poem 24 the speaker takes up the same wheedling stance he does toward Aurelius in poem 15, and the same one the *servus callidus* of Roman comedy uses to ingratiate himself with a superior character whom he tries to deceive. Calling the boy *flosculus* flatters him and allows Catullus to cast himself as his protector.[24] Furthermore, he repeatedly emphasizes the boy's financial interests in what is ultimately an erotic matter, in much the same way as the *servus callidus* focuses on money with an eye toward acquiring the beloved. He says that he would rather Juventius give away all the riches of Midas than to let himself be loved by the man (*mallem divitias Midae dedisses / isti, cui neque servus est neque arca, / quam sic te sineres ab illo amari*, 4–6). The speaker does not offer any money or attempt to bargain with the boy, merely

---

[22] Fordyce (1961, 155); cf. Kroll (1959, 45), who argues for identification with some Juventii of Verona, and see also Hubbard (2004/5, 182), who incorrectly compares Gallus in Verg. *Ecl.* 10 as evidence for using a real name in poetry, since they do not perform the same role (Gallus is not a beloved, but an active *amator*, closer in status to poetic speakers of Latin poetry such as Catullus and the elegists, who share the same name as their authors).

[23] On the poetic convention of using pseudonyms for the beloved, see Randall (1979), Wyke (1987), Holzberg (2001), and Heslin (2011). Remarkably, scholars recognize pseudonyms as common features of many of Catullus' named figures (e.g., *Mentula* = *Mamurra*, *Lesbius* = *Clodius*) but have resisted this idea in the case of Juventius; see Hutchinson (2003, 211).

[24] Quinn (1970, 164).

discussing what the boy can do (*dedisses*, 4; *te sineres*, 6) and thus suggesting that Catullus has no stake of his own in this decision – though to the reader this stance is obviously a disingenuous one. Finally, as with Aurelius, the speaker knowingly sympathizes with Juventius' predicament. He agrees with the boy that the man is pretty (*est*, 7), but he has reservations about this relatively small positive point in light of the larger financial issues at stake.

And this matter is primarily about money, as the speaker emphasizes that this other man is a poor choice because he is not the most promising buyer. While it does not refer directly to Juventius by name, poem 106 can also be seen to stand in the background of this situation:

> cum puero bello praeconem qui videt esse,
>     quid credit, nisi se vendere discupere?

> When someone sees an auctioneer with a pretty boy,
>     what does he think, except that he wants to sell himself?

The boy is essentially selling himself, at least in the speaker's eyes, and Catullus' professed aim in poem 24 is to make sure that Juventius does not make a poor choice. Of course, poems 48 and 99 reveal that his tacit goal is to claim the boy for himself, and his plan to achieve this relies on making Juventius doubt the financial status of Catullus' rivals and implying that he has more to offer the *puer*.

Recently, Shawn O'Bryhim has argued that poem 23 alludes repeatedly to Roman comedy and that Catullus uses these comic elements to portray Furius as the penniless *adulescens amator* and Juventius as a *meretrix* whom the "young man in love" needs money to purchase.[25] Indeed, if, as I have argued, Catullus consistently portrays Juventius as an object over whom competing lovers are engaged in a competition for control, his points take on greater significance beyond the boundary of that poem alone. We already saw in the previous chapter how Catullus appropriates the image of the comic *adulescens* to represent himself in other erotic contexts. With the addition of poem 23, we can see that Catullus essentially represents himself, Furius, and Aurelius as three Roman comic rivals striving to possess Juventius, who seems to be playing them off one another like the shrewd *mala meretrix*. In poem 24, Catullus tries to redirect the *puer*'s erotic/financial attention away from these other men, emphasizing their poverty. This, of course, requires eliding over his own *paupertas*, which Catullus shows in poem 13 is substantial: "your Catullus' wallet is full of

---

[25] O'Bryhim (2007, 135–36).

cobwebs; but instead you'll receive pure love" (*nam tui Catulli | plenus sacculus est aranearum. | sed contra accipies meros amores*, 7–9). The speaker's cobwebs match those of Furius in poem 23, whose deficiencies include, besides a slave and a strongbox, a spider as well (*araneus*, 2). He does, however, at least have something Furius lacks: a *servus*, in the shape of the "clever slave" he performs as in poem 24. His intertextual invocation of this Plautine stock character is a wink to the audience, revealing the sleight of hand he uses to get the *puer* – or, barring that, to deprive his competition of financial and sexual satisfaction.

## Patrons and Parasites (Poem 49)

Of the three intratextual allusions to the comic schtick I explore in this chapter, the two examined thus far seem a sensible set: one about deceiving Aurelius and wresting control over Juventius, the other about deceiving Juventius and asserting superiority over Aurelius and Furius. The schtick's last appearance in the corpus, though, seems utterly remote from these homosocial and homoerotic squabbles, namely, poem 49, Catullus' panegyric of Cicero. Nevertheless, I think the same Plautine deception and assertion of control over a rival in a superior position undergirds his engagement with Cicero as well, and with similar humorous effects.

In poem 49 Catullus deferentially praises Cicero while undercutting his own qualities:

> disertissime Romuli nepotum,
> quot sunt quotque fuere, Marce Tulli,
> quotque post aliis erunt in annis,
> gratias tibi maximas Catullus
> agit pessimus omnium poeta,          5
> tanto pessimus omnium poeta,
> quanto tu optimus omnium patronus.

> Most learned of Romulus's grandsons,
> all who are and all who were, Marcus Tullius,
> and all afterward who will be in other years,
> Catullus gives the greatest thanks to you –
> Catullus the worst poet of all;
> as much the worst poet of all
> as you are the best patron of all.

Interpretations of poem 49 falls into two distinct camps: the first argues that the speaker is being genuine, humbling himself before the great orator for some unnamed benevolent act performed by Cicero for Catullus' benefit; the second argues that the speaker is exaggerating ironically and that his sheer hyperbole cannot be reconciled with any sincere gratitude.[26] Both are plausible on their face, but I think the Plautine deception schtick that can be seen to stand behind the opening three lines encourages the more humorous and deceptive reading, which is also more in keeping with Catullus' approach elsewhere.[27]

The pose that the speaker strikes is consistently wheedling: his hyperbolic thanks (*gratias tibi maximas*, 4), his extreme humility and self-deprecation (*pessimus omnium poeta*, 5–6), and his elevation of Cicero with the highest praise (*tu optimus omnium patronus*, 7) serve to set up the speaker as a sycophantic confidante on par with a Plautine slave. Furthermore, the speaker's tongue-in-cheek juxtaposition of himself as worst poet and Cicero as best patron of all conceals multiple jokes. By calling himself a *poeta* and Cicero a *patronus*, the speaker emphasizes that poetry is not the orator's best suit, diminishing Cicero's literary merit.[28] Next, Catullus uses an ambiguous genitive in *omnium*, implying both that Cicero is the best *patronus* out of all *patroni* (i.e., understanding *omnium* as a partitive genitive) and that he is the best *patronus* to call if you are guilty or disreputable, because he will advocate for any- and everyone without scruple (i.e., *omnium* as an objective genitive).[29] He wheedles Cicero with praise and compliments, all the while ironically mocking him, at least to those who can read between the lines of the poem. The speaker uses irony to invert the relative positions of Cicero and himself, temporarily advancing in the zero-sum game of social jockeying that dominates both first-century BCE Roman society and Catullus's poetry.

This clever malevolence on the part of the speaker highlights one final comic allusion in this poem. As I discuss in the Introduction, Catullus infuses false modesty and nugatory play into poem 1, where he downplays to his dedicatee Cornelius Nepos the significance of his work – but also wants his addressee to play along and recognize that Catullus means his work to be taken more seriously than he represents it. He performs the same gesture in poem 49, adding a special marker that suggests he does not expect or want Cicero to be in on the same nugatory jokes that he and his

---

[26] See Fredericksmeyer (1973) for representative bibliography of both arguments, with Tatum (1988), Batstone (1993), and Thomson (1998, 323–24) for more recent work.

[27] Karakasis (2014) also sees a comic allusion here and argues for sincerity in poem 49; while I disagree, I find his interpretation worth considering simultaneously, particularly for the possible ways in which he incorporates Cicero's own oratorical use of Roman comedy.

[28] Gugel (1967) and Thomson (1967, 227, and 1998, 324).

[29] Schmidt (1914) and Collins (1952).

close friends enjoy. Catullus calls himself "the worst poet" (*pessimus ... poeta*, 49.6), using a term laden with comic baggage. As I noted at the start of this chapter, Plautus frequently employs *pessimus* and related vocabulary of *malitia* to mark out what Anderson names "Heroic Badness," a special quality that he attributes to the *servus callidus*, who uses his native cunning, quick wit, and disarming charm to exploit his social superiors and explode the status quo.[30] A brief summary of its essential features in Plautus is in order. In its broadest sense, it is rebellion for rebellion's sake, a temporary triumph of play over the chafing constraints of society. While badness with a lowercase "b" implies inherent flaws and unfitness for some purpose ("bad egg," "bad taste," "bad attitude"), Badness, signified by the Latin word *malitia*, involves "ill intentions and willful deceitfulness" achieved through *dolus*, that is, trickery, guile, and general wiliness.[31]

Comic "clever slaves" use *malitia* to their advantage to gain control over someone with greater social standing, because the sides are so unbalanced. Here the speaker takes a page from their books, marking himself as a representative of Heroic Badness in poem 49 and gaining the upper hand over Cicero, whose standing and reputation in Rome were beyond Catullus' own. But he also expands its usage, deploying it against Aurelius, Furius, and Juventius in social and erotic situations to assert his own superiority over them. But why should such a lowly character and the stereotypically disreputable tool of *malitia* be particularly appealing as a means to achieve this? One answer, I think, lies in the structural overlap between the plots of Roman comedy and the reality in which the Roman audience watching them lived.

Although more than a century had elapsed since Plautus was writing, and though Roman comedy centers on different socioeconomic classes than Catullus' poetry, the same issues that Plautus' plays explored in the third and second centuries BCE persisted well into the first century BCE. And many of the social problems that affect slaves and sex laborers in Plautus' comedies likewise afflicted affluent young men like Catullus, albeit of course on a different scale and with different repercussions. Catullus' world was, in effect, a continuous play centered on Roman struggles for superiority across traditional boundaries, and his poetry reflects concerns about personal identity and individual status time and

---

[30] Anderson (1993, 88–106); see also Segal (1987), who predates Anderson's coinage but still explores the concept, and McCarthy (2000, 3–34 and passim), for whom comic *malitia* presents a distinctive component of Plautus' technique, as well as Fantham (2008), who argues that by the first century BCE it had developed a strong association with comic rogues.

[31] Fantham (2008).

again. One path to success in this series of social performances lay in accepting, even embracing one's relative inferiority, and using the tools available to make the most of one's position as subjugated individual, essentially to cast oneself as versatile comic hero rather than inflexible and doomed tragic protagonist. In this way, Plautine Heroic Badness was an optimal weapon in Roman social struggles. And Kathleen McCarthy argues that one of the most accessible ways for Romans to cope with this constant struggle was through humor, and particularly the self-consciously clever and malevolent humor of an inferior individual aimed at knocking superiors down a notch, if only temporarily.[32] The "clever slave" of Roman comedy embodies this kind of humorous subversion: when Romans watched Chrysalus or Pseudolus on stage, regardless of their own status, they saw a universalized, idealized, and triumphant avatar of themselves sketched in the clearest and simplest terms, a Platonic form of self-assertion in a society in which control was usually in the hands of someone else. Fitzgerald nicely summarizes McCarthy's major points:[33]

> Doubtless slaves at Rome did resist and manipulate their masters to the best of their ability, but Plautus' clever slaves are not just portraits, however exaggerated, of that resistance. These lovable tricksters in their imaginary Greek setting can be read, among other things, as fantasy projections of the free, not so much portraits of slaves as others through whom the free could play out their own agenda. Slavery, as a polar opposite of the free state, could be the place where the free imagined escaping from the demands of "liberal" comportment and indulging in revolt against their own superiors.

The slave protagonist's Heroic Badness represents a fortiori freedom for any and everyone, since if a slave – the character most subject to the will of others – can triumph over his social betters, then certainly those equal or superior to him (i.e., the entire audience) can similarly gain control over their own lives.

It should not be surprising that this celebration of Heroic Badness that Plautus exploits so well and fully should permeate Catullus' poetry.[34] In the late Republic, elite culture in Rome was circumscribed by rigid hierarchies based on ancestry, class, rank, wealth, sex, gender, and any number of criteria for which individuals were constantly judged, appraised, and assigned relative social roles. All Romans had "bosses," so to speak –

---

[32] McCarthy (2000, 25–34); see also Fitzgerald (2000, 32–50).    [33] Fitzgerald (2000, 11).
[34] Pace Quinn (1972, 220), who asserts: "But the skinflint father and the witty slave are the result of the exigencies of plot-construction: their function is to produce the bewildering sequence of hopeless complication hard on the heels of hopeless complication. Their absence from the pages of Catullus isn't surprising, therefore."

others whose evaluations of their behavior and character defined the groups to which they were allowed to belong – and Romans were in one way or another subject to the authority or dominance of others and had to jockey for position against their peers and superiors.[35] Similar insecurities about the status quo and one's place within it that Rome's social system engenders stand prominently in many of Catullus' poems, particularly those such as 21, 24, and 49 that explore poetic rivalry, erotic competition, and social one-upmanship. In these moments the speaker takes a page from Plautus' book, adopting the universalizing *servus callidus* and his distinctively humorous *malitia* to find ways to advance his own interests over those of Aurelius, Furius, Juventius, and Cicero.

---

[35] See McCarthy (2000, 17–29), as well as Fitzgerald (2000, 69–86), who focuses primarily on slavery as a means for understanding social hierarchy during the early Empire, and Wallace-Hadrill (1989) for a discussion of Roman social hierarchies and competition in these periods.

# CHAPTER 4

# Naughty Girls
## Comic Figures and Gendered Control in Catullus

What makes a "good" Roman woman? To answer this question, likely our best source is the dead – or, to be more precise, those who commemorated them. In describing the qualities of the ideal "good" woman, the sponsors of Roman funerary monuments return again and again to the same circumscribed set of traits. Take, for example, the epitaph of Claudia, from a generation or two before Catullus was born (*CIL* 6.15346):[1]

> hospes, quod deico paullum est: asta ac pellege.
> heic est sepulcrum hau pulcrum pulcrai feminae.
> nomen parentes nominarunt Claudiam.
> suom mareitom corde deilexit souo.
> gnatos duos creavit. horunc alterum
> in terra linquit, alium sub terra locat.
> sermone lepido, tum autem incessu commodo.
> domum servavit. lanam fecit. dixi. abei.

> Stranger, what I have to say is short. Stop and read.
> This is the unlovely tomb of a lovely woman.
> Her parents named her with the name Claudia.
> She cherished her husband in her heart.
> She produced two sons. Of these, she leaves
> one behind on the earth; the other she puts under it.
> Her speech was charming; moreover, her gait was agreeable.
> She kept her home. She spun wool. I have finished speaking. Go.

We might compare the epitaph of Amymone, who died around Catullus' lifetime (*CIL* 6.34045):

> hic iacet Amymone uxor Barbari pulcherrima
> pia, frugi, casta, lanifica, domiseda.

---

[1] Krostenko (2001a, 71–72) discusses some of the vocabulary used here and its relevance for social ideals in first-century BCE Rome.

> Here lies Amymone, wife of Barbarus; the most beautiful,
> she was dutiful, frugal, chaste, made wool, and stayed home.

And as a final example, that of a freedwoman named Veratia Salvia (*CIL* 6.19838):

> seic florem aetatis tenuit veratia caste
>   nulla ut perciperet gaudia dedecoris
> coniuge namque uno vixit contenta probate
>   cetera digna bonis femina facta tulit.

> Veratia kept the flower of her age so chastely
>   that no delight in dishonor took hold of her:
> for she lived content with one esteemed spouse.
>   A woman worthy of good things, she endured the opposite.

As Werner Riess notes, it is telling that "seven to ten adjectives were capable of representing thousands of women of so many different generations and social classes."[2] From the noble mother of the Gracchi to foreigners and freedwomen, emphasis consistently remains on how these women performed a particular set of roles that included being beautiful but modest, a steadfast supporter of her family's men but utterly absent from the public civic life in which those men participated, and – perhaps most significant of all – willing to endure whatever was necessary for the success of others, even at cost to herself. Riess concludes that grave markers were "not a medium to challenge the gendered assignments of social norms and roles, but one to make them firm, steadfast, even immobile ... They not only subjected women to male rule and dominance, but also stabilized Roman social relations and thus Roman power in general by making the gender hierarchy permanent."[3]

Such "good women," *lanificae* and *univirae*, appear abundantly in Roman epitaphs, and they also show up in the fantasies of other Roman poets, but they are not really to be found in Catullus' world.[4] With a few exceptions, Catullus is interested in women who break that mold, and the more forcefully they do, the more fascinating they are to him. For him, the feminine ideal seems to have been not the *bona mulier*, but the *pessima puella*, the "naughty girl." Something similar can be said of Roman comedy, whose *malae meretrices* are often the stars of the show, and to

---

[2] Riess (2012, 493). See also Hallett (1973).    [3] Riess (2012, 500–501).

[4] Chaste, wool-working women appear in Prop. 1.3.41–46, Tib. 1.3.83–88, Ov. *Am.* 1.13.23–26, etc. Significantly, Catullus' only *lanificae* are the Parcae, on whose aged lips bits of wool cling grotesquely (*laneaque aridulis haerebant morsa labellis*, 64.314) and whose prophetic threads presage widespread murder, desecration, and the abandonment of mortals by the gods.

whom Catullus alludes throughout his poetic corpus. Indeed, in the Introduction I briefly discussed how he casts Varus' girlfriend in poem 10 as a *mala meretrix* who uses her cleverness to undercut his own attempt to perform as a comic *miles gloriosus*. In this chapter, I explore other poems in which women are explicitly marked as "bad" and argue that, in each case, Catullus uses their *malitia* as a way to consider and display tensions that arise when men and women compete for control. These women take on characteristics of comedy's *meretrices callidae*, or "clever sex laborers," while he aligns himself with familiar antagonistic stock types such as the "harsh father" or "braggart soldier," figures through whom traditional aristocratic values and male concerns are caricatured.

In the previous chapter, I examined how Catullus' speaker performs as the *servus callidus*, or "clever slave," of Roman comedy in several poems, particularly when he jockeys for position against aristocratic male competitors. The comic slave was interesting to him, I think, for much the same reason he was so popular on the stage: his exploits represent Saturnalian freedom, an opportunity for Romans to fantasize about what they might do if they were unbound by *mores maiorum* and obligations to social superiors that hold them to traditional behavioral norms.[5] The *servus callidus* allows the poet to ponder, "What if I could do and say whatever I wanted to others with more control in any given situation, and get away with impunity to boot?" As I noted in the previous chapter, the trait that gives the "clever slave" this power is "Heroic Badness," as Anderson has termed it: an indifference to the rules of Roman society, pleasure in cleverness and trickery, and desire to subvert authority for the sake not of personal gain but of the temporary triumph of pleasure over business.[6] In this chapter, we will see that Heroic Badness belongs not to the *servus callidus* alone but also to other incarnations of the subaltern, particularly the *meretrix callida*, or "clever sex laborer."

These lower-class women have much in common with Roman comedy's *servi callidi*, as Gratwick observes: "The *meretrix* is exotic, extravagant, and amoral rather than immoral. She is presented as the intellectual equal of the clever slave, being *docta, astuta, callida, faceta, mala, nequam*, and taking the same detached view of love as he."[7] Sex laborers in Roman comedy act as counterparts to "clever slaves," who share similar methods but different anxieties. They both use Heroic Badness as a tool to assert

---

[5] On the *servus callidus* and Saturnalian inversion, see Segal (1987); for the paradoxical role of the *servus callidus* in aristocratic audience's fantasies of freedom, see McCarthy (2000, 3–34).
[6] Anderson (1993, 88–106).   [7] Gratwick (1982, 110).

control over their own lives, but while the *servus callidus* struggles against his servile status and citizens who wield social and legal authority, the *meretrix callida* is faced with the difficulties that being a woman in Rome automatically entails.

It might seem odd that Catullus – an aristocratic male citizen– would show an interest in the challenges of being a woman and make women the protagonists in some of his poems, but it is well established that his work is defined by a certain affinity with the feminine, especially in contrast to masculine Roman ideals such as *negotium* and *virtus*.[8] Additionally, women in Catullus' poetry occupy positions similar to the "clever slave": because they are not allowed to participate in public spheres, they are also free from the social restrictions and expectations that bind their male counterparts in, for example, patron–client relationships and political maneuvers. No Roman male citizen would envy the lack of self-determination that women face, and neither would he welcome the very real dangers and degradations of slavery, but there is nevertheless a certain appeal to servile and female disengagement from the strictures of free male competition. If the audience of a Roman comedy and Catullus could enjoy watching "clever slaves" exercise their roguish freedom, that could also motivate their joy in seeing "clever sex laborers," whose Plautine *malitia* helps them overcome their social superiors. The figure of the *meretrix callida* becomes for Catullus an embodiment of the anti-traditional values that he embraces throughout his poetry – *urbanitas*, *venustas*, and *lepos* – and not only that, but a useful exemplary model for navigating the complexities of social competition.

Rei observes that, "in the plays of Plautus, the discourse of the body is linked to the discourse of social status" and that social inferiority is connected "on the one hand with the vulnerability of slaves to physical and sexual abuse by their masters, and on the other hand with the expected role of the sexually passive and socially submissive woman."[9] But there is a major difference in Plautine comedy between the roles that free, aristocratic women such as the "dowered wife," or *uxor dotata*, play and those that we see lower-class *meretrices* performing. Free women of the upper classes, even when they oppose male characters or grumble about their treatment at the hands of their husbands, never take any action that violates traditional mores. While they are oppressed by male hegemony,

---

[8] See Wiseman (1985, 115–24), Skinner (2007), and Stevens (2013, 203–56) on feminine interests and discourse in Catullus' poetry.
[9] Rei (1998, 92).

they are nevertheless (often unwilling) participants in the same set of values and traditions as men in Roman comedy. For example, Cleostrata, the wife in *Casina*, works to stop her husband Lysidamus from sleeping with Casina, but at the end of the play she forgives him and gladly returns to their domestic status quo. Rei notes that "she both reasserts her own virtue and rescues her husband from the threatening implications of his humiliation. Husband and wife are reunited in order to affirm domestic stability.... The questions raised in the course of the action about the upper-class male's control over his subordinates have been resolved in his favor."[10]

Lower-class and slave women, however, gain nothing from such restoration of traditional values. In fact, quite the opposite: whereas citizen wives in Roman comedy can, and often must, ensure domestic stability to protect their standing as *matronae* and to avoid the perils of divorce, domestic bliss and perfect Roman mores would put *meretrices* and the like out of business and in impossible financial straits.[11] For them, male dominance represents a catch-22: as women, they are automatically prone to sexual and social assaults when they interact with men, but since they are also wholly dependent on men for their living, refusals to engage would exclude them from the resources controlled by men. "Clever sex laborers" must strike the difficult balance between subjecting themselves to male authority and asserting their own independence, to play the game while bending the rules that put them at a disadvantage so they can have a chance to win, if only momentarily. Heroic Badness gives women in Roman comedy a tool set to achieve this goal by acting naughty enough to be desirable while being Naughty enough to use male desire and pride to their advantage.[12]

One of the key differences between servile Heroic Badness and female *malitia* centers on this intermediate position in which comic women find themselves. When a "clever slave" uses Heroic Badness, he makes an active choice to interfere in the business of free citizens and to align himself with rebellious "bad" slaves rather than obedient "good" slaves, a vital

---

[10] Rei (1998, 104).

[11] See Rei (1998) on the roles of free and unfree women in Plautus' plays. James (2003, 35–107) outlines the many material difficulties of socially and financially dependent women in Roman comedy and elegy.

[12] Rei (1998, 94): "Female tricksters in particular are referred to and proudly refer to themselves as *malae* ('bad') in this context. It is important, however, to qualify Anderson's observation by pointing out that the trickster's *malitia* sidesteps ethical evaluation: the term is always used in reference to his or her theatrical skill at circumventing power through disguise and role-play."

distinction that we will examine more closely in the next section. While he is subject to verbal and physical abuse from his master, he is not seen per se as a target, since aristocratic males do not, in Roman comedy at least, seek out slaves for the express purpose of dominating them. It is possible for the comic slave to keep his head down and do what he is told without inviting abuse from his social superiors, so becoming a *servus callidus* and using Heroic Badness represent active choices to antagonize the authorities. The comic *meretrix*, however, does not have the luxury of avoiding the dominance of others, since her livelihood derives from submitting herself to the sexual and social power of men. Additionally, her sex automatically makes her a target, as women in Rome are expected to be physically inferior and sexually passive. Sex laborers do not need to seek out negative attention from male citizens, because men will always come to them for the purpose of dominating them.

For comic *meretrices callidae*, Heroic Badness offers a way to redirect and escape abuse and attempts at domination by men. Unlike *servi callidi*, who use *malitia* actively to invert the social hierarchy and temporarily make their superiors inferior, *meretrices* use it as a form of comic aikido to grab male aggression and use its momentum to turn it against their would-be assailants. The final act of Plautus' *Bacchides* offers a clear example. Before this point, the *adulescentes amatores* Mnesilochus and Pistoclerus have fallen in love with two *meretrices*, sisters named Bacchis, to the chagrin (and monetary loss) of their fathers Nicobulus and Philoxenus. The women have never themselves wronged the two old men, but these *senes duri* blame the sex laborers rather than their sons and rush toward their house to scare them away, threatening to break in the doors with axes (*heus Bacchis, iube sic actutum aperiri fores, / nisi mavoltis fores et postis comminui securibus*, 1118–19). Nicobulus calls the women *pessumae* (1123) and one of them *ista mala* (1162), marking them as Heroically Bad. Of course, the *meretrices* have embraced their Badness from the beginning of the play (*ne tibi lectus malitiam apud me suadeat?*, 54), and they flip the tables on Nicobulus, naming him "best old man in the world" (*senex optume quantum est in terra*, 1170) and so aligning him with the side of law and order that Roman comedy dooms to failure.[13] These women use Heroically Bad jokes and wordplay throughout this scene, and before long they overwhelm both men. By the end of the scene Nicobulus admits that he has been twisted to the dark side (*tua sum opera et propter te improbior*, 1201), and one of the sisters closes the play by highlighting the

---

[13] See Anderson (1993, 101–3).

women's success in turning the *senes*' attempted assault against them
(1207). For these and other comic *meretrices callidae*, the anti-value of
*malitia* provides a means to self-defense, and something similar can be seen
in Catullus' appropriation of female Heroic Badness. In poems 55/58b and
36/37 he tries to abuse women and has his attack turned against himself,
and to these examples we will turn now.

### Lessons from the Ladies at Pompey's Theater (Poems 55 and 58B)

Situated near the end of Catullus' polymetrics among poems often dis-
missed as failed experiments or notebook scraps, poem 55 and its companion 58b have drawn comparatively little notice from scholars.[14] When
read, attention is usually given to their text-critical problems, their unusual
meters, or the light they shed the topography of the city of Rome in the
late Republic.[15] But I would argue that these poems represent not only one
of the most interesting interactions in the corpus but also a key moment
for understanding how Catullus represents gender and power, which
I argue he explores through Plautine Heroic Badness and an allusion to a
scene in Plautus' *Amphitruo*. To begin, in poem 55 Catullus recounts an
outing in Rome spent searching fruitlessly all over the city for his elusive
friend Camerius:[16]

---

[14]  Failed experiments or posthumously published scraps: Merrill (1893, 89 and 93), Barwick (1928),
    Wheeler (1934, 252 n. 35), Fordyce (1961, 225, 232, and 409–10), Clausen (1976, 40), Skinner
    (1981, 74–76), Thomson (1998, 335–6 and 344); for arguments *contra*, see Peachy (1972) and
    MacLeod (1973).

[15]  Bibliography on the poems' text-critical issues is massive, but see, esp., Copley (1952), Bianco
    (1964), Khan (1967), Foster (1971), Peachy (1972, 258–61), Camps (1973), Goold (1974, 15–21),
    Németh (1978), Harrison and Heyworth (1999, 98–101), and Kokosziewicz (2007). On the
    poems' odd meter, a mixture of deca- and hendecasyllables, see Ellis (1889, 188), Peachy (1972,
    261–63), and Goold (1974, 15–21). On topography in the poems: Ellis (1889, 189–95), Wiseman
    (1979, 1980a, and 1980b), and Richardson (1980).

[16]  The text is Thomson's (1998) except: in line 9 where I prefer the manuscripts' *ipse*, defended
    credibly by Foster (1971), over Munro's (1905, 129–31) unnecessary emendation *usque*; and in line
    13, where I follow Copley (1952) in assigning this and the preceding line to the *puella*, for reasons
    discussed later. I do not aim to solve the poem's textual difficulties, which have fueled an
    overwhelming bibliography, but a few remarks are necessary. Khan (1967, 121) and Foster
    (1971) persuasively argue that *avelte* in line 9 derives from corrupt dittography of *quas vultu* in
    line 8 directly above, obscuring the original opening, which is irrecoverable. Camps (1973, 131–32)
    asserts that whatever *avelte* displaced was a "verb of command, entreaty or enquiry," likely an
    imperative (e.g., "Give him back!," cf. *reflagitate:* / "*moecha putida, redde codicillos*" at 42.10–11);
    Riese (1884), Goold (1983), and Kokoszkiewicz (2007) propose an indicative verb of accusation
    (e.g., "You took him!," cf. *tam bellum mihi passerem abstulistis,* 3.15). The sense, at any rate, is clear:
    the speaker implies the women are hiding Camerius. The end of line 11 is also lost, but Ellis' (1889)
    supplement adopted by Thomson seems reasonable; for alternatives, which mostly amount to the
    same idea, see Harrison and Heyworth (1999, 101).

oramus, si forte non molestum est,
demonstres ubi sint tuae tenebrae.
te in Campo quaesivimus minore,
te in Circo, te in omnibus libellis,
te in templo summi Iovis sacrato.                                    5
in Magni simul ambulatione
femellas omnes, amice, prendi,
quas vultu vidi tamen sereno.
†avelte† (sic ipse flagitabam):
"Camerium mihi, pessimae puellae!"                                  10
quaedam inquit, nudum reduc<ta pectus,>
"en hic in roseis latet papillis,
sed te iam ferre Herculei labos est."
tanto te in fastu negas, amice?
dic nobis ubi sis futurus, ede                                      15
audacter, committe, crede luci.
nunc te lacteolae tenent puellae?
si linguam clauso tenes in ore,
fructus proicies amoris omnes.
verbosa gaudet Venus loquella.                                      20
vel, si vis, licet obseres palatum,
dum vestri sim particeps amoris.

I beg you, if perhaps it isn't a bother,
to reveal what shadows you're hiding in.
I searched for you in the Lesser Campus,
in the Circus, in all the bookshops,
in the sacred temple of Jove the Highest.
In the Colonnade of Magnus as well,
my friend, I caught hold of all those little ladies,
who, as I looked them over, were unfazed.
I confronted them like this: "<Hand over>
my Camerius, you naughty girls!"
One of them, drawing apart her bare breasts,
said: "Look, he's hiding here in my rosy tits!
But it's a labor of Hercules for you to take him."
Do you keep your distance so disdainfully, friend?
Tell me where I can find you, proclaim it
boldly, confide it, entrust it to the light of day.
Are milky-white girls holding you up now?
If you keep your tongue shut up in your mouth,
you throw away all the fruits of love.
Venus rejoices in chatty gossip.
Or, if you like, you can zip your lips,
as long as I can partake in your love.

The poem opens with a politeness marker common to Plautine dialogues: *si forte non molestum est* (1), which comic characters regularly use to initiate a request for information.[17] While the phrase appears elsewhere and can be understood without any reference to comedy, it can be seen to evoke comic connotations for an audience attuned to comedy's formulaic language. We might compare the expression, "Honey, I'm home!," which can be used without allusive intent or as an intertextual reference to 1950s sitcoms like *I Love Lucy* or *Leave It to Beaver* and stereotypes of normative family dynamics.

When the speaker shifts into the past to narrate his search, he confirms that we are entering a theatricalized version of Rome that has been adapted to the setting of Roman comedy. As he recounts how he traveled breathlessly all over the city, he portrays himself as a character performing the stock routine of the "wild-goose chase," a familiar schtick that appears several times in Plautus' and Terence's plays.[18] In this scene, a character comes on stage to deliver a monologue in which he lists the many urban places he has searched for a person to whom he must deliver a message. The character, usually a slave, also complains about his exhaustion from his search. While the schtick is regular – indeed, common enough that Plautus has characters riff on it metatheatrically – there is one especially close and significant incarnation of it to which Catullus can be seen to allude here, namely, a scene in Plautus' *Amphitruo* in which the play's eponymous hero performs the role. Before this point in the play, Jupiter has disguised himself as Amphitruo, who has been away at war, and spends an extended night with Amphitruo's wife Alcumena. Unaware of the divine mischief, Amphitruo returns home only to grow confused and infuriated as Alcumena says she slept with him the previous night, believing that she is trying to cover up an affair. Distrusting her claims of fidelity and seeking grounds for divorce, Amphitruo stalks away to find his shipmate and Alcumena's relative Naucrates, who he asserts will testify that Amphitruo was on the ship all night and so could not have slept with

---

[17] See Bagordo (2001, 115–16) on the phrase's comic connotations and Ferri (2008, 22 and 25) on its use in comedy as a negative politeness marker. The comic *loci similes* are noted by Riese (1884), Kroll (1959), and Agnesini (2004, 87); cf. Pl. *Epid.* 460–61, *Per.* 599, *Poen.* 50–51, *Rud.* 120–21, *Trin.* 932; cf. also Ter. *Ad.* 806, Afr. Fr. 95–6 R, and Lucil. 987.

[18] Riese (1884), Kroll (1959), Condorelli (1965, 464–65), and Agnesini (2004) note this parallel but leave it unexamined, attributing the coincidence to the passive influence of Roman cultural patrimony rather than to comic allusion. On the schtick, see Christenson (2000, 293) and cf. Pl. *Amph.* 1009–14, *Mer.* 805–8, Ter. *Ad.* 713–18. The fruitless search motif occurs also at Pl. *Epid.* 719–20, *Per.* 1–6, *Rud.* 223–28, and Ter. *Andr.* 355–61.

Alcumena. He fails to find Naucrates and returns from the harbor to complain (1009–19):

> Naucratem quem convenire volui in navi non erat,
> nec domi neque in urbe invenio quemquam qui illum viderit.          1010
> nam omnis plateas perreptavi, gymnasia et myropolia;
> apud emporium atque in macello, in palaestra atque in foro,
> in medicinis, in tonstrinis, apud omnis aedis sacras
> sum defessus quaeritando: nusquam invenio Naucratem.
> nunc domum ibo atque ex uxore hanc rem pergam exquirere,          1015
> quis fuerit quem propter corpus suom stupri compleverit.
> nam me quam illam quaestionem inquisitam hodie amittere
> mortuom satiust. sed aedis occluserunt. eugepae,
> pariter hoc fit atque ut alia facta sunt. feriam fores.

> That Naucrates whom I wanted to find wasn't on the ship,
> and I can't find anyone at his house or in the city who's seen him.
> See, I crept all around every street, the gyms and the perfume shops;
> at the market and in the grocer's, in the wrestling school and in the forum,
> around the doctors, the barbers, at every sacred shrine.
> I'm worn out with searching: I can't find Naucrates anywhere.
> Now I'll go home and keep asking my wife about this to find out
> who it was that was worth filling her body with adulterous shame.
> Because I'd rather die than let go of this investigation already
> under way. But they've locked up the house! Just great! Well,
> that's about how the rest of this has been. I'll knock on the doors.

Amphitruo's "wild-goose chase" soliloquy is paralleled closely by Catullus' account in poem 55: both use the same verb to describe their behavior (*quaeritando*, 1014; cf. *quaesivimus*, 55.3), and Amphitruo's complaint *sum defessus quaeritando* finds a remarkably strong echo in poem 58b – a companion piece to poem 55 to which we will return shortly – which ends as the speaker says he is "weary with searching (*defessus . . . essem . . . quaeritando*, 8–10). And both recount the many urban locales they have visited before admitting their failure.[19]

Significantly, though, neither man is acting as we would expect him to do normally, because this stock routine is strongly associated with servile characters, and running around frantically is a marker of low status both on the stage and in real life, as Quintilian states (*Inst.* 11.3.111–12):

> plus autem adfectus habent lentiora, ideoque Roscius citatior, Aesopus gravior fuit quod ille comoedias, hic tragoedias egit. eadem motus quoque

---

[19] Condorelli (1965) and Agnesini (2004, 79–89).

observatio est. itaque in fabulis iuvenum senum militum matronarum gravior ingressus est, servi ancillulae parasiti piscatores citatius moventur.

Slower verbal delivery, however, has greater force; for that reason Roscius was faster, Aesopus more solemn, since the former performed comedies, the latter tragedies. This same observation is also true of movement. And so in plays the gait of young men, old men, soldiers, and matrons is more solemn, while slaves, maids, parasites, and fishermen move more quickly.

*Amphitruo* is, of course, a bizarre play, because it is the only extant Roman comedy that features a cast of mythological figures rather than of stock characters with generic names. But whatever role Amphitruo is playing, he surely is not supposed to be read as a slave, parasite, or fisherman. In fact, at the start of the play, whenever he appears before other characters on stage, Amphitruo maintains the façade of the *miles gloriosus*, or "braggart soldier." Plautus readies the audience for his military braggadocio hundreds of lines before he steps foot on stage. The first thing his slave Sosia does when he appears is to publicize his master's accomplishments in war (186–261), in much the same way other *milites gloriosi* are aggrandized by hangers-on in Roman comedy. He recounts how Amphitruo conquered King Pterelas in single combat (*ipsusque Amphitruo regem Pterelam sua optruncavit manu*, 252) and won his foe's golden drinking-cup in recognition of his manly courage (*post ob virtutem ero Amphitruoni patera donata aurea est*, 260). While this might seem a genuine accomplishment, Sosia's speech is a send-up of the Roman triumph, the *spolia opima*, and the stereotypical self-promoting general, revealing Amphitruo as the comic *miles gloriosus*.[20] Humorously, Sosia has no actual knowledge of any of the deeds for which he praises his master, since he admits from the start he was running away the whole time and is spinning a tale for his mistress (197–200):

> ea nunc meditabor quo modo illi dicam, quom illo advenero.
> si dixero mendacium ... solens meo more fecero.
> nam quom pugnabat maxume, ego tum fugiebam maxume;
> 200 verum quasi affuerim tamen simulabo atque audita eloquar.

Now I'll think about how I'll tell her these things when I arrive there.
If I wind up telling a lie, I'll only be doing what I do in my usual way.
See, when he was fighting hardest, that's when I was fleeing the hardest!
Still, I'll pretend like I really was there and tell her what I've heard.

---

[20] On these parodic elements and their effects on the audience's perception of Amphitruo as the *miles gloriosus*, see Janne (1933), Halkin (1948), Galinsky (1966), Beard (2003 and 2007, 253–56), and Polt (2013).

Sosia's disingenuous encomium of Amphitruo is comparable to the famous scene at the opening of Plautus' *Miles gloriosus*, where the parasite Artotrogus praises the bombastic Pyrgopolynices to his face but confesses to the audience that he is faking everything (9–71). Amphitruo's martial glory is more show than substance.[21]

When Amphitruo finally appears on stage, these hints that his assumption of authority is doubtful are verified by the concrete *miles gloriosus* persona he puts on: he abuses Sosia for almost an entire scene (551–89) and then emphasizes how impressed his wife Alcumena will be with his victory (654–58). He boasts about his role as a general (*auspicio meo atque [in]ductu*, 657), the impossible odds against him (*quos nemo posse superari ratust*, 656), and the speed of his success (*primo coetu*, 657), revealing his ridiculous self-importance and disregard for others, both key traits of the *miles gloriosus*.[22] His virility and military prowess are also undercut by his costume, as Amphitruo is not wearing the typical mask of the soldier, but that of the *senex durus*, or "harsh old man." Later in the play Mercury mocks his age (*senecta aetate a me mendicas malum*, 1032), and after Jupiter knocks him out with a thunderbolt the *ancilla* Bromia wonders who the old man lying outside their house is (*quis hic est senex qui ante aedis nostras sic iacet?*, 1072).[23] As he greets Alcumena, he becomes hostile in short order, showing the worst traits of the *miles gloriosus* and *senex durus* (798–847). Amphitruo criticizes his wife like the typical "harsh old men," questioning her chastity (shown to be impeccable throughout the play) while abusing her aggressively in ways characteristic of "braggart soldiers."[24] At the end of the scene, Amphitruo threatens divorce as the penalty for Alcumena's perceived infidelity if he can find Naucrates (848–52), and at this moment he shows the full extent of his identity as the "harsh old man," since the *patria potestas* of the *senex* gives him power

---

[21] Marshall (2006, 171–72) explores Artotrogus' insincerity and Pyrgopolynices' ridiculousness in the *Miles Gloriosus* scene.

[22] Christenson (2000, 255). On the traits of "braggart soldiers," see Duckworth (1952, 264–65); cf. also the *miles gloriosus* of *Epidicus*, who wants to find someone to whom he can recount his battles instead of someone who will talk about himself (*pol ego magis unum quaero meas quoi praedicem / quam illum qui memoret suas mihi*, 453–54).

[23] Christenson (2000, 308–9) discusses Amphitruo's costuming and identification as *senex*.

[24] On Alcumena's chastity, see Duckworth (1952, 150 and 256–57) and Hunter (1985, 126–27); see also Christenson (2000, 37–45 and 2001) and Owens (2001), who note that Alcumena's *virtus* is paradoxical, considering her sexual appetite and (unwitting) adultery. On the husband's typical verbal abuse of his wife in comedy, see Duckworth (1952, 242–43 and 282–85) and Braund (2005), who points out that the *senex* rarely criticizes his wife to her face.

over the family unit and the ability to dissolve familial relations.[25] In combining the extremes of the two stock types, the *miles gloriosus* and *senex durus*, Amphitruo becomes his play's primary *agelast*, the comic blocking figure endowed with a socially superior position.

As we learn with his "wild-goose chase" scene, though, all his hyperaggression amounts to nothing but posturing before his slave and his wife to assert power over social inferiors who are already vulnerable to him. This comic hubris sets him up to be defeated by the protagonists from among the clever stock types, and indeed the "wild-goose chase" scene represents a pivotal moment in the play when the audience catches Ampitruo's internal inferiority and readies us for his impending comeuppance. Amphitruo behaves in such servile fashion only because he thinks no one is looking, metatheatrically unaware that he has begun performing as if he were a *servus bonus*.

Catullus performs a similar character turn in poem 55, concealing his servile character beneath the façade of an aggressive *miles gloriosus* and *senex durus* in largely the same way as Amphitruo. At the end of line 7 he reaches the final destination in his frantic search, where he slows down and the central action of the poem – a confrontation between him and a handful of sex laborers – takes place in the Portico of Pompey. While this was one of the standard haunts of *meretrices* in Rome, and we could understand Catullus' choice to zoom in on this space as a way to lend realistic color to his description of the city, we must also remember that poem 55 is not a travel guide to Catullus' everyday experience of Rome.[26] The Portico exists in the artificially constructed space of poetry, where Catullus sets it alongside an assemblage of other selectively chosen locations, characters, and situations, like a textual capriccio.[27] And as part of this poetic construct, the Portico not only imbues poem 55 with a sense of physical urban space, but also brings to bear some cultural and literary connotations that have so far been overlooked. After all, the Portico was the greater part of the immense and sumptuous theater complex Pompey built in 55 BCE – not long before this poem must have been written – as the city's

---

[25]  Rosenmeyer (1995) and Braund (2005) note the aberrance of divorce in Roman comedy and the complex power dynamics operating here.

[26]  McGinn (2004, 22 n. 54): "The portico at the Theater of Pompey was such a familiar venue for the solicitation of clients that the association was elevated to a literary topos: Catull. 55.6–10; Prop. 4.8.75; Ov. *Ars* 1.67, 3.387; Mart. 11.47.3."

[27]  Edwards (1996), Boyle (2003, 1–63), Welch (2005), and Huskey (2006) analyze the selective representation and constructedness of urban space in poetry after Catullus. See also Neumeister (1993) and Schmitzer (2001) for interpretations of literary itineraries set in the city of Rome.

first permanent venue for dramatic performance after more than a century and a half of failed attempts and strife among Rome's elite. Moreover, its inaugural program was filled with lavish spectacles and revivals of Roman drama's classics, even drawing Clodius Aesopus, one of the first century BCE's greatest actors, out of retirement for an encore performance, and Cicero implies that members of the elite were expected to attend.[28] This space must have been meaningful to Catullus, and together with the allusions we have seen so far, it metatheatrically marks this scene as a little drama, in much the same way as we saw poem 10's entrances *a foro* and *a peregre* operate in the Introduction.

When he first runs into the sex laborers, Catullus takes a condescending tone with them, calling them "little ladies" (*femellas*, 7) and accosting them (*simul omnes prendi*, 6–7) before berating them without provocation (*usque flagitabam*, 9).[29] Catullus' self-portrayal here is not flattering or sympathetic, and indeed he acts like the brutish Amphitruo does when he rebukes Alcumena and tries to shame her into admitting to crimes she did not commit. The verb he uses in line 9 is, I think, especially telling. Catullus is performing a sort of *flagitatio*, a form of "folk-justice" in which a wronged party ritually and publicly shames a wrongdoer in order to enforce compliance and restitution. Earlier in the corpus he uses this technique to abuse a woman whom he has accused of stealing his *tabellae* in poem 42, where he urges his hendecasyllables to pursue her (*persequamur eam et reflagitemus*, 6). He then orders them to surround her and shout insults until she returns the goods (10–12):

> circumsistite eam et reflagitate:
> "moecha putida, redde codicillos,
> redde, putida moecha, codicillos!"

> Stand around her and shout:
> "Filthy slut, give back the tablets,
> give back the tablets, filthy slut!"

---

[28] On the dating and form of Pompey's theater complex, see Coarelli (1971–72) and Sear (2006, 57–61). Thomson (1998, 3–4) discusses this and other datable references in Catullus' poetry. On the inaugural program and experience of Pompey's Theater, see Beacham (1999, 49–71, and 2007, 218–23), Erasmo (2005, 83–90), and Temelini (2006); Cic. *Fam.* 7.1 sketches its opening festivities.

[29] The word *femellas* (7), attested only here, is almost certainly colloquial and derogatory; see Ellis (1889) and Thomson (1998), who note that Isidore interprets *femellarius* as "womanizer," suggesting that *femella* connotes sexual looseness and female objectification (both appropriate to the speaker's tone and surrounding context of poem 55). The verb *prehendere* frequently implies aggression and violence; cf. parallels in Ellis (1889) and Fordyce (1961). Williams (1968, 197) notes the verb (*re*)*flagitare* is semi-technical and implies, if not violence, then at least hostility; see also Usener (1901), Fraenkel (1961, 46–51), and Williams (1968, 196–99).

In the end his tactic fails and she remains unmoved (*sed nil proficimus, nihil movetur*, 21), so the speaker humorously resorts to disingenuous compliments instead.

Sander Goldberg has argued persuasively that Catullus' *flagitatio* in poem 42 alludes to another passage of Roman comedy, the scene in Plautus' *Pseudolus* where the eponymous slave and the *adulescens* Calidorus try to force the *leno* Ballio to give up the *meretrix* Philocomasium (357–59):[30]

> CALID: Pseudole, assiste altrim secus atque onera hunc maledictis.
> PSEUD: licet.
> numquam ad praetorem aeque cursim curram, ut emittar manu.
> CALID: ingere mala multa. PSEUD: iam ego te differam dictis meis.

> CALID: "Pseudolus, stand on the other side and heap insults on him."
> PSEUD: "Sure.
> I'd never run so fast, even to the praetor to be set free."
> CALID: "Pile on lots of abuses." PSEUD: "Now I'll tear you apart with my words!"

Ballio endures, even revels in invective, and eventually their *flagitatio* falls flat when Pseudolus admits, "We're pouring our words into a broken pot, we're wasting our effort" (*in pertusum ingerimus dicta dolium, operam ludimus*, 369).

The situation in poem 55.7–13 is not quite the same as that in poem 42, but they do share the basic structure of the *flagitatio* and its comic implications. But if the speaker's use of "folk-justice" in poem 42 can be viewed as justifiable because this woman has apparently wronged him, the same cannot be said of the abuse in poem 55, where he clearly does not stand on the side of justice.[31] That his quarrel with the sex laborers represents the same kind of *flagitatio* is clear from his explicit use of ritual vocabulary (*sic ipse flagitabam*, 9) and command that the women return something to him (*Camerium mihi, pessimae puellae*, 10). The women, though, are innocent bystanders, and at no point does he show any reason to suspect they have seen his friend, let alone that they had anything to do with his disappearance. Importantly, his blustering character presented in

---

[30] Goldberg (2005, 108–13); see also Usener (1901), Fraenkel (1961, 46–51), Williams (1968, 196–99), Augello (1991), and Goldberg (2000) for comments on *flagitatio*, Roman comedy, and Catull. 42.

[31] Pace Fraenkel (1961, 46–51) and Williams (1968, 197), who claim the *flagitatio* was primarily a tool for justice and not merely a method for forcing compliance, Selden (1992, 484) rightly observes that "the insult (or flattery) that the poet levels at the girl packs its punch regardless of the truth or falsehood of his claims. Thus, the poet does not hesitate to present contradictory assessments of the girl's morals in order to exert the type of verbal pressure that contingencies require."

these lines stands in direct contrast to the slavish version of the speaker in the preceding three lines. In this way he mirrors the two-faced Amphitruo, who tries to conceal his internal servility with the façade of socially dominant stock types. As we saw, Amphitruo's verbal abuse of his wife casts him as a mixture of the *miles gloriosus* and *senex durus* characters, and some of their traits can be seen in the Catullan speaker's harassment of these women.

The crux of poem 55 comes at its exact center, when one of the sex laborers breaks her silence and responds to the speaker's attacks. If there was any doubt about the superficiality of the speaker's domineering façade, these women remove it with their reactions to his bullying: they stand with a calm demeanor as he performs his *flagitatio* (*quas vultu vidi tamen sereno*, 8), undercutting his self-importance and showing that not even the most vulnerable people in Rome take his bluster seriously. The Portico's setting also contributes special theatrical connotations for the women, since it was filled with statuary representing various female figures, including the Muses, Marvels of Nature, and Conquered Nations, as well as poets and (most significantly for poem 55) famous sex laborers. Evans argues convincingly that this last group of statues portrayed heroines of Greek new comedy, such as Menander's Lais and Glykera, Philemon's Neaira, and Timocles' Phryne, and we can imagine the images of these illustrious literary *hetairai* offered strength and inspiration to the living sex laborers in poem 55 who worked in the Portico alongside them. Indeed, Kuttner observes that "the call-girls' implacable *vultus serenus* evokes the garden-statues of courtesans," and their calm reaction to the speaker's aggression shows that they have learned how to deal with socially superior men as well as their comic predecessors had done.[32] Additionally, he demands that they give Camerius back, calling them the "worst girls" (*pessimae puellae*, 10). As I observed in poem 49 in the previous chapter, the adjective *pessimus* in Roman comedy acts as a marker of Heroic Badness, that primary trait of Plautine rogues such as the *servus callidus* or *meretrix callida*, and here it alerts us to the sex laborer's *malitia* and *calliditas*, as well as an imminent comic inversion.

The climax of the poem comes when one of the *pessimae puellae* steps forward to enact her Heroic Badness, performing her role as the "clever sex laborer" of Roman comedy. The bold *meretrix callida* bares her breasts, and at first we (and the speaker) might assume she is trying to use her

---

[32] Kuttner (1999, 351) and Evans (2009).

sexuality to mollify the male aggressor, but she then turns this expectation on its head by cracking a joke about Catullus and Camerius (11–13):

> quaedam inquit, nudum reduc<ta pectus,>
> "en hic in roseis latet papillis,
> sed te iam ferre Herculei labos est."

> One of them, drawing apart her bare breasts,
> said: "Look, he's hiding here in my rosy tits!
> But it's a labor of Hercules for you to take him."

Her reply can be seen to contains a clever mythological joke. Editors have usually assigned the line after the reference to the sex laborer's breasts (*sed te iam ferre Herculei labos est*, 13) to the speaker, but Copley argues persuasively, to my mind, that it belongs to the *puella* and marks the end of her sassy reply. If it is a labor of Hercules to retrieve Camerius from the girl's body, then she has cast herself as Hippolyta, the queen of the Amazons whose girdle Hercules had to retrieve as his ninth labor.[33] Plautus' Heroically Bad characters often compare themselves to mythological figures to aggrandize themselves, so the *puella*'s self-identification as an Amazon queen recasts her as a powerful female leader whose words can control hyperaggressive men.[34]

Of course, if the *puella* is Hippolyta, that makes the speaker Hercules, which is a far less flattering comparison than we might at first assume. On the one hand, Hercules is the paragon of ancient virility and domination, and thus exactly the sort of figure the speaker seems to aspire to become in behaving like Amphitruo's *miles gloriosus* type. On the other hand, the real Hercules actually retrieved Hippolyta's ζώνη, while poem 55 suggests that Catullus talks the talk but can't walk the walk: he departs the Portico of Pompey empty-handed. What is more, while characters in Roman comedy regularly compare themselves with Hercules, they usually focus on Hercules' suffering rather than his victory.[35] At the start of Plautus' *Persa*, for example, the slave Toxilus performs breathlessly as he compares his great exertions trying to find someone – similar to the "wild-goose chase" scene in *Amphitruo* – to the labors of Hercules (1–6):

---

[33] Copley (1952). Although speculative (and rejected by, e.g., Peachy [1972], Wiseman [1976, 15], and Gärtner [2007, 24]), Copley suggests the *puella* intentionally "mishears" *Camerium* as καμάριον, which, he argues, on somewhat loose evidence, is a colloquial term for brassiere; if he is right, the *puella* also demonstrates the clever bilingual wordplay of the Plautine rogue.

[34] On mythological comparisons in Plautus, see Anderson (1993, 94–95) and Fraenkel (2008 [1922], 45–71).

[35] Slater (2000, 31 n. 2) notes the frequency of Hercules comparisons; see also Fraenkel (2008 [1922], 7–8). Cf. Pl. *Bac.* 663, *Epid.* 178–79, *Men.* 199–201, *St.* 232–33 and 386.

qui amans egens ingressus est princeps in Amoris vias
superavit aerumnis suis aerumnas Herculei.
nam cum leone, cum excetra, cum cervo, cum apro Aetolico,
cum avibus Stymphalicis, cum Antaeo deluctari mavelim,
quam cum Amore: ita fio miser quaerendo argento mutuo          6
nec quicquam nisi "non est" sciunt mihi respondere quos rogo.

The penniless paramour who first stepped upon the ways of Love
outdid the labors of Hercules with his own labors.
Why, I'd rather struggle with the Lion, with the Hydra, with the Stag,
with the Aetolian Boar, with the Stymphalian Birds, with Antaeus
than with Love! I'm becoming miserable with searching for loan money,
and no one I ask knows how to say anything to me but "Haven't got it."

The labor of Hippolyta's girdle also appears in *Menaechmi*, where
Epidamnian Menaechmus steals one of his wife's *pallae* to give his mistress
Erotium, likening his deed to Hercules' (199–201):[36]

                               nimio ego hanc periculo
  surrupui hodie. meo quidem animo ab Hippolyta succingulum
  Hercules haud aeque magno umquam apstulit periculo.

                         I've stolen this today
at incredible risk. To my mind, Hercules really hardly ever faced as
great a risk when he stole the girdle from Hippolyta.

Hippolyta in comedy thus represents a mythological exemplum for a
powerful woman whom a man must overcome. And even though
Menaechmus successfully captures his wife's piece of clothing, his theft
ultimately fails when the unnamed *matrona* later denies him access to his
own house until he returns it (662), as does the *meretrix* Erotium when he
comes to her house empty-handed (692).[37] The conflict between Hercules
and Hippolyta in Roman comedy therefore comes to stand in not for the
triumph of the Hercules *comparandum* as much as for his struggle and
ultimate failure to exercise masculine authority over socially vulnerable
women. In Catullus' poem 55, the sex laborer's comic comparison of
herself to Hippolyta and, by extension, of the speaker to Hercules characterizes their confrontation in the same way. He is no supervirile hero, and
at the end of his *flagitatio* of the women in Pompey's Portico we find him
just as he began, politely and submissively addressing his missing friend.

---

[36] On this passage, see Gratwick (1993, 159). Copley (1952, 297 n. 4) also links the *Menaechmi*
passage to Catull. 55, but he merely cites it as a *locus similis* without analyzing its implications.
[37] Braund (2005) and Duffalo (2013, 21–28) offer insightful readings of *Menaechmi*, a bizarre play in
that it violates norms of Roman comedy in ways that parallel *Amphitruo* and poem 55.

Catullus' mythological failure recurs in poem 58b, with which poem 55 forms a pair on the same topic and alluding to the same comic scene. Here the speaker describes his exhaustion in a slightly different way than he does in 55, listing famous exempla known for their speed but whose powers would be useless in helping him find Camerius.[38]:

> non custos si fingar ille Cretum,
> non si Pegaseo ferar volatu,
> non Ladas ego pinnipesve Perseus,
> non Rhesi niveae citaeque bigae;
> 5  adde huc plumipedas volatilesque,
> ventorumque simul require cursum:
> quos vinctos, Cameri, mihi dicares,
> defessus tamen omnibus medullis
> et multis languoribus peresus
> 10  essem te mihi, amice, quaeritando.

> Not if I should be fashioned the guardian of the Cretans,
> not if I should be borne on Pegasus' flight,
> not if I should be Ladas or wing-footed Perseus,
> not Rhesus' snowy and swift chariot;
> add to this those feather-footed and flying ones,
> and likewise look for the course of the winds,
> even if you were to chain them up and call them mine,
> Camerius, still I'd be weary in all my marrow
> and worn out by great fatigue
> in seeking for you, friend.

Catullus tries to aggrandize himself with these epic comparisons, but everything falls flat when he finally reveals the goals to which he would put the powers of these exempla: the apodosis in lines 8–10, where he complains about how tired he has become in looking around Rome for his buddy, shows that all his mythological bluster is merely a tempest in a teacup. As we saw above, such bathetic use of myth is a standard piece in the toolbox of Heroically Bad comic figures, but here Catullus undercuts the significance of these comparisons by admitting that they would fail to help him complete this minor task. Unlike characters such as Pseudolus,

---

[38] The text is Thomson's (1998), except at lines 2 and 3, where I see no reason to accept Muret's conjectured transposition. On differences in the tones of poems 55 and 58b, see Comfort (1935), Condorelli (1965), Khan (1967), and Benediktson (1986). The relationship between poems 55 and 58b is vexed, with some arguing that 58b should be inserted into 55 and others that they are separate poems; besides those just cited, see Peachy (1972), Macleod (1973), and Goold (1974, 15–21). I am inclined to read them as two pieces that balance and contrast with one another (just as poems 2 and 3, 5 and 7, etc.), but it makes little difference for my interpretation.

who likens himself to Ulysses and then pulls off a victory against the odds through pure cleverness, Catullus frames his comparison in negative terms: the contrafactual confirms that he isn't a Perseus or Bellerophon, and even if he were, still he would put on a disappointing performance.

To return to poem 55, it is significant, I think, that the speaker has no reply for the *puella* and concludes his narrative of this embarrassing moment by turning back to Camerius. He even seems to show the sex laborers respect, since he asks if the "milky-white girls are holding you up now" (*nunc te lacteolae tenent puellae*, 17). The adjective *lacteolae* points the reader back to the sex laborer's breasts, which the speaker draws attention to at lines 11–12 (*nudum pectus* and *roseis papillis*), and the allusion to the girdle of Hippolyta. No wonder Camerius is missing: the speaker implies that these women can go toe-to-toe with any man short of Hercules himself. These comic *pessimae puellae* leave him nearly as speechless as Camerius himself.[39] The women have the last word with no negative consequence for themselves. As we saw both in the prior chapter and at the beginning of this chapter, for Heroic Badness to function properly in Plautine comedy, the socially inferior character who expresses it must not suffer as a result, since that would spoil the fun. The *servus callidus* and *meretrix callida* always get away with their clever quips, and while they often discuss the potential for retribution and the dangers to which their low status exposes them, the socially superior butts of their schemes and jokes suffer embarrassment without doling out the punishments we might expect in a nonliterary context. Heroic Badness gives characters a temporary reprieve from the consequences of their subversion and restraints that keep traditional Roman power structures in place, and Catullus imports this carnivalesque quality into his poems through these comic allusions.

## Watching It Burn (Poems 37 and 36)

Let us turn to one more set of poems where conflict between the speaker and a woman is mediated through Plautine stock types and Heroic Badness. Whereas we have seen how Catullus explores gendered competition in public civic spheres in poem 55, we can also see comic *malitia* operating in amatory and erotic contexts, such as poems 36 and 37, where the speaker and Lesbia compete for dominance in their relationship.

---

[39] Stevens (2013, 4–5) discusses aspects of speech and silence in this poem, though he comes to different conclusions about the speaker's power to speak relative to others.

In poem 37 the speaker addresses a seedy tavern and its sleazy patrons, who seem to have accepted his *puella* into their sexual coterie:

> salax taberna vosque contubernales,
> a pilleatis nona fratribus pila,
> solis putatis esse mentulas vobis,
> solis licere, quidquid est puellarum,
> 5     confutuere et putare ceteros hircos?
> an, continenter quod sedetis insulsi
> centum an ducenti, non putatis ausurum
> me una ducentos irrumare sessores?
> atqui putate: namque totius vobis
> 10    frontem tabernae sopionibus scribam.
> puella nam mi, quae meo sinu fugit,
> amata tantum quantum amabitur nulla,
> pro qua mihi sunt magna bella pugnata,
> consedit istic. hanc boni beatique
> 15    omnes amatis, et quidem, quod indignum est,
> omnes pusilli et semitarii moechi;
> tu praeter omnes, une de capillatis,
> cuniculosae Celtiberiae fili,
> Egnati, opaca quem bonum facit barba
> 20    et dens Hibera defricatus urina.

> Saucy tavern, and you tentmates
> at the ninth column from the Capped Brothers,
> you think you're the only ones who have cocks,
> that you alone can fuck whatever girls you want
> and think everyone else is a goat?
> Or, because you sit there witless,
> one or two hundred, you don't think that I'll dare
> to fuck over two hundred men sitting together?
> Well, think about this: I'll draw pricks
> all over your tavern's front wall.
> For my girl, who flew from my lap,
> who is loved more than any other will be loved,
> for whom many great wars have been fought by me,
> has prostituted herself there. All you great and
> good men love her and, what's the real shame,
> so do all the petty back-alley lovers.
> And you beyond all others, paragon of long-haired
> fops, son of rabbity Spain, Egnatius,
> whom your dark beard makes well bred,
> and your teeth brushed with Spanish piss.

The speaker rails against the tavern's patrons, whom he threatens with *irrumatio* for their sexual appetites and for their alleged liaisons with his *puella.* The most important aspect of the poem for my purposes is how the speaker characterizes the men, himself, and his girl. Johnson and Nappa argue that the speaker recasts the men as fellow-soldiers (*contubernales*, 1) and suggests that he himself is also a soldier, albeit not in the normal sense.[40] He confirms this self-identification by asserting that he has fought many wars for his girl (*pro qua mihi sunt magna bella pugnata*, 13). The speaker is a soldier of love whose *militia amoris* centers exclusively on the possession and control of his *puella*, who has become little more than a prize on par with the litter-bearers he falsely claims as his own in poem 10.

But the speaker is not just any soldier: he is the greatest soldier, superior to all the men in the *salax taberna*, at least in his eyes. David Wray argues the term *contubernales*, in addition to its normal martial meaning of "tentmates," connotes the sexual partners of slaves. The men in the tavern are soldiers against whom the speaker fights in his battle for love and sex, but by using this double entendre the speaker asserts his own authority over them: they may all be *milites*, but the speaker projects his sexual escapades as far above the low relationships of slaves. Moreover, the pair of sexually charged threats (*non putatis ausurum / me una ducentos irrumare sessores*, 6–7; *namque totius vobis / frontem tabernae sopionibus scribam*, 9–10) further subordinates the men to the speaker's power, both social and sexual.[41] He thus effectively portrays himself as the most virile soldier, one whose wars have been the greatest and whose social and sexual potency are unassailable.

But this sexual invective is part of a weak façade, which is uncovered by the absurd pitch of the speaker's braggadocio. Wray notes the disparity between appearance and reality in the poem: "The Catullus of Poem 37 ... seems to be as much at pains to paint himself as a comically absurd blusterer as many readers have been at pains to give him back his high moral seriousness and his *simpatico* as a tender lover roughly wronged." Wray goes on to show that the speaker is not only a *miles*, but specifically the Plautine *miles gloriosus*, mirroring the behavior and traits of the archetypical Pyrgopolynices from Plautus' *Miles Gloriosus*. His summary is worth quoting in full here:[42]

> Given that this poem opens by setting a burlesque, even carnivalesque context through a pair of puns involving military imagery, given that the

---

[40] Johnson (1999, 86) and Nappa (2001, 63).

[41] Wray (2001, 85); see also Skinner (1979) and Nappa (2001, 64–68) on the sexual dynamics in these threats.

[42] Wray (2001, 84 and 85–86).

characterization of the "barflies" as *contubernales* reads both as playful fiction (since they are no soldiers) and as bawdy comedic gag (by the sexual reference pitched at the lowest social register), and given that Catullus' Priapic threat to irrumate two hundred men is on its face a venting of wildly absurd braggadocio, it seems at least worth suggesting that the claim to have "fought many wars" for the *puella* be taken not as a veiled reference to be fitted by the reader into the collection's novelistic narrative, but rather as a line spoken "in character," as an instance of Catullus "getting into" the ridiculous stock role of *miles gloriosus* ("Braggart Soldier") in which his miniature mime has cast him.

We see his sexual invective as well in his description of the *puella*, who he says sits in the tavern (*consedit istic*, 14), implying she has become a sex laborer practicing her trade there.[43] But his comparison of the girl to a runaway (*puella nam mi, quae meo sinu fugit*, 11) marks a shift in the poem from simple invective to hybrid Plautine performance. Wray concludes, if the speaker is the *miles gloriosus*, the *puella* is not merely a low-class sex laborer, but the comic *virgo* or *meretrix*, the object of the "braggart soldier's" affection who wants to escape from him in order to return to her *amator adulescens* in many of Plautus' comedies.[44] As in other poems we have explored, when the speaker takes on the qualities of antagonistic stock types, his antagonists are cast in comic roles as well.

The speaker, then, sets up a relationship between himself and his girl that is similar to the one between the comic *miles gloriosus* and *meretrix*. This relationship, with all its Plautine character, stands strongly in the background of poem 36, which can be fruitfully understood as a complement to poem 37. In this poem the speaker describes a vow that his girl makes in order to reconcile them and stop him from writing invective. She promises to dedicate the poems of the worst poet to the sacred fire. But the girl had a trick up her sleeve, and she seems to have meant the speaker's poetry as the work of the worst poet:

>  annales Volusi, cacata carta,
>  votum solvite pro mea puella.
>  nam sanctae Veneri Cupidinique
>  vovit, si sibi restitutus essem
> 5 desissemque truces vibrare iambos,
>  electissima pessimi poetae
>  scripta tardipedi deo daturam

[43] Thomson (1998, 302); see also Adams (1983, 329–30), who cites instances where the verb *sedere* used of woman implies they are low-class sex laborers (e.g., Mart. 2.17.1 and 6.66.2).
[44] Wray (2001, 86).

infelicibus ustulanda lignis,
et hoc pessima se puella vidit
iocose lepide vovere divis.                                                    10
nunc, o caeruleo creata ponto,
quae sanctum Idalium Uriosque apertos
quaeque Ancona Cnidumque harundinosam
colis quaeque Amathunta quaeque Golgos
quaeque Dyrrachium Hadriae tabernam,                                           15
acceptum face redditumque votum,
si non illepidum neque inuenustum est.
at vos interea venite in ignem,
pleni ruris et inficetiarum
annales Volusi, cacata carta.                                                  20

Annals of Volusius, shitty sheets,
fulfill a vow for my girl.
For she vowed to sacred Venus and Cupid,
if I were restored to her
and stopped hurling my harsh iambs,
then the choicest works of the worst poet
would be given to the slow-footed god
to be burned by the unlucky kindling.
And that worst girl saw that she made
this vow with a charming joke.
Now, O goddess born from the blue-green sea,
who dwell on sacred Idalia and spreading Urii,
and who dwell in Ancona and reedy Cnidos,
and who dwell in Amathus and Golgi,
and who dwell in the Dyrrachian tavern of the Adriatic,
mark this vow accepted and paid,
if it is not uncharming and ungraceful.
But you meanwhile into the fire with you,
full of roughness and lacking polish,
Annals of Volusius, shitty sheets.

Wray traces the many points of contact between poems 36 and 37 that reinforce their connection to one another, and Thomson argues persuasively that we should understand poem 37 (among others) as the *truces iambos* (5) that are the target of the *puella*'s frustration. Like poems 55 and 58b, these two form a complementary cycle whose poems play off one another and correspond in form, vocabulary, and tone.[45]

---

[45] Thomson (1998, 298) and Wray (2001, 75).

As in poem 37, the speaker here tries to assert his dominance by acting like the "braggart soldier" that he pretends to be while assailing everyone in the *salax taberna*. Wray remarks that "everything in Catullus' stance here bespeaks a hypermasculine, aggressive mastery – a mastery that expresses itself both in scatological *convicium* ('verbal abuse') against Volusius and in the performance of verbal wit and exquisite poetic form."[46] Indeed, the speaker's domination of Volusius' poetry through its consignment to the flames, the inversion of the girl's vow by means of his own prayer to Venus in lines 11–17, and the insult of *pessima puella* (9) directed at Lesbia all indicate an attempt on the part of the speaker to gain control of the situation. But while Wray says this poem marks the speaker's successful recovery of power, I suggest that poem 36 follows the same formula for female Plautine *malitia* that we have seen in poems 55 and 58b, and indeed that comic allusions are at play in this poem's gendered conflict as well.

Like poem 55, poem 36 consists of a narrative set in the past framed by a present address, in roughly the same proportions as in poem 55. The opening two lines outline his current request, followed by a description of a past event that runs until the exact midpoint of the poem, when the speaker returns to the present. He reveals he has been writing "sharp iambs," such as poem 37, where he tries to assert dominance over other men and the *puella* by acting like a *miles gloriosus*. The speaker's girl vows to burn the poems of the worst poet (*pessimi poetae*, 6) to end his harsh insults and mollify him. The phrase *pessimus poeta*, however, is ambiguous, refusing to identify the target by name and giving the *puella* an opportunity to combat the speaker's invective. The girl seems to have spoken tongue-in-cheek (*et hoc pessima se puella vidit / iocose lepide vovere divis*, 9–10), and the speaker's description of events, albeit vague, implies that she meant he was the worst poet and the poems she would consign to the fire are his offending iambs. As in poem 55, the woman is marked by the vocabulary of Heroic Badness (*pessima*, 9), highlighting another instance of Plautine *malitia*. Further, the juxtaposition of *pessimus poeta* (6) as a supposedly bad author with *pessima puella* (9) as Heroically Bad gives the woman added authority, putting her on par with the speaker, who claims the same title in poem 49. Running away from the speaker did not work for the woman in poem 37, but her clever subversion of his aggressive poetry in poem 36 grants her a temporary victory over the posturing of the speaker as *miles gloriosus* as his equal.

---

[46] Wray (2001, 79).

Of course, there is an added dimension to this poem not present in the other instances of Plautine *malitia* we have explored, namely, a recovery by the speaker. In poem 36 he comes full circle, returning to the present and fulfilling the vow he makes at the start of the poem (*annales Volusi, cacata carta, / votum solvite pro mea puella*, 1–2). At the very end he consigns Volusius' poetry to the flames (*at vos interea venite in ignem, / pleni ruris et inficetiarum / annales Volusi, cacata carta*, 18–20). The speaker makes this new vow in the hopes of recovering something of his urbane composition, thinking that he will become witty and charming again (*si non illepidum neque invenustum est*, 17) by appropriating his *puella*'s joke at his expense as his own humorous jab against Volusius. Note that this same phrase appears in poem 10, albeit applied to Varus' girl instead (*non sane illepidum neque invenustum*, 4). Catullus seems to have taken a lesson from women such as poem 10's naughty *puella*, using her as a model for virtues of *urbanitas*. He is embarrassed, but he redirects the mockery against another poet and in the process saves his own *iambi* from the flames. By making Volusius' poems the work of the worst poet, he adds an extra dimension to the meaning of the vow's *pessimus poeta*. His *puella* initially makes him seem bad, but through a clever turn he takes on Heroic Badness, adopting Plautine *malitia* in a way similar to the ironic inversion in poem 49, where he transforms his status as "bad poet" (*pessimus poeta*, 5–6) into that of Heroically Bad rogue.

We can see, then, a mixture of iambic threats and Plautine farce in poems 37 and 36. The speaker levels invectives such as poem 37 against his *puella* and adopts the characteristics of the *miles gloriosus*. But the *puella* in poem 36 is not a passive *meretrix*, as he depicts her in poem 37. She vows to dedicate the poems of the worst poet to the fire if the speaker will cease writing such *truces iambos* (5), but in a sudden turn we can infer that her vow is a double entendre: she means to burn the speaker's own work. Immediately before this revelation, he calls her *pessima puella* (9), prefiguring her Heroic Badness as he does the *malitia* of poem 55's *quaedam femella* and of poem 10's *puella*. All three employ Plautine Heroic Badness, often the only resource that characters in inferior positions have in Plautus and Catullus – but a formidable one nevertheless. The speaker, perhaps taking his cue from these repeated embarrassing lessons about cleverness and social control, tries Plautine *malitia* for himself in poem 37 successfully. The *puella* asserts her power over the speaker, but he redirects it against Volusius, regaining what he had lost in this zero-sum game of Roman social domination.

# Epilogue
## The Show Goes On: From Roman Comedy to Latin Love Elegy

About sixty years ago, Kenneth Quinn declared a "Catullan Revolution," arguing that Catullus and his peers radically broke from prior poetic traditions to create a new type of poetry centered on *personality*: a subjective, meditative lyric consisting of short pieces that seem not to have been meant for an audience to hear, as earlier poetry had been, but to make readers feel they were *over*hearing conversations not intended for their ears.[1] Nevertheless, Quinn stressed that this sensation was illusory: Catullus' poems were not memorializations of his own life, but constructed introspections needing no knowledge beyond the poem's *ipsissima verba* to be understood as art. Quinn's New Critical stance held that that there was only the poem itself, legible in isolation from its social and historical context and prior poetic traditions, especially the Greek ones on which Catullan *Quellenforschung* had focused. Quinn gestured, if half-heartedly, at the potential importance of Roman poetic traditions, including Roman comedy, for Catullus, remarking that "the differences of style and attitude which made Roman comedy distinct from tragedy and epic had latent in them the power to contribute to a transformation of Roman poetry" and that "this stream provided not only realism ... but also idealizations of love as an important activity, and of youth and friendship in opposition to old men and old men's notions of what constitutes the serious business of life." But Quinn also denied that Catullus saw Roman comedy as having a unique identity, placing the *fabula palliata* under a nebulous umbrella of the "comic-satiric tradition" whose "shapelessness and incoherence of form is remote from the exquisite concentration of the new poetry."[2]

---

[1] Quinn (1959). Wray (2001, 18–35) offers an even-handed assessment of how Quinn's ideas here shaped Catullan studies.

[2] Quinn (1959, 10–12 and 17). For criticism of Quinn on this point, see, e.g., Putnam (1961).

I do not mean to cite Quinn here as a straw man, and I acknowledge that he did much to help break the field away from the *Catullroman* ("Story of Catullus") and biographical readings that had been dominant. Preceded by Havelock and Cherniss and aided by contemporary work of Kernan and Anderson, Quinn played a pivotal role in opening questions and approaches based on persona theory.[3] Still, in the decades since, scholars have revised his theses and brought greater nuance to readings of Catullus that recognize the importance of his context. Each poem is deeply embedded in first-century BCE Roman culture and enmeshed in literary traditions that Catullus was exposed to and drew on, both actively and subconsciously. As a corollary, his poetry is not merely about his inner life and artistic production, but also how he chooses to perform as an individual within a larger collective and how he uses knowledge of that collective to engage with others. We are, Catullus saw, the roles we play, including both the novel – thoughts, feelings, and behaviors unique to ourselves – and the cliched – thoughts, feelings, and behaviors we have observed others display and imitate ourselves. A world where we all behave entirely uniquely would be illegible, a chaos of signs meaningful only to us individually. We need the common, the predictable, and the banal to speak with one another. Human communication relies on the interplay of these two elements, of public theme and private variation.

I have tried throughout this book to argue that Catullus' work is not so much poetry of *personality* as of *personal drama*, with "personal" here meaning both *personalis*, that is, related to one's private as opposed to public life, and "defined and conveyed by *personae*," masks worn by Roman actors to identify their stock characters. Catullus, I argue, performs his individuality by borrowing these readily recognizable signs and characters from Roman comedy. One of my chief goals has been to show that, while Catullus was indeed a revolutionary in many ways, in others he was channeling a comedic tradition that was hackneyed and as old as Latin literature itself, at least as Romans conceived of it.[4] Of course, this choice of continuity was itself revolutionary, involving the transformation of the

---

[3] Havelock (1938), Cherniss (1943), Kernan (1959), and Anderson (1964 and 1982). For a brief account of the development of persona theory in Catullan scholarship, see Polt (2018).

[4] Complex pre-textual literary traditions had long existed in Italy, but the Romans enjoyed and promoted a fiction that Livius Andronicus, who wrote and staged the first play in Rome, was the founder of Latin literature; see Goldberg (2005, 1–18), Habinek (2005), Citroni (2013), and Feeney (2016). Livy (7.2) reports that *ludi scaenici* were first introduced to Rome in the fourth century BCE by Etruscan dancers but that Andronicus' contribution of plays with scripted plots was a watershed; cf. Cic. *Brut.* 71–75 and Hor. *Ep.* 2.1.119–61 for different versions of this literary history. For conflicting narratives of Roman drama's origins, see also Beare (1939) and Wiseman (1994, 1–22).

public voice of the stage and a genre focused on the quotidian and low-class into tools to examine and interrogate private concerns of the Roman elite. This experiment in theatricality paralleled his appropriation of the vocabulary of public alliance (*amicitia, fides, pietas, officium,* etc.), which has long been seen as one of Catullus' most groundbreaking gestures.[5] As he borrowed from the store of homosocial political concepts that were familiar to his peers to describe intimate, subjective experiences of hetero-erotic love, so too he drew on the shared vocabulary of public theater to make sense of private relations and thoughts.

This choice had a larger impact on subsequent authors than, I think, has been recognized. Catullus' experiments in adapting Roman comedy to his personal poetry paved the way for later poets to do something similar, as I suggest above the "pre-neoterics" did for Catullus, and I hope the examples of Catullus' use of Roman comedy I illustrate here – by no means exhaustive and to which others have already added soon after the bulk of this book was written – will encourage scholars to keep looking for the *palliata* in Imperial literature, especially less obvious elements of the genre.[6] I want to close by noting one such path between Roman comedy and subsequent literature – namely, Latin love elegy – that Catullus can be seen to have pioneered but to which his contribution has largely been overlooked.

Sharon James and others have argued persuasively that Latin love elegy's essential erotic plot is based on the conflict between the *adulescens amator* and *meretrix* in Roman comedy, and particularly its focus on the competition between lover and beloved for sexual access, behavioral control, and the economic interests of both parties.[7] In sum, the elegiac *puella*, just as the comic *meretrix*, works to minimize the amount of sex that she has with her male suitors in the hopes of extracting from them valuable gifts that will sustain her both now and after she grows too old to attract attention and financial support from men. The elegiac poet, just as the *adulescens amator*, strives to minimize the cost of sex with the *puella*. The resulting

---

[5] On the vocabulary of public alliance, see, esp., Ross (1969, 80–95), Minyard (1985, 22–29), and Fitzgerald (1995, 115–20).

[6] For further readings of Roman comedy in Catullus, see Hanses (2015, 38–41 and 107–36) on poems 1–8 and 32 and Maynes (2016) on 67. For receptions of comedy in the Empire, see, e.g., Augoustakis (2014) and Hanses (2014; 2015, 152–284; 2016). Lowe (2019) has recently linked the comic *praeco* and *leno*, which appear in Catullus (discussed briefly in Chapter 3) and Roman elegy. See also Spencer (2017) for intriguing arguments that Acts 12:12–17 may be informed by the *servus currens* schtick.

[7] James (1998, 2003, 2012, and 2016); see also, e.g., Konstan (1986), Yardley (1972 and 1987), Myers (1996), and Herrmann (2011).

tension drives much of both genres' interest and narrative. Women who have sex too freely will find themselves viewed as cheap. The lover's logic is, Why buy the cow when you can get the milk for free? The rarer the sex, the higher the value, the more lavish the gifts the woman can expect. But if she makes the lover think that his prize is unattainable, then he could lose interest, and with that she would lose her income stream. Conversely, men who will never pay are wasting her time. The *puella* needs to hook whales, not minnows, and time spent dangling bait for small fish represents lost chances, and the clock rapidly ticks as she ages out of the erotic profession. The man must always recall, and be reminded periodically by the canny woman, that there are other fish in the sea for her to catch; likewise, the woman needs to know how to keep a man hooked or, if he has become more trouble than he's worth, when to cut the line.

Scholars have generally viewed this allusive relationship between the two genres fairly directly, with elegists reading and adapting the plays of Plautus and Terence to their love poetry as an innovation of their own. But I think Catullus was an exemplary figure for the elegists who first showed how Roman comedy could enter sustained personal poetry, and I argue here that Catullus was, with respect to the erotic and economic conflict outlined above, a proto-elegist.[8] Indeed, in one understudied cycle of his poems Catullus limned the essential elements of Roman elegy's appropriation of Roman comedy's "greedy girl" motif, serving as a bridge between the two genres and a window through whom Ovid and other elegists viewed Plautus and Terence. Before we get to that cycle, however, it would be useful to sketch briefly how Latin love elegy appropriates Roman comedy's erotic discourse, and to do that Ovid's first book of *Amores* offers a clear test case. As has been well established, in *Amores* 1.6 the elegiac speaker plays the role of the comic *exclusus amator*, or "the shut-out lover," which we saw in Chapter 2 Lucretius also adapts from Roman comedy.[9] Similarly, in *Amores* 1.8 the speaker laments that his *puella* has excluded him on the advice of the *lena*, the older and more experienced woman who teaches the *meretrix* in Roman comedy how to maximize profit and minimize sexual activity with suitors.[10] Finally, in *Amores* 1.10

---

[8] On the vexed relationship between Catullus and the Latin love elegists and Catullus' identity as a proto-elegiac poet, see Miller (2007).

[9] See Copley (1956, 28–42), McKeown (1979, 82), Brown (1987, 135 and 297–303), and Yardley (1987).

[10] This poem's allusions to Roman comedy have been discussed at length by Gutzwiller (1985), Myers (1996), and James (2003, 52–68).

the speaker complains that his *puella* has fundamentally changed their relationship by demanding presents (9–18):

> ... animique resanuit error,
> 10    nec facies oculos iam capit ista meos.
>       cur sim mutatus quaeris? quia munera poscis.
>         haec te non patitur causa placere mihi.
>       donec eras simplex, animum cum corpore amavi;
>         nunc mentis vitio laesa figura tua est.
> 15    et puer est et nudus Amor; sine sordibus annos
>         et nullas vestes, ut sit apertus, habet.
>       quid puerum Veneris pretio prostare iubetis?
>         quo pretium condat, non habet ille sinum!

> ... and my mind's mistake has been cured,
>   and your looks don't captivate my eyes now.
> Why am I changed, you ask? Because you demand gifts.
>   This reason does not allow you to please me.
> While you were ingenuous, I loved you, mind and body.
>   Now your figure has been marred by a fault in your brain.
> Love is a child, and naked as well; his years are unsullied
>   and he wears no clothes, so that he's exposed.
> Why are you making Venus' child sell himself for money?
>   Where would he even put the cash? He hasn't got pockets!

His focus on clothes here recalls the traditional complaints in Roman comedy by the *adulescens amator* of the need to acquire expensive outfits for the *meretrix*, usually paid for by squandering his father's estate, as we saw Lucretius allude to in Chapter 2. Ovid goes on to compare the *puella* explicitly and unfavorably to *meretrices* who must satisfy the demands of *lenones*, perhaps alluding to Ballio's threats against the sex laborers in Plautus' *Pseudolus* (21–24):[11]

> stat meretrix certo cuivis mercabilis aere
>   et miseras iusso corpore quaerit opes;
> devovet imperium tamen haec lenonis avari
>   et, quod vos facitis sponte, coacta facit.

> A prostitute, buyable by anyone, stands for sale at a fixed price
>   and seeks filthy lucre by using her body on command.
> Still, this woman curses the greedy pimp's commandment
>   and does under duress what you do of your own free will.

---

[11] Cf. Pl. *Ps.* 172–229; see also Goldberg (2005, 108–13) and Chapter 4 for Catullus' allusions to this scene in poems 42 and 55.

He closes by likening their relationship to scenes of corruption in Roman civic life, particularly the courtroom (38–46):

> nec bene conducti vendunt periuria testes
>   nec bene selecti iudicis arca patet;
> turpe reos empta miseros defendere lingua,
>   quod faciat magni, turpe tribunal, opes;            40
> turpe tori reditu census augere paternos
>   et faciem lucro prostituisse suam.
> gratia pro rebus merito debetur inemptis;
>   pro male conducto gratia nulla toro.
> omnia conductor solvit mercede solute;               45
>   non manet officio debitor ille tuo.

> It's not good when witnesses are hired to sell false testimony,
>   not good when the purse of a chosen judge lies open.
> It's shameful to defend wretched clients with a bought tongue.
>   shameful for a court to enrich itself,
> shameful to grow your family's accounts with a bed's revenue
>   and to prostitute your looks for profit.
> Favors should be given deservedly for unbought deeds.
>   No thanks are owed for a bed that has been ill hired.
> The buyer cuts all ties when the sale is complete;
>   he no longer remains in debt by his obligations to you.

As Myers, James, and others note, one of the primary sources behind Ovid's representation of the elegiac lover in *Amores* 1.4 and 1.6 and of the *lena* in *Amores* 1.8 is the *amator adulescens* and *lena* of Plautus' *Asinaria*, and we can fruitfully read *Amores* 1.10 as yet another extended allusion to the conflict between these characters.[12] Shortly after the play begins, the *adulescens* Diabolus complains he has been made an *exclusus amator* by the *meretrix* Philaenium and her mother, the *lena* Cleareta (127–30):[13]

> DIA: sicine hoc fit? foras aedibus me eici?
> promerenti optume hoccin preti redditur?
> bene merenti mala es, male merenti bona es;
> at malo cum tuo ...

> DIA: So that's how it is? I've been tossed out of doors?
> Is this the cost of deserving the very best by you?
> You're good to those who ill deserve it, bad to those who deserve well;
> But it'll go badly for you ...

---

[12] Yardley (1987), Myers (1996), James (2006 and 2012), and Piazzi (2013).

[13] The *amator* here is not explicitly named in the text, and scholars disagree whether the part belongs to the play's main *adulescens* Argyrippus or his rival Diabolus; see Porter (2016). I follow de Melo's assignment, but it makes no difference for my purposes.

Significantly, both Ovid and Diabolus define their relationships with the *puella* in terms of just deserts (*promerenti*, 128; *bene merenti ... male merenti*, 129; *gratia pro rebus merito debetur*, 1.10.43): they want rewards granted for good behavior rather than for money. One good turn deserves another, and they claim gifts sully love. Diabolus ironically uses a financial term, "cost" (*preti*, 128), to describe his exclusion rather than the actual price the beloved demands, and Ovid repeatedly implies that the real toll is emotional rather than fiscal: "It's not the giving I despise and hate, but the fact that a price is asked" (*nec dare, sed pretium posci dedignor et odi*, 63).[14]

Diabolus then rushes to Cleareta's house, where he finds the *lena* and proceeds to argue with her about his erotic and financial arrangements with Philaenium (167–75, 187–93):

> DIA: qui modus dandi? nam numquam tu quidem expleri potes;
> modo quom accepisti, haud multo post aliquid quod poscas paras.
> CLE: qui modi est ductando, amando? numquamne expleri potes?
> 170  modo remisisti, continuo iam ut remittam ad te rogas.
> DIA: dedi equidem quod mecum egisti. CLE: et tibi ego misi mulierem:
> par pari datum hostimentum est, opera pro pecunia.
> DIA: male agis mecum. CLE: quid me accusas si facio officium meum?
> nam nec fictum usquam est nec pictum nec scriptum in poematis
> 175  ubi lena bene agat cum quiquam amante quae frugi esse volt.
>        . . .
> si ecastor nunc habeas quod des, alia verba praehibeas;
> nunc quia nil habes, maledictis te eam ductare postulas.
> DIA: non meum est. CLE: nec meum quidem edepol ad te ut mittam
>        gratis.
> 190  verum aetatis atque honoris gratia hoc fiet tui,
> quia nobis lucro fuisti potius quam decori tibi:
> si mihi dantur duo talenta argenti numerate in manum,
> hanc tibi noctem honoris causa gratis dono dabo.

> DIA: What limit to giving? Why, you really can never be satisfied.
> When you've gotten something, hardly a second later you plot some new demand.
> CLE: What limit to taking her away, to loving? Can't you ever be satisfied?
> When you've sent her back, right away you ask me to send her back to you.
> DIA: Well, I've given what we agreed on. CLE: And I've sent you the woman:
> an even trade and payment made, services rendered for money earned.

---

[14] See Zagagi (1980, 106–20) and Porter (2016, 316–28) on Diabolus' framing of the financial relationship with the *meretrix* using "aristocratic notions of reciprocity."

DIA: You're dealing badly with me. CLE: Why are you chiding me if I do
  my job?
Why, it's never been sculpted, never been painted, never been written in
poems
where a madame who wants to make money deals respectably with any
lover.
. . .

By Castor, if you still had anything to give, you'd be speaking differently;
because you've got nothing, you expect to take her away through abuse.
DIA: That's not my way. CLE: And by Pollux it's certainly not my way to
  send
her to you for free. But I'll do this, in recognition of your youth and
offering,
since you've been more profitable to us than to your own propriety:
if two talents of silver are counted out and placed in my hand,
I'll give you her for the night – free of charge, in recognition of your
offering.

Many of the structural, topical, and thematical parallels are obvious, but
I want to focus here on the peculiar vocabulary that Diabolus, Cleareta,
and Ovid use to portray their erotic transactions. Building on the "aristocratic notions of reciprocity" expressed in their use of (*pro*)*merenti*, these
passages further frame their heteroerotic relations by using terms borrowed
from the vocabulary of homosocial public alliance. Ovid begins his rebuke
of the *puella* with her demand for *munera* (1.10.11), which Strong observes
"is a crucial choice of word: it means both 'gifts' and the duties owed by a
public official to his town in the form of public entertainments and
endowments."[15] Later, when Diabolus composes a contract to limit
Philaenium's interactions with other men, he angrily bellows that an older
suitor is trying to "perform a young man's duty with his girlfriend,
snatching a tart from her lover and throwing silver coins at her madame"
(*apud amicam munus adulescentuli | fungare . . . | praeripias scortum amanti
atque argentum obicias | lenae*, 812–15). Both works also discuss the erotic
relationship in terms of *officia*, which are *stricto sensu* mutual services
performed to create and renew *amicitia*, a relationship of reciprocal obligations between Roman men of equal social standing.[16] Ovid's speaker
argues that a man who gives women gifts is useless once they have had sex,
since "he no longer remains in debt by his obligations to you" (*non manet*

---

[15] Strong (2016, 235 n. 81).
[16] "Friendships are formed so that common advantage may be ruled by reciprocal obligations"
(*amicitiae comparantur ut commune commodum mutuis officiis gubernetur*, Cic. *S. Rosc.* 111); see
Gibson (1995) and Platter (1995) for a fuller discussion of *officium*.

*officio debitor ille tuo*, 1.10.46). He thus implies that women who forgo gifts earn *officium*, a service that binds men to them, and he closes by saying that poor lovers in particular should not pay for sex with money, but with *officium . . . studiumque fidemque* (1.10.57). Notably, this assertion adds another idea from the public sphere, as *fides* properly denotes reciprocal trust that binds formal pacts, for example, diplomatic treaties, patron–client relations, and marriage.[17]

Cleareta defines her treatment of Diabolus as *officium*, though one that similarly inverts traditional norms of the public sphere: she claims that it is the well-recognized *officium* of *lenae* to squeeze money from prospective *amatores* (173–75). Further, she offers to let Diabolus sleep with Philaenium if he pays two talents, a deal she claims to make "in recognition of your *honos*" (*honoris gratia*, 190; *honoris causa*, 193). Monti notes that this too is a loaded term borrowed from the public sphere and intimately tied to the concepts of *officium* and *fides*:[18]

> Honos has religion as its proper sphere of application since it means the homage paid to the gods and usually indicates a sacrifice or ritual offering. It thus belongs to the *fides* and *pietas* of the worshipper to perform *honores* to the gods for the benefactions they confer. Transferred to the political sphere, *honor* is used to designate the payment of the debt that results from receiving an *officium* or a *beneficium*, and again belongs to the domain of *fides* and *pietas*.

Ovid not only uses the scenario and content of this comic scene as an allusive touchstone for the conflict with his *puella*, but even borrows the vocabulary of public alliance that Diabolus and Cleareta use to contest the significance of each other's heteroerotic expectations. He was not, however, doing so out of whole cloth. Besides the similar use of Roman comedy and the motif of the "greedy girl" that scholars have observed in the other elegists, I think Ovid also drew on Catullus' poetry as a blueprint for how to read love affairs of the *fabula palliata* into sustained personal poetry. In particular, Ovid arguably viewed the conflict between *adulescens amator* and *lena/meretrix* through the window of Catullus' poem 110, which alludes to the same scene of the *Asinaria*. I want to close by examining how this poem can be seen as a proto-elegiac forerunner of the Latin love elegists' appropriation of Roman comedy.

---

[17] See Ross (1969, 85) and Caston (2012, 141–55).     [18] Monti (1981, 26).

## Catullus' Comic Economics and Elegy's "Greedy Girl"
## (Poem 110)

In poem 110, Catullus rebukes a woman named Aufillena for refusing to give him sexual favors in exchange for his apparently unending supply of gifts:

> Aufillena, bonae semper laudantur amicae:
>     accipiunt pretium, quae facere instituunt.
> tu, quod promisti, mihi quod mentita inimica es,
>     quod nec das et fers saepe, facis facinus.
> aut facere ingenuae est, aut non promisse pudicae,
>     Aufillena, fuit; sed data corripere
> fraudando officiis, plus quam meretricis avarae <est>
>     quae sese toto corpore prostituit.

> Aufillena, good girlfriends are always praised:
>     they receive a payment for what they agree to do.
> You, because you promised, because you lied to me, unfriendly girl,
>     because often you don't give but keep on taking, you do wrong.
> An upright girl would've done it, a modest girl wouldn't have promised,
>     Aufillena. But snatching up what's been given by reneging
> on your obligations: that's beyond what a greedy prostitute
>     who puts her whole body on sale does.

In the past century of scholarship, interpretation of this poem has been spare but consistent, and Brian Arkins encapsulates the usual view: "Aufillena . . . contracts to have sexual intercourse with Catullus, but fails to keep her side of the bargain." Wiseman reaches a similar conclusion, adding praise for the speaker: "Nothing is more certain about the persona of Catullus than that he cared deeply about fair transactions. Even at the lowest level, with Aufillena the dishonest tart, he uses language of contract and obligation."[19] In other words, poem 110 is generally read as an account of the broken contract of a sex laborer. More recently, though, Thomson has noted that "there is really nothing here to say that Aufillena takes money for her favours; she is not, in fact, called a *meretrix*. What she has done is to take Catullus' presents and subsequently deny him a sexual

---

[19] Arkins (1982, 10–12) and Wiseman (1985, 105). See Merrill (1893, 219), who calls Aufillena a "courtesan"; Persson (1914, 116–20); Fordyce (1961, 398), who says, "Aufillena is accused of taking money for her favours and then breaking her bargain"; Quinn (1970, 449), who says, "Aufillena, like Silo, the *leno* of Poem 103, does not stick to a bargain"); and Garrison (2004, 163 and 165), who calls her "a professional *amica*" and "just a tart, and a dishonest one at that."

relationship."[20] Catullus closes the poem by making clear that Aufillena is not a sex laborer, since he says her behavior is "beyond what a greedy prostitute who puts her whole body on sale does" (*plus quam meretricis avarae <est> / quae sese toto corpore prostituit*, 7–8). Aufillena appears in two other poems, and in both Catullus implies she belongs to the same social circles as he and his peers.[21] He is using the vocabulary of sex labor to represent their relationship, but there is no reason to trust that this gesture is any different from what he does with other women, such as the *puella* in poem 10, whom he calls a *scortum* and depicts as a comic *meretrix mala*.[22]

Aufillena shares another point of contact with Flavius' girlfriend in poem 10: she is also represented as a comic character, in this case a mixture of the *meretrix mala* and the *lena*. Phyllis Forsyth suggests that Aufillena's name represents an example of etymological wordplay: she is Aufil-*lena*, an embodiment of the *lena* of Roman comedy.[23] Indeed, her name can be seen as a metapoetic marker for the presence of allusions to Roman comedy here, similar to the function of Marrucinus' stolen *pallium* in poem 12, as we saw in the Introduction. Poem 110 mirrors the situation of one of Roman comedy's most common stock scenes, where an *adulescens amator*, having given many gifts to a *meretrix* without receiving access to her, breaks down and rebukes her or her *lena* for refusing his generosity. In fact, it overlaps remarkably with the same instance of this routine from Plautus' *Asinaria* that I showed Ovid alluding to in *Amores* 1.10.

Catullus opens the poem with a line worthy of the most tediously decent Latin textbooks: "good girlfriends are always praised" (*bonae semper laudantur amicae*, 1). After setting up the rewards for women who behave well, he proceeds to lay out what constitutes the behavior of good women and to contrast it with Aufillena's: "they receive payment" (*accipiunt pretium*, 2), and do what they agree to do. Catullus is focused on business transations, using vocabulary and concepts reminiscent of the accounting

---

[20] Thomson (1998, 547); ironically, Quinn (1959, 74–75) advises that "we must be on our guard against the Victorian commentator who tends to treat as a prostitute every mistress who is not her lover's social equal."

[21] In Catull. 100 Aufillena and her brother are positive objects of attention, and in 111 Catullus says to Aufillena, "for a woman to live content with one man is worth the highest of all praises for brides" (*viro contentam vivere solo / nuptarum laus ex laudibus eximiis*, 1–2), extolling her as a married *univira* and mother (*matrem*, 4) before implying that her husband is also her uncle and her sons are her brothers. See Forsyth (1980/81) on the social dynamics here; invective aside, actual *meretrices* are not depicted as having brothers, husbands, uncles, and sons.

[22] On similar traditions of assuming the *puella* of Catull. 10 is a sex laborer and reasons to reject them, see Skinner (1989, 16), as well as my discussion of the poem in the Introduction.

[23] Forsyth (1980/81); for Catullus' etymological wordplay, see Chapter 3.

vocabulary we saw in poem 5 in Chapter 2, where Catullus tots up kisses as if on an abacus. Indeed, both poems frame sex and eroticism in terms borrowed from the distinctly male-dominated world of finance, transvaluing the traditionally homosocial and the distinctly heteroerotic. Poem 110 continues in this vein, boiling down their relationship to one that is purely transactional, centering on give-and-take (*das et fers*, 4; *data corripere*, 6). He adds to these commercial ideas a set of charged political terminology that transports eroticism to male spheres of social interaction. He calls Aufillena "unfriendly" (*inimica*, 3) contrasting her with the *bonae amicae* he commends at the start. This adjective can be seen to depict the woman merely as hostile, but the wordplay also evokes the concept of *amicitia*, which Ross and Gibson argue is about homosocial civic and political relationships rather than a heteroerotic ones.[24] Finally, he accuses Aufillena of "reneging on her obligations" (*fraudando officiis*, 7), yet another example of the vocabulary of public alliance being deployed for erotic purposes that we saw above with Ovid's *Amores* 1.10 and Plautus' *Asinaria*. Indeed, all of Catullus' realignment of these sorts of terms and concepts drawn from masculine public spheres of behavior finds parallels in Plautus' scene where Diabolus confronts Cleareta.[25]

Near the start of the scene, Diabolus complains, "Well, I've given what we agreed on" (*dedi equidem quod mecum egisti*, 171). After Cleareta says that she's given him everything that was due to him, "services rendered for money earned" (*opera pro pecunia*, 172), he responds, "You're dealing badly with me" (*male agis mecum*, 173). The parallels begin to come into focus. Catullus opens by complaining that Aufillena has been not been good to him, and Diabolus ends this passage by saying the *lena* has dealt with him badly. Both men imply that they understood the relationship as a transaction of give-and-take, with Catullus' speaker saying that good women receive a payment for what they agree to do and Diabolus that he has given payment for what they agreed on. Catullus' speaker says Aufillena snatches up gifts and refuses to give anything back, and Diabolus complains about his limitless gifts and the *lena*'s constant demands for more (167–68). But while the Catullan speaker and Diabolus argue they should be protected by official rules that regulate business transactions, the *lena* Cleareta makes it clear that fairness has nothing to do with being a successful madame or *meretrix*. She asks, "Why are you chiding me if I do my job?" (*quid me accusas si facio officium meum*, 173), which Catullus

---

[24] Ross (1969, 86–87) and Gibson (1995).
[25] See also Krostenko (2001a, 274–76) on *facis facinus* as a comic phrase.

nods to with his accusation that Aufillena is "reneging on her obligations" (*fraudando officiis*, 7). Her crucial phrase here is "deals respectably" (*bene agat*, 175), the exact opposite of Diabolus' accusation that the *lena* is "dealing badly" with him (*male agis*, 173). According to Cleareta, her approach follows the rules just as much as anyone else's, except that she is not expected to be fair, since she is a *lena* and so not bound by male norms. Being bad is her *officium*, as is extracting as much from foolish lovers as she can. She points out that now that Diabolus is not giving the women anything else but still expects sexual favors, he "demands to take her away through abuse" (*maledictis te eam ductare postulas*, 188). This is the situation in Catullus' poem 110, where the speaker no longer wants to give Aufillena gifts without getting sex in return and resorts to poetic invective as a way to force her to conform to his expectations.

Significantly, the speaker's treatment of Aufillena here mirrors his approach elsewhere in the corpus where he uses Roman comedy to depict women who offer resistance to his desires. As in poems 10, 42, 55, and 36, Catullus uses comic allusions alongside invective to demonstrate his failed attempts to assert control over women in inferior positions. And significantly in each case, the women are depicted as being "bad" or "the worst" (*mala, pessima*), marking them not only as refusing to conform to Roman male notions of ideal womanhood but also as comic figures who can use Heroic Badness to push back against abusive men. The same values are on display here in poem 110, as well as in the *Asinaria* scene to which it alludes. Diabolus says he deserves the best (*promerenti optume*, 128), and though he deserves well (*bene merenti*, 129), Philaenium is being bad to him but good to those who deserve ill (*mala es, male merenti bona es*, 129). He then accuses Cleareta of dealing badly with him (*male agis*, 173), which she bears as a mark of honor and an obligation to her profession and sex. It's her *officium* to treat men badly. After all, "it's never been sculpted, never been painted, never been written in poems, that a madame who wants to make money deal respectably with any lover" (*nec fictum usquam est nec pictum nec scriptum in poematis / ubi lena bene agat cum quiquam amante quae frugi esse volt*, 174–75). Cleareta is celebrating her comic Heroic Badness directly in front of the man whom she has duped with her *malitia*. In alluding to this scene, Catullus also highlights these same antivalues, showing them being used against him by Aufillena just as we saw they were by other women in Chapter 4. "Good" sex laborers always receive praise (*bonae semper laudantur amicae*, 110.1), but she is decidedly "bad," that is, dismissing his desires and being a hostile sex laborer (*inimica*, 3) – the *meretrix mala* of Roman comedy.[26] As with the other examples, comic allusions in this poem help to give readers a fuller picture of the dramatic scenario beyond what the speaker himself reveals. Recognizing Plautine Heroic Badness in the background, as well as the comic ways in which the poet undermines his own speaker's claims to fairness, we can see this poem is not as straightforwardly transactional as seems on first glance. Catullus' comic allusions complicate the picture and offer a corrective to biographical readings that would otherwise encourage readers to assume that the speaker is a reliable narrator, performing the same work as we saw in poems 10, 55, 36, and elsewhere.

One of the few scholars to note the comic gestures in poem 110, Roy Gibson, remarks, "Here Catullus anticipates the elegist's strategy of trying to coerce the beloved by assimilating her to a *meretrix*."[27] In many ways, I think Ovid took his cues directly from Catullus in adapting Roman comedy's "greedy girl" motif. Catullus compares Aufillena unfavorably to real *meretrices* while simultaneously aligning her with comic *lenae*, and Ovid likewise compares Corinna unfavorably to *meretrices* who must obey their *leno* (*Amores* 1.10.21–24). There is also significant overlap in the themes, topics, and terms they both use as they rework Plautus' scene. But it is also clear that Catullus and Ovid saw the different potential that Roman comedy held for their individual poetic projects. Catullus and the elegists, for example, all represent poetry as a type of gift, *munus*, they present to others, but only the elegists offer it as a replacement for monetary gifts to woo their *puellae*; Catullus' poetic *munera* are eroticized too, but they are given exclusively to male addressees, never as an enticement for women to have sex with him.[28] In adapting the *adulescens amator* in poem 110, Catullus borrows the comic lover's complaints and abuse, whereas the elegists innovate further by voluntarily embracing poverty and turning their poetry into an object of gift-exchange. The elegists seemed to have learned from Catullus that abuse isn't enough. If you want to catch flies, honey works better than vinegar.

I think this difference is symptomatic of the major distinction between Catullus' and the elegists' use of Roman comedy. For Catullus, it was fundamentally a tool of invective, whether to flagellate women who offered resistance, to jockey against men with whom he saw himself in

---

[26] Strong (2016, 33–35) notes that *amica* is a standard euphemism for *meretrix*.
[27] Gibson (1995, 78 n. 12); Skinner (2003, 203 n. 55) also hints that Ovid may have had Aufillena in mind at *Tr.* 2.429–30.
[28] Cf. Catull. 14, 65.19, 68.10, 68.32, 68.149–50 (*carmine munus / pro multis ... officiis*), 110, and see White (1993, 89) and James (2003, 71–107).

competition, or to critique himself for his erotic shortcomings. We have seen multiple examples of each situation throughout this book, as well as examined how his approach to Roman comedy departed from that of his contemporaries, particularly Cicero and Lucretius. But while Catullus offered a crucial exemplum for subsequent poets of how to see one's life in the mirror of Roman comedy, his deployment of Roman comedy is embedded in his own time and defined by his own needs and concerns. The elegists in turn took his appropriation of Roman comedy as a model but made it their own, just as Catullus did with his predecessors, making the *fabula palliata* speak to the anxieties and interests of the Augustan age. This supreme adaptability is, I think, a testament to the enduring vitality and relevance of Roman comedy long after the curtain came down on its heyday in the third and second centuries BCE.

# Bibliography

Adams, J. N. 1972. "Latin Words for 'Woman' and 'Wife.'" *Glotta* 50:234–55.
    1982. *The Latin Sexual Vocabulary*. Baltimore: Johns Hopkins University Press.
    1983. "Words for 'Prostitute' in Latin." *RhM* 126:321–58.
Adler, E. 1981. *Catullan Self-Revelation*. New York: Arno Press.
Agnesini, A. 2004. *Plauto in Catullo*. Bologna: Pàtron.
Allen, J. 2001. *Inference from Signs: Ancient Debates about the Nature of Evidence*.
    Oxford University Press.
Anderson, W. S. 1964. "Anger in Juvenal and Seneca." *California Publications in
    Classical Philology* 19:127–96.
    1982. *Essays on Roman Satire*. Princeton University Press.
    1984. "Love Plots in Menander and His Roman Adapters." *Ramus* 13:124–34.
    1993. *Barbarian Play: Plautus' Roman Comedy*. University of Toronto Press.
Arkins, B. 1982. *Sexuality in Catullus*. Hildesheim: Olms.
Asmis, E. 2004. "Epicurean Economics." In J. T. Fitzgerald, D. Obbink, and G.
    S. Holland (eds.), *Philodemus and the New Testament World*. Leiden: Brill,
    131–76.
Astin, A. E. 1978. *Cato the Censor*. Oxford University Press.
Augello, G. 1991. "Catullo e il folklore." In *Studi di Filologia Classica in Onore di
    Giusto Monaco*. Universitá di Palermo, Facoltá di Lettere e Filosofia,
    723–35.
Augoustakis, A. 2014. "*Plautinisches im Silius*? Two Episodes from Silius Italicus'
    Punica." In Perysinakis and Karakasis (2014), 259–76.
Baehrens, E. 1876. *Catulli veronensis liber*. Leipzig: Teubner.
Bagordo, A. 2001. *Beobachtungen zur Sprache des Terenz, mit Besonderer
    Berücksichtigung der Umgangssprachlichen Elemente*. Göttingen: Vandenhoeck
    and Ruprecht.
Bailey, C. 1947. *Titi Lucreti Cari de rerum natura libri sex*. Oxford University
    Press.
Baldwin, B. 1979. "Cover-Names and Dead Victims in Juvenal." *Athenaeum*
    45:304–12.
Baker, R. J. 1981. "Propertius' Monobiblos and Catullus 51." *RhM* 124:312–24.
    1983. "Catullus and Sirmio." *Mnemosyne* 36:316–23.
Baraz, Y. 2012. *A Written Republic: Cicero's Philosophical Politics*. Princeton
    University Press.

Barsby, J. 1999a. *Terence: Eunuchus*. Cambridge University Press.

    1999b. "Love in Terence." In *Amor: Roma: Love and Latin Literature*. Cambridge University Press, 5–29.

    2001. *Terence*. 2 vols. Cambridge, MA: Harvard University Press.

Barton, C. 1993. *The Sorrows of the Ancient Romans: The Gladiator and the Monster*. Princeton University Press.

Bartsch, S. 1994. *Actors in the Audience: Theatricality and Doublespeak from Nero to Hadrian*. Cambridge, MA: Harvard University Press.

    2006. *The Mirror of the Self: Sexuality, Self-Knowledge, and the Gaze in the Early Roman Empire*. University of Chicago Press.

Barwick, K. 1928. "Zu Catull c. 55 und 58a." *Hermes* 63:66–80.

Batstone, W. W. 1993. "Logic, Rhetoric, and Poesis." *Helios* 20:143–72.

    1998. "Dry Pumice and the Programmatic Language of Catullus 1." *CPh* 93:125–35.

    2005. "Plautine Farce and Plautine Freedom." In W. Batstone and G. Tissol (eds.), *Defining Genre and Gender in Latin Literature*. New York: Lang, 13–46.

    2007. "Catullus and the Programmatic Poem: The Origins, Scope, and Utility of a Concept." In M. B. Skinner (ed.), *A Companion to Catullus*. Malden, MA: Blackwell, 235–53.

Beacham, R. C. 1999. *Spectacle Entertainments of Early Imperial Rome*. New Haven: Yale University Press.

    2007. "Playing Places: The Temporary and the Permanent." In M. McDonald and J. M. Walton (eds.), *The Cambridge Companion to Greek and Roman Theatre*. Cambridge University Press, 202–26.

Beard, M. 2003. "The Triumph of the Absurd: Roman Street Theatre." In C. Edwards and G. Woolf (eds.), *Rome the Cosmopolis*. Cambridge University Press, 21–43.

    2007. *The Roman Triumph*. Cambridge, MA: Harvard University Press.

Beare, W. 1939. "The Italian Origins of Latin Drama." *Hermathena* 29:30–53.

Benediktson, D.T. 1986. "Catullus 58B Defended." *Mnemosyne* 39:305–12.

Bernek, R. 2004. "Catull c. 10 – Tragikomödie eines Aufschneiders. Intertextuelle Verbindungen zwischen Catull und der (römischen) Komödie." In M. Janka (ed.), *ΕΓΚΥΚΛΙΟΝ ΚΗΠΙΟV (Rundgärtchen) zu Poesie, Historie und Fachliteratur der Antike. Festschrift für Hans Gärtner*. Munich: Saur, 81–100.

Berno, F. R. 2004. "One *truncus*, Many Kings. Priam, Agamemnon, Pompey (Vergil, Seneca, Lucan), Part 1." *Maia* 56:79–84.

Bernstein, F. 1998. *Ludi publici: Untersuchungen zur Entstehung und Entwicklung der Öffentlichen Spiele im Republikanischen Rom*. Stuttgart: Steiner.

Bessone, F. 2013. "Latin Precursors." In T. S. Thorsen (ed.), *The Cambridge Companion to Latin Love Elegy*. Cambridge University Press, 39–58.

Betensky, A. 1980. "Lucretius and Love." *CW* 73:291–9.

Bianco, O. 1964. "Catullo, c. 55 e 58a." *RCCM* 6:33–44.

Bieber, M. 1959. "Roman Men in Greek Himation (Romani Palliati): A Contribution to the History of Copying." *Proceedings of the American Philosophical Society* 103:374–417.

Bloomer, M. 1997. *Latinity and Literary Society at Rome*. Philadelphia: University of Pennsylvania Press.

Booth, J. 1997. "All in the Mind: Sickness in Catullus 76." In S. M. Braund and C. Gill (eds.), *The Passions in Roman Literature and Thought*. Cambridge University Press, 150–68.

Boyle, A. J. 2003. *Ovid and the Monuments: A Poet's Rome*. Bendigo: Aureal Publications.

2006. *Roman Tragedy*. London: Routledge.

Bowersock, G. W. 1994. *Fiction as History: Nero to Julian*. Berkeley: University of California Press.

Brachtendorf, J. 1997. "Cicero and Augustine on the Passions." *Revue des Études Augustiniennes* 43:289–308.

Bradley, M. 2015. "Foul Bodies in Ancient Rome." In M. Bradley (ed.), *Smell and the Ancient Senses*. New York: Routledge, 133–45.

Braund, D. 1996. "The Politics of Catullus 10: Memmius, Caesar, and the Bithynians." *Hermathena* 160:45–57.

Braund, S. M. 1988. *Beyond Anger: A Study of Juvenal's Third Book of Satires*. Cambridge University Press.

2005. "Marriage, Adultery, and Divorce in Roman Comic Drama." In W. S. Smith (ed.), *Satiric Advice on Women and Marriage: From Plautus to Chaucer*. Ann Arbor: University of Michigan Press, 39–70.

Brown, B. 1996. *The Material Unconscious: American Amusement, Stephen Crane, and the Economies of Play*. Cambridge, MA: Harvard University Press.

Brown, R. 1987. *Lucretius on Love and Sex: A Commentary on De rerum natura IV, 1030–1287 with Prolegomena, Text, and Translation*. Leiden: Brill.

Buchheit, V. 1976. "Sal et lepos versiculorum (Catull c. 16)." *Hermes* 104:331–47.

Bungard, C. 2014. "To Script or Not to Script: Rethinking Pseudolus as Playwright." *Helios* 41:87–106.

Butler, S. 2015. "Making Scents of Poetry." In M. Bradley (ed.), *Smell and the Ancient Senses*. New York: Routledge, 74–89.

Byrne, S. N. 2000. "Horace *Carm.* 2.12, Maecenas, and Prose History." *Antichthon* 34:18–29.

Cairns, F. 1969. "Catullus 1." *Mnemosyne* 22:153–58.

1973. "Catullus' *Basia* Poems (5, 7, 48)." *Mnemosyne* 26:15–22.

1974. "*Venusta Sirmio*: Catullus 31." In A. J. Woodman and D. A. West (eds.), *Quality and Pleasure in Latin Poetry*. Cambridge University Press, 1–17.

2003. "Catullus in and about Bithynia: Poems 68, 10, 28, and 47." In D. Braund and C. Gill (eds.), *Myth and Culture in Republican Rome: Studies in Honour of T. P. Wiseman*. University of Exeter Press, 165–90.

Cameron, A. 1993. *The Greek Anthology: From Meleager to Planudes*. Oxford University Press.

1995. *Callimachus and His Critics*. Princeton University Press.

Camps, W. A. 1973. "Critical and Exegetical Notes." *AJPh* 94:131–46.

Caston, R. R. 2012. *The Elegiac Passion: Jealousy in Roman Literature*. Oxford University Press.

2014. "Reinvention in Terence's *Eunuchus*." *TAPhA* 144:41–70.

Champlin, E. 2003. "Agamemnon at Rome: Roman Dynasts and Greek Heroes." In D. Braund and C. Gill (eds.), *Myth, History and Culture in Republican Rome: Studies in Honour of T. P. Wiseman*. University of Exeter Press, 295–319.

Chaplin, J. D. 2000. *Livy's Exemplary History*. Oxford University Press.

Cherniss, H. F. 1943. "The Biographical Fashion in Literary Criticism." *University of California Publications in Classical Philology* 12:279–92.

Christenson, D. M. 2000. *Plautus: Amphitruo*. Cambridge University Press.

2001. "Grotesque Realism in Plautus' *Amphitruo*." *CJ* 96:243–60.

2019. "Metatheatre." In M. Dinter (ed.), *The Cambridge Companion to Roman Comedy*. Cambridge University Press, 136–50.

Churchill, J. B. 2001. "The Lucky Cato, and His Wife." *Phoenix* 55:98–107.

Cilliers, L., and F. P. Retief. 2000. "Poisons, Poisoning and the Drug Trade in Ancient Rome." *Akroterion* 45:88–100.

Cinaglia, V. 2014. *Aristotle and Menander on the Ethics of Understanding*. Leiden: Brill.

Citroni, M. 2013. "Horace's *Epistle* 2.1, Cicero, Varro, and the Ancient Debate about the Origins and the Development of Latin Poetry." In J. Farrell and D. Nelis (eds.), *Augustan Poetry and the Roman Republic*. Oxford University Press, 180–204.

Clark, A. C. 1905. *M. Tulli Ciceronis orationes*. Vol. 1. Oxford University Press.

Clark, C. A. 2008. "The Poetics of Manhood? Nonverbal Behavior in Catullus 51." *CPh* 103:257–81.

Clausen, W. 1964. "Callimachus and Latin Poetry." *GRBS* 5:181–96.

1976. "*Catulli Veronensis Liber*." *CPh* 71:37–43.

Clay, D. 1998. "The Theory of the Literary Persona in Antiquity." *MD* 40:9–40.

Coarelli, F. 1971–72. "Il complesso Pompeiano del Campo Marzio e la sua decorazione scultorea." *RPAA* 44:99–122.

Coffee, N. 2013. "Ovid Negotiates with His Mistress: Roman Reciprocity from Public to Private." In M. L. Satlow (ed.), *The Gift in Antiquity*. Hoboken: Wiley-Blackwell, 77–95.

Collins, J. H. 1952. "Cicero and Catullus." *CJ* 48:11–17, 36–41.

Comfort, H. 1935. "Parody in Catullus LVIIIa." *AJPh* 56:45–59.

Commager, S. 1965. "Notes on Some Poems of Catullus." *HSPh* 70:83–110.

Condorelli, S. 1965. "I due carmi a Camerio." *Helikon* 5:463–80.

Connor, P. J. 1974. "Catullus 8: The Lover's Conflict." *Antichthon* 8:93–96.

Connors, C. 1997. "Scents and Sensibility in Plautus' *Casina*." *CQ* 47:305–9.

Conte, G. B. 1994. *Latin Literature: A History*. Baltimore: Johns Hopkins University Press.

Copley, F. O. 1951. "Catullus, c. 1." *TAPhA* 82:200–206.

1952. "Catullus 55, 9–14." *AJPh* 73:295–97.

1956. *Exclusus Amator: A Study in Latin Love Poetry*. Madison: University of Wisconsin Press.

Cornell, T. 2013. *The Fragments of the Roman Historians*. Oxford University Press.

Cotton, H. M. 1986. "The Role of Cicero's Letters of Recommendation: *Iustitia versus Gratia?*" *Hermes* 114:443–60.

Courtney, E. 1993. *The Fragmentary Latin Poets*. Oxford University Press.

Craig, C. P. 1995. "Teaching Cicero's Speech for Caelius: What Enquiring Minds Want to Know." *CJ* 90:407–22.

Csapo, E. G. 1993. "A Case Study in the Use of Theatre Iconography as Evidence for Ancient Acting." *Antike Kunst* 36:41–58.

Curley, D. 2013. *Tragedy in Ovid: Theater, Metatheater, and the Transformation of a Genre*. Cambridge University Press.

Damon, C. 1995. "Greek Parasites and Roman Patronage." *HSPh* 97:181–95.

1997. *The Mask of the Parasite: A Pathology of Roman Patronage*. Ann Arbor: University of Michigan Press.

Davis, J. E. 2014. "Terence Interrupted: Literary Biography and the Reception of the Terentian Canon." *AJPh* 135:387–409.

de Melo, W. 2011–2013. *Plautus*. 5 vols. Cambridge, MA: Harvard University Press.

Dettmer, H. 1997. *Love by the Numbers: Form and Meaning in the Poetry of Catullus*. New York: Lang.

Deuling, J. K. 1999. "Catullus and Mamurra." *Mnemosyne* 52:188–94.

Dickie, M. 1993. "Malice, Envy, and Inquisitiveness in Catullus 5 and 8." *PLLS* 7:9–26.

Duckworth, G. 1952. *The Nature of Roman Comedy: A Study in Popular Entertainment*. Princeton University Press.

Duffalo, B. 2013. *The Captor's Image: Greek Culture in Roman Ecphrasis*. Oxford University Press.

Duncan, A. 2006. *Performance and Identity in the Classical World*. Cambridge University Press.

Dutsch, D. 2008. *Feminine Discourse in Roman Comedy: On Echoes and Voices*. Oxford University Press.

Dyck, A., ed. 2010. *Cicero: Pro Sexto Roscio*. Cambridge University Press.

ed. 2013. *Cicero: Pro Marco Caelio*. Cambridge University Press.

Dyson, M. 1973. "Catullus 8 and 76." *CQ* 23:127–43.

Earl, D. C. 1960. "Political Terminology in Plautus." *Historia* 9:235–43.

Edwards, C. 1996. *Writing Rome: Textual Approaches to the City*. Cambridge University Press.

Elder, J. P. 1951. "Notes on Some Conscious and Subconscious Elements in Catullus' Poetry." *HSPh* 60:101–36.

1967. "Catullus I, His Poetic Creed, and Nepos." *HSPh* 71:143–49.

Elderkin, G. W. 1934. "The *Curculio* of Plautus." *AJA* 38:29–36.

Ellis, R. 1889. *A Commentary on Catullus*. Oxford University Press.

Erasmo, M. 2005. *Roman Tragedy: Theatre to Theatricality.* Austin: University of Texas Press.

Ernout, A., ed. 1961. *Plaute. Comédies.* Vol. 7. Paris. Les Belles Lettres.

Evans, J. D. 2009. "Prostitutes in the Portico of Pompey? A Reconsideration." *TAPhA* 139:123–45.

Fantham, E. 1972. *Comparative Studies in Republican Latin Imagery.* University of Toronto Press.

    1977. "Philemon's *Thesauros* as a Dramatisation of Peripatetic Ethics." *Hermes* 105:406–21.

    2002. "*Orator and/et actor.*" In P. Easterling and E. Hall (eds.), *Greek and Roman Actors: Aspects of an Ancient Profession.* Cambridge University Press, 362–76.

    2008. "With Malice Aforethought: The Ethics of *malitia* on Stage and at Law." In I. Sluiter and R. M. Rosen (eds.), *Kakos: Badness and Anti-Value in Classical Antiquity.* Leiden: Brill, 319–34.

Fantuzzi, M., and R. Hunter. 2004. *Tradition and Innovation in Hellenistic Poetry.* Cambridge University Press.

Farrell, J. 2009. "The Impermanent Text in Catullus and Other Roman Poets." In W. A. Johnson and H. N. Parker (eds.), *Ancient Literacies.* Oxford University Press, 164–85.

Feeney, D. 2016. *Beyond Greek: The Beginnings of Latin Literature.* Cambridge, MA: Harvard University Press.

Ferguson, J. 1985. *Catullus.* Lawrence: Coronado.

Ferri, R. 2008. "Politeness in Latin Comedy: Some Preliminary Thoughts." *MD* 61:15–28.

    2014. "The Reception of Plautus in Antiquity." In M. Fontaine and A. C. Scafuro (eds.), *The Oxford Handbook of Greek and Roman Comedy.* Oxford University Press, 767–81.

Finch, C. E. 1960. "Machiavelli's Copy of Lucretius." *CJ* 56:29–32.

Fitzgerald, W. 1984. "Lucretius' Cure for Love in the *De rerum natura.*" *CW* 78:73–86.

    1992. "Catullus and the Reader: The Erotics of Poetry." *Arethusa* 25:419–43.

    1995. *Catullan Provocations: Lyric Poetry and the Drama of Position.* Berkeley: University of California Press.

    2000. *Slavery and the Roman Literary Imagination.* Cambridge University Press.

Flury, P. 1968. *Liebe und Liebessprache bei Menander, Plautus und Terenz.* Heidelberg: Carl Winter.

Fontaine, M. 2010. *Funny Words in Plautine Comedy.* Oxford University Press.

    2014. "Dynamics of Appropriation in Roman Comedy: Menander's *Kolax* in Three Roman Receptions (Naevius, Plautus and Terence's *Eunuchus*)." In S. D. Olson (ed.), *Ancient Comedy and Reception: Essays in Honor of Jeffrey Henderson.* Berlin: De Gruyter, 180–202.

Fordyce, C. J. 1961. *Catullus: A Commentary.* Oxford University Press.

Forsyth, P. Y. 1980/81. "Quintius and Aufillena in Catullus." *CW* 74:220–23.

    1986. *The Poems of Catullus.* Lanham: University Press of America.

Forsythe, G. 1994. Review of Gruen (1992). *BMCR* 94.02.11.

Foster, J. 1971. "Catullus, 55. 9–12." *CQ* 21:186–87.

Fowler, D. P. 2007. "Lucretius and Politics." In M. R. Gale (ed.), *Oxford Readings in Lucretius*. Oxford University Press, 397–431.

Fraenkel, E. 1961. "Two Poems of Catullus." *JRS* 51:46–53.

2008 [1922]. *Plautine Elements in Plautus*. Oxford University Press.

Frank, R. I. 1968. "Catullus 51: *Otium* vs. *Virtus*." *TAPhA* 96:233–39.

Frazer, R. M., Jr. 1966. "Nero the Artist-Criminal." *CJ* 62:17–20.

Fredericksmeyer, E. A. 1970. "Observations on Catullus 5." *AJPh* 91:431–45.

1973. "Catullus 49, Cicero, and Caesar." *CPh* 68:268–78.

Gaisser, J. H. 2009. *Catullus*. Malden, MA: Wiley-Blackwell.

Gale, M. 2007. "Lucretius and Previous Poetic Traditions." In S. Gillespie and P. Hardie (eds.), *The Cambridge Companion to Lucretius*. Cambridge University Press, 59–75.

Galinsky, G. K. 1966. "Scipionic Themes in Plautus' *Amphitruo*." *TAPhA* 97:203–35.

Garani, M. 2016. "The Negation of Fame: Epicurus' Meta-*Fama* and Lucretius' Response." In S. Kyriakidis (ed.), *Libera Fama: An Endless Journey*. Newcastle upon Tyne: Cambridge Scholars Publishing, 28–44.

Garrison, D. H. 2004. *The Student's Catullus*. Norman: University of Oklahoma Press.

Gärtner, T. 2007. "Kritisch-exegetische Überlegungen zu Catullgedichten." *AAntHung.* 47:1–41.

Garton, C. 1972. *Personal Aspects of the Roman Theatre*. University of Toronto Press.

Geffcken, K. 1973. *Comedy in the Pro Caelio. With an Appendix on the In Clodium et Curionem*. Leiden: Brill.

Gellar-Goad, T. H. M. 2018. "Trouble at Sea in Juvenal 12, Persius 6 and the Proem to Lucretius, *De rerum natura* 2." *CCJ* 64:49–69.

Gibson, R. K. 1995. "How to Win Girlfriends and Influence Them: *Amicitia* in Roman Love Elegy." *PCPhS* 41:62–82.

Gilula, D. 1989. "Greek Drama in Rome: Some Aspects of Cultural Transposition." In H. Scolnicov and P. Holland (eds.), *The Play out of Context*. Cambridge University Press, 99–109.

Goldberg, S. 1978. "Plautus' *Epidicus* and the Case of the Missing Original." *TAPhA* 108:81–91.

1987. "Quintilian on Comedy." *Traditio* 43:359–67.

2000. "Catullus 42 and the Comic Legacy." In G. Vogt-Spira and E. Stärk (eds.), *Dramatische Wäldchen. Festschrift für Eckard Lefèvre*. Hildesheim: Olms, 475–89.

2005. *Constructing Literature in the Roman Republic*. Cambridge University Press.

Goldschmidt, N. 2013. *Shaggy Crowns: Ennius' Annales and Virgil's Aeneid*. Oxford University Press.

Goold, G. P. 1974. *Interpreting Catullus*. London: H. K. Lewis & Co.

1983. *Catullus*. London: Duckworth.

Gratwick, A. S. 1982. "Drama." In E. J. Kenney and W. V. Clausen (eds.), *The Cambridge History of Classical Literature, vol. 2: Latin Literature.* Cambridge University Press, 77–137.

1993. *Plautus: Menaechmi.* Cambridge University Press.

Graver, M. 2002. *Cicero on the Emotions: Tusculan Disputations 3 and 4.* University of Chicago Press.

Green, E. 1940. "Furius Bibaculus." *CJ* 35:348–56.

Griffin, J. 1981. "Genre and Real Life in Latin Poetry." *JRS* 71:39–49.

1985. *Latin Poets and Roman Life.* London: Duckworth.

Grimm, R. E. 1963. "Catullus 5 Again." *CJ* 59:15–22.

Gruen, E. S. 1992. *Culture and National Identity in Republican Rome.* Ithaca, NY: Cornell University Press.

Gugel, H. 1967. "Cicero und Catull." *Latomus* 26:686–88.

Gutzwiller, K. 1985. "The Lover and the *Lena*: Propertius 4.5." *Ramus* 14:105–15.

2000. "The Tragic Mask of Comedy: Metatheatricality in Menander." *CA* 19:102–37.

Habinek, T. 2005. *The World of Roman Song: From Ritualized Speech to Social Order.* Baltimore: Johns Hopkins University Press.

Halkin, L. 1948. "La parodie d'une demande de triomphe dans l'*Amphitryon* de Plaute." *AntCl* 17:297–304.

Hall, J. 2009. *Politeness and Politics in Cicero's Letters.* Oxford University Press.

Hallett, J. P. 1973. "The Role of Women in Roman Elegy: Counter-cultural Feminism." *Arethusa* 6:103–24.

Hanchey, D. 2013. "Cicero, Exchange, and the Epicureans." *Phoenix* 67:118–34.

Hankinson, R. J. 2013. "Lucretius, Epicurus, and the Logic of Multiple Explanations." In D. Lehoux, A. D. Morrison, and A. Sharrock (eds.), *Lucretius: Poetry, Philosphy, Science.* Oxford University Press, 69–98.

Hanses, M. 2014. "*Plautinisches im Ovid:* The *Amphitruo* and the *Metamorphoses*." In Perysinakis and Karakasis (2014), 225–58.

2015. "The Life of Comedy after the Death of Plautus: The Palliata in Roman Life and Letters." Diss., Columbia University.

2016. "Juvenal and the Revival of Greek New Comedy at Rome." In C. W. Marshall and T. Hawkins (eds.), *Athenian Comedy in the Roman Empire.* London: Bloomsbury.

Hardy, C. 2005. "The Parasite's Daughter: Metatheatrical Costuming in Plautus' *Persa*." *CW* 99:25–33.

Harries, B. 2007. "Acting the Part: Techniques of the Comic Stage in Cicero's Early Speeches." In J. Booth (ed.), *Cicero on the Attack: Invective and Subversion in the Orations and Beyond.* Swansea: Classical Press of Wales, 129–48.

Harrison, S. J., and S. J. Heyworth. 1999. "Notes on the Text and Interpretation of Catullus." *CCJ* 44:85–109.

Harrison, S., T. D. Papanghelis, and S. Frangoulidis, eds. 2018. *Intratextuality and Latin Literature.* Berlin: De Gruyter.

Havelock, E. A. 1938. *The Lyric Genius of Catullus.* Oxford University Press.

Haywood, M. S. 1984. "Epibaterion: A Study of Ancient Arrival Poetry." Diss., University of Liverpool.

Heath, M. 1989. "Aristotelian Comedy." *CQ* 39:344–54.

Hellegouarc'h, J. 1963. *Le vocabulaire Latin des relations et des partis politiques sous la République.* Paris: Les Belles Lettres.

Hemelrijk, E. A. 2004. "Masculinity and Femininity in the *Laudatio Turiae.*" *CQ* 54:185–97.

Herrmann, K. 2011. *Nunc Levis est Tractanda Venus: Form und Funktion der Komödienzitate in der Römischen Liebeselegie.* Frankfurt am Main: Lang.

Hershkowitz, D. 1995. "Pliny the Poet." *G&R* 42:168–81.

Heslin, P. 2011. "Metapoetic Pseudonyms in Horace, Propertius, and Ovid." *JRS* 101:51–72.

Heyworth, S. J. 2015. "Lutatius Catulus, Callimachus and Plautus' *Bacchides.*" *CQ* 65:390–95.

Higbie, C. 2011. "Cicero the Homerist." *Oral Tradition* 26:379–88.

Hinds, S. 1998. *Allusion and Intertext: Dynamics of Appropriation in Roman Poetry.* Cambridge University Press.

Holford-Strevens, L. 2002. "*Horror vacui* in Lucretian Biography." *LICS* 1:1–23.

Hollis, A. S. 2007. *Fragments of Roman Poetry, c. 60 BC–AD 20.* Oxford University Press.

Holzberg, N. 2001. "Lesbia, the Poet, and the Two Faces of Sappho: 'Womanufacture' in Catullus." *CCJ* 46:28–44.

Hubbard, T. K. 2004/5. "The Invention of Sulpicia." *CJ* 100:177–94.

Huffman, C. A. 2005. *Archytas of Tarentum: Pythagorean, Philosopher, and Mathematician King.* Cambridge University Press.

Hughes, J. J. 1997. "*Inter tribunal et scaenam*: Comedy and Rhetoric in Rome." In W. J. Dominik (ed.), *Roman Eloquence: Rhetoric in Society and Literature.* New York: Routledge, 182–97.

Hunter, R. 1980. "Philemon, Plautus and the *Trinummus.*" *MH* 37:216–30.

———. 1985. *The New Comedy of Greece and Rome.* Cambridge University Press.

Huskey, S. 2006. "Ovid's (Mis)Guided Tour of Rome: Some Purposeful Omissions in *Tr.* 3.1." *CJ* 102:17–39.

Hutchinson, G. O. 2003. "The Catullan Corpus, Greek Epigram, and the Poetry of Objects." *CQ* 53:206–21.

Iddeng, J. W. 2005. "How Shall We Comprehend the Roman *I*-Poet? A Reassessment of the *Persona*-Theory." *C&M* 56:185–205.

Innocenti, B. 1994. "Towards a Theory of Vivid Description as Practiced in Cicero's *Verrine* Oration." *Rhetorica* 12:355–81.

James, S. L. 1998. "Introduction: Constructions of Gender and Genre in Roman Comedy and Elegy." *Helios* 25:3–16.

———. 2003. *Learned Girls and Male Persuasion: Gender and Reading in Roman Love Elegy.* Berkeley: University of California Press.

2006. "A Courtesan's Choreography: Female Liberty and Male Anxiety at the Roman Dinner Party." In C. A. Faraone and L. McClure (eds.), *Prostitutes and Courtesans in the Ancient World*. Madison: University of Wisconsin Press, 224–51.

2012. "Elegy and New Comedy." In B. K. Gold (ed.), *A Companion to Roman Love Elegy*. Malden, MA: Wiley-Blackwell, 253–68.

2016. *"Fallite Fallentes*: Rape and Intertextuality in Terence's *Eunuchus* and Ovid's *Ars amatoria*." *EuGeStA* 6:86–111.

Janan, M. 1994. *When the Lamp Is Shattered: Desire and Narrative in Catullus*. Carbondale: Southern Illinois University Press.

Janko, R. 1984. *Aristotle on Comedy: Towards a Reconstruction of Poetics II*. London: Duckworth.

Janne, H. 1933. "L'*Amphitruon* de Plaute et M. Fulvius Nobilior." *RBPhil* 34:515–31.

Jocelyn, H. D. 1979. "Catullus 58 and Ausonius, Ep. 71." *LCM* 4:87–91.

Johnson, M. 1999. "Catullus 37 and the Theme of Magna Bella." *Helios* 26:85–96.

Johnson, W. R. 2009. *A Latin Lover in Ancient Rome: Readings in Propertius and His Genre*. Columbus: Ohio State University Press.

Karakasis, E. 2014. "Cicero *Comicus* – Catullus *Plautinus*: Irony and Praise in Cat. 49 Re-examined." In Perysinakis and Karakasis (2014), 197–224.

Kaster, R. 2001. "Controlling Reason: Declamation in Rhetorical Education at Rome." In Y. L. Too (ed.), *Education in Greek and Roman Antiquity*. Leiden: Brill, 317–37.

Kenney, E. J. 1970. "Doctvs Lucretivs." *Mnemosyne* 23:366–92.

Kernan, A. 1959. *The Cankered Muse: Satire of the English Renaissance*. New Haven: Yale University Press.

Ketterer, R. C. 1986a. "Stage Properties in Plautine Comedy I." *Semiotica* 58:193–216.

1986b. "Stage Properties in Plautine Comedy II." *Semiotica* 59:93–135.

1986c. "Stage Properties in Plautine Comedy III." *Semiotica* 60:29–72.

Khan, H. A. 1967. "An Interpretational Crux: Catullus LV and LVIIIa." *AC* 36:116–31.

Kokoszkiewicz, K. M. 2007. "Catullus 14B, 16, 41, 43, 55, 58B: Adnotationes criticae." *Mnemosyne* 60:608–27.

Konstan, D. 1972. "Two Kinds of Love in Catullus." *CJ* 68:102–6.

1986. "Love in Terence's *Eunuch*: The Origins of Erotic Subjectivity." *AJPh* 107:369–93.

Kroll, W. 1959. *Catull*. Stuttgart: Teubner.

Kronenberg, L. 2009. *Allegories of Farming from Greece and Rome: Philosophical Satire in Xenophon, Varro, and Virgil*. Cambridge University Press.

Krostenko, B. 2001a. *Cicero, Catullus, and the Language of Social Performance*. University of Chicago Press.

2001b. *"Arbitria Vrbanitatis*: Language, Style, and Characterization in Catullus cc. 39 and 37." *CA* 20:239–72.

Kuttner, A. L. 1999. "Culture and History at Pompey's Museum." *TAPhA* 129:343–73.

Kutzko, D. 2006. "Lesbia in Catullus 35." *CPh* 101:405–10.

Lada-Richards, I. 2005. "'In the Mirror of the Dance': A Lucianic Metaphor in Its Performative and Ethical Contexts." *Mnemosyne* 58:335–57.

Laurens, P. 1965. "A propos d'une image catullienne (c. 70, 4)." *Latomus* 24:545–50.

Lavigne, D. E. 2010. "Catullus 8 and Catullan *Iambos*." *SyllClass* 21:65–92.

LeFèvre, E. 1982. *Maccus Vortit Barbare: vom Tragischen Amphitryon zum Tragikomischen Amphitruo.* Wiesbaden: Steiner.

1997. *Plautus' Pseudolus.* ScriptOralia 101. Tübingen: Narr.

1999. "Plautus' *Amphitruo* zwischen Tragödie und Stegreifspiel." In T. Baier (ed.), *Studien zu Plautus' Amphitruo.* ScriptOralia 111. Tübingen: Narr, 11–50.

Leigh, M. 2004. *Comedy and the Rise of Rome.* Cambridge University Press.

2013. *From Polypragmon to Curiosus: Ancient Concepts of Curious and Meddlesome Behaviour.* Oxford University Press.

Leo, F. 1912. *Plautinische Forschungen*, 2nd ed. Berlin: Weidmann.

Levy, H. L. 1941. "Catullus, 5, 7–11 and the Abacus." *AJPh* 62:222–24.

Lintott, A. 1999. *The Constitution of the Roman Republic.* Oxford University Press.

Lowe, D. 2019. "Loud and Proud: The Voice of the *Praeco* in Roman Love Elegy." In S. Matzner and S. Harrison (eds.), *The Poetics of the Weaker Voice in Latin Literature.* Oxford University Press, 149–68.

Lowe, J. C. B. 1983. "The *Eunuchus*: Terence and Menander." *CQ* 33:428–44.

1989. "The *Virgo Callida* of Plautus, *Persa*." *CQ* 39:390–99.

MacLeod, C. W. 1973. "Parody and Personalities in Catullus." *CQ* 23:294–303.

Maltby, R. 1997. "The Language of Early Latin Epigram." *Sandalion* 20:43–56.

Manuwald, G. 1999. "Tragödienelemente in Plautus' *Amphitruo* – Zeichen von Tragödienparodie oder Tragikomödie?" In T. Baier (ed.), *Studien zu Plautus' Amphitruo.* ScriptOralia 111. Tübingen: Narr, 177–202.

2011. *Roman Republican Theatre: A History.* Cambridge University Press.

2014. "Cicero, an Interpreter of Terence." In S. Papaioannou (ed.), *Terence and Interpretation.* Cambridge University Press, 179–200.

Manwell, E. 2007. "Gender and Masculinity." In M. B. Skinner (ed.), *A Companion to Catullus.* Malden, MA: Wiley-Blackwell, 111–28.

Marshall, C. W. 2006. *The Stagecraft and Performance of Roman Comedy.* Cambridge University Press.

Marsilio, M., and K. Podlesney. 2006. "Poverty and Poetic Rivalry in Catullus (c. 23, 13, 16, 24, 81)." *AClass* 49:167–81.

Mastronarde, D. J. 1990. "Actors on High: The Skene Roof, the Crane, and the Gods in Attic Drama." *CA* 9:247–94.

May, J. 1988. *Trials of Character: The Eloquence of Ciceronian Ethos.* Chapel Hill: University of North Carolina Press.

Mayer, R. G. 2003. "Persona Problems. The Literary Persona in Antiquity Revisited." *MD* 50:55–80.

Maynes, C. 2016. "Comic Callimacheanism in Catullus 67." *TAPhA* 146:281–323.

Mayor, A. 2014. "Mithridates of Pontus and His Universal Antidote." In P. Wexler (ed.), *History of Toxicology and Environmental Health, vol. 1: Toxicology in Antiquity*. Amsterdam: Academic Press.

McCarthy, K. 2000. *Slaves, Masters, and the Art of Authority in Plautine Comedy*. Princeton University Press.

McCormick, P. J. 1981. "Reading and Interpreting Catullus 8." In S. Kresic (ed.), *Contemporary Literary Hermeneutics and Interpretation of Classical Texts*. Ottawa University Press, 317–26.

McGinn, T. A. J. 2004. *The Economy of Prostitution in the Roman World*. Ann Arbor: University of Michigan Press.

McKeown, J. C. 1979. "Augustan Elegy and Mime." *CCJ* 25:71–84.

  1987. *Ovid: Amores. Text, Prolegomena, and Commentary*. Vol. 1. Liverpool: Francis Cairns.

Merrill, E. T. 1893. *Catullus*. Cambridge, MA: Harvard University Press.

Miller, P. A. 1988. "Catullus, c. 70: A Poem and Its Hypothesis." *Helios* 15:127–32.

  2007. "Catullus and Roman Love Elegy." In M. B. Skinner (ed.), *A Companion to Catullus*. Malden, MA: Wiley-Blackwell, 399–417.

Minarini, A. 1987. *Studi Terenziani*. Bologna: Pàtron.

Minyard, J. D. 1985. *Lucretius and the Late Republic: An Essay in Roman Intellectual History*. Leiden: Brill.

Monti, R. C. 1981. *The Dido Episode and the Aeneid: Roman Social and Political Values in the Epic*. Leiden: Brill.

Moore, T. J. 1991. "*Palliata Togata*: Plautus, *Curculio* 462–86." *AJPh* 112:343–62.

  1995. "How Is It Played? Tragicomedy as a Running Joke: Plautus' *Amphitruo* in Performance." *Didaskalia* Suppl. 1. www.didaskalia.net/issues/supplement1/moore.html.

  1998. *The Theater of Plautus: Playing to the Audience*. Austin: University of Texas Press.

  2012. *Music in Roman Comedy*. Cambridge University Press.

  2013. "Meter and Music." In A. Augoustakis and A. Traill (eds.), *A Companion to Terence*. Malden, MA: Wiley-Blackwell, 89–110.

Moore-Blunt, J. 1974. "Catullus XXXI and Ancient Generic Composition." *Eranos* 72:106–18.

Moretti, G. 2006. "Lo spettacolo della Pro Caelio: oggetti di scena, teatro e personaggi allegorici nel processo contro Marco Celio." In G. Petrone and A. Casamento (eds.), *Lo Spettacolo della Giustizia: le Orazioni di Cicerone*. Palermo: Flaccovio, 139–64.

Morgan, L. 2010. *Musa Pedestris: Metre and Meaning in Roman Verse*. Oxford University Press.

Morgan, M. G. 1977. "Nescio Quid Febriculosi Scorti: A Note on Catullus 6." *CQ* 27:338–41.

Morrelli, A. 2007. "Hellenistic Epigram in the Roman World: From the Beginnings to the End of the Republican Age." In P. Bind and J. Bruss (eds.), *Brill's Companion to Hellenistic Epigram.* Leiden: Brill, 521–41.

Morris, E. P. 1909. "An Interpretation of Catullus VIII." *Transactions of the Connecticut Academy of Arts and Sciences* 15:139–51.

Muecke, F. 1986. "Plautus and the Theater of Disguise." *CA* 5:216–29.

Müller, R. 2013. "Terence in Latin Literature from the Second Century BCE to the Second Century CE." In A. Augoustakis and A. Traill (eds.), *A Companion to Terence.* Malden, MA: Wiley-Blackwell, 363–79.

Munro, H. A. J. 1905. *Criticisms and Elucidations of Catullus.* London: G. Bell.

Murgia, C. 2002. "Critica Varia." In J. F. Miller, C. Damon, and K. S. Myers (eds.), *Vertis in Usum: Studies in Honor of Edward Courtney.* Stuttgart: Teubner, 67–75.

Myers, K. S. 1996. "The Poet and the Procuress: The *Lena* in Latin Love Elegy." *JRS* 86:1–21.

Nappa, C. 2001. *Aspects of Catullus' Social Fiction.* Frankfurt am Main: Lang.

Németh, B. 1978. "Some Notes to the Textual Criticism of Catullus' c. 55." *ACD* 14:37–42.

Neumeister, C. 1993. *Das Antike Rom: ein Literarischer Stadtführer.* Munich: C. H. Beck.

Newman, J. K. 1983. "Comic Elements in Catullus 51." *ICS* 8:33–36.

1990. *Roman Catullus and the Modification of the Alexandrian Sensibility.* Hildesheim: Weidmann.

Nicgorski, W. 2002. "Cicero, Citizenship, and the Epicurean Temptation." In D. Allman and M. Beaty (eds.), *Cultivating Citizens: Soulcraft and Citizenship in Contemporary America.* Oxford University Press, 3–28.

Nielsen, R. M. 1987. "Catullus and *Sal* (Poem 10)." *AC* 56:148–61.

Nugent, G. 1994. "*Mater* Matters: The Female in Lucretius' *De rerum natura.*" *Colby Quarterly* 30:179–205.

Nussbaum, M. C. 1994. *The Therapy of Desire: Theory and Practice in Hellenistic Ethics.* Princeton University Press.

O'Bryhim, S. 2007. "Catullus 23 as Roman Comedy." *TAPhA* 137:133–45.

2017. "Catullus' Mullets and Radishes (c. 15.18–19)." *Mnemosyne* 70:323–30.

O'Hara, J. J. 1996. "Sostratus Suppl. Hell. 733: A Lost, Possibly Catullan-Era Elegy on the Six Sex Changes of Tiresias." *TAPhA* 126:173–219.

Orlin, E. 2010. *Foreign Cults in Rome: Creating a Roman Empire.* Oxford University Press.

Otto, A. 1890. *Die Sprichwörter und Sprichwörtlichen Redensarten der Römer.* Hildesheim: Olms.

Owens, W. 2001. "Plautus' Satire of Roman Ideals." In E. Tylawsky and C. Weiss (eds.), *Essays in Honor of Gordon Williams: Twenty-Five Years at Yale.* New Haven: Yale University Press, 213–27.

Palmer, A. 2014. *Reading Lucretius in the Renaissance*. Cambridge, MA: Harvard University Press.

Parker, H. N. 1989. "Crucially Funny or Tranio on the Couch: The *servus callidus* and Jokes about Torture." *TAPhA* 119:233–46.

1996. "Plautus vs. Terence: Audience and Popularity Re-examined." *AJPh* 117:585–617.

Pascucci, G. 1979. "*Praeneoterica*: Lutazio, Callimaco e Plauto." In *Studi di Poesia Latina in Onore di Antonio Traglia*. Vol. 1. Rome: Edizioni di Storia e Letteratura, 109–26.

Peachy, F. 1972. "Catullus 55." *Phoenix* 26:258–67.

Pease, A. S. 1955–1958. *M. Tulli Ciceronis De Natura Deorum*. 2 vols. Cambridge, MA: Harvard University Press.

Pedrick, V. 1986. "*Qui Potis Est, Inquis?* Audience Roles in Catullus." *Arethusa* 19:187–209.

1993. "The Abusive Address and the Audience in Catullan Poems." *Helios* 20:173–96.

Peek, P. S. 2002. "Feeding Aurelius' Hunger: Catullus 21." *AClass* 45:89–99.

Pelling, C. B. R. 1988. *Plutarch: Life of Antony*. Cambridge University Press.

Penwill, J. L. 1994. "Image, Ideology and Action in Cicero and Lucretius." *Ramus* 23:68–91.

Persson, P. 1914. "Zur Interpretation von Catull c. CX." *Eranos* 14:116–29.

Perutelli, A. 1990. "Lutazio Catulo Poeta." *RFIC* 118:257–81.

Perysinakis, I. N., and E. Karakasis, eds. 2014. *Plautine Trends: Studies in Plautine Comedy and Its Reception. Festschrift in Honour of Prof. D. K. Raios*. Berlin: De Gruyter.

Phillips, T. 2013. "Callimachus on Books: *Aetia* fr. 7.13–14." *ZPE* 187:119–21.

Piazzi, L. 2013. "Latin Love Elegy and Other Genres." In T. S. Thorsen (ed.), *The Cambridge Companion to Latin Love Elegy*. Cambridge University Press, 224–38.

Platter, C. L. 1995. "*Officium* in Catullus and Propertius: A Foucauldian Reading." *CPh* 90:211–24.

Pohlenz, M. 1914. *M. Tulli Ciceronis Tusculanae Disputationes*. Leipzig: Teubner.

Polt, C. B. 2013. "The Humour and Thematic Centrality of the *Patera* in Plautus' *Amphitruo*." *G&R* 60:232–45.

2018. "'I found someone'... or Did I? Teaching Persona Theory through Popular Music." *CW* 112:627–47.

Porter, J. R. 2016. "Devil in the Details: The Young Man of Plautus, *Asinaria* 127–248 Once Again." *Logeion* 6:308–58.

Potkay, A. 2007. *The Story of Joy: From the Bible to Late Romanticism*. Cambridge University Press.

Powell, J. G. F. 1988. *Cicero: Cato Maior de Senectute*. Cambridge University Press.

2006. *M. Tulli Ciceronis De Re Publica; De Legibus; Cato Maior De Senectute; Laelius De Amicitia*. Oxford University Press.

Pratt, N. T., Jr. 1956. "Numerical Catullus 5." *CPh* 51:99–100.

Preston, K. 1916. *Studies in the Diction of the Sermo Amatorius of Roman Comedy*. University of Chicago Press.

Putnam, M. C. J. 1961. Review of Quinn (1959). *CPh* 56:204–7.

1964. "Catullus 25.5." *CPh* 59:268–70.

Quinn, K. 1959. *The Catullan Revolution*. Melbourne University Press.

1970. *Catullus: The Poems*. London: Macmillan.

1972. *Catullus: An Interpretation*. London: Batsford.

Ramminger, A. 1937. "Motivgeschichtliche Studien zu Catulls Basiagedichten." Diss., Würzburg.

Ramsey, J. T. 2003. *Cicero: Philippics I–II*. Cambridge University Press.

Rand, E. K. 1932. "The Art of Terence's Eunuchus." *TAPhA* 63:54–72.

Randall, J. G. 1979. "Mistresses' Pseudonyms in Latin Elegy." *LCM* 4:27–35.

Rei, A. 1998. "Villains, Wives, and Slaves in the Comedies of Plautus." In S. R. Joshel and S. Murnaghan (eds.), *Women and Slaves in Greco-Roman Culture*. New York: Routledge, 92–108.

Richardson, L., Jr. 1963. "*Fvri et Avreli, comites Cavlli*." *CPh* 58:93–106.

1980. "Two Topographical Notes." *AJPh* 101:53–56.

Richlin, A. 1984. "Invective against Women in Roman Satire." *Arethusa* 17:67–80.

1992. "The Meaning of *irrumare* in Catullus and Martial." *CPh* 76:40–46.

2014. "Talking to Slaves in the Plautine Audience." *CA* 33:174–226.

2017. *Slave Theater in the Roman Republic: Plautus and Popular Comedy*. Cambridge University Press.

Riese, A. 1884. *Die Gedichte des Catullus*. Leipzig: Teubner.

Riess, W. 2012. "*Rari exempli femina*: Female Virtues on Roman Funerary Inscriptions." In S. L. James and S. Dillon (eds.), *A Companion to Women in the Ancient World*. Malden, MA: Wiley-Blackwell.

Roller, M. B. 1998. "Pliny's Catullus: The Politics of Literary Appropriation." *TAPhA* 128:265–304.

2004. "Exemplarity in Roman Culture: The Cases of Horacius Cocles and Cloelia." *CPh* 99:1–56.

2009. "The Exemplary Past in Roman Historiography and Culture." In A. Feldherr (ed.), *The Cambridge Companion to Roman Historians*. Cambridge University Press, 214–30.

Rollo, A. 2017. "La tradition des passages grecs dans le De vita Caesarum de Suétone entre le Moyen Âge et la Renaissance." *Annuaire de l'École Pratique des Hautes Études (EPHE), Section des Sciences Historiques et Philologiques. Résumés des Conférences et Travaux* 148:51–68.

Roman, L. 2006. "A History of Lost Tablets." *CA* 25:351–88.

Rosenmeyer, P. A. 1995. "Enacting the Law: Plautus' Use of the Divorce Formula on Stage." *Phoenix* 49: 201–17.

Rosivach, V. J. 1980. "Lucretius 4.1123–1140." *AJPh* 101:401–3.

1986. "Love and Leisure in Roman Comedy and the Amatory Poets." *AC* 55:175–89.

2012. *When a Young Man Falls in Love: The Sexual Exploitation of Women in New Comedy*. New York: Routledge.

Ross, D. O. 1969. *Style and Tradition in Catullus*. Cambridge, MA: Harvard University Press.

Rudd, N. 1955. "The Poet's Defence (2): A Study of Horace *Serm.* 1.4." *CQ* 5:149–56.

1989. *Horace: Epistles Book II and Epistle to the Pisones ("Ars Poetica")*. Cambridge University Press.

Russell, A. 2016. *The Politics of Public Space in Republican Rome*. Cambridge University Press.

Sandy, G. N. 1971. "Catullus 16." *Phoenix* 25:51–57.

Saylor, C. F. 1975. "The Theme of Planlessness in Terence's *Eunuchus*." *TAPhA* 105:297–311.

Scheidel, W. 1994. "Libitina's Bitter Gains: Seasonal Mortality and Endemic Disease in the Ancient City of Rome." *AncSoc* 25:151–75.

2003. "Germs for Rome." In C. Edwards and G. Woolf (eds.), *Rome the Cosmopolis*. Cambridge University Press, 158–76.

Schiesaro, A. 2007. "Lucretius and Roman Politics and History." In S. Gillespie and P. Hardie (eds.), *The Cambridge Companion to Lucretius*. Cambridge University Press, 41–58.

Schlam, C. C. 1968. "The Curiosity of the Golden Ass." *CJ* 64:120–25.

Schmidt, B. 1914. "Die Lebenszeit Catulls und die Herausgabe seiner Gedichte." *RhM* 69:267–83.

Schmidt, K. 1902. "Die Griechischen Personennamen bei Plautus II." *Hermes* 37:535–90.

Schmitzer, U. 2001. "Literarische Stadtführungen – von Homer bis Ammianus Marcellinus und Petrarca." *Gymnasium* 108:515–37.

Seager, R. 1974. "*Venustus, Lepidus, Bellus, Salsus*: Notes on the Language of Catullus." *Latomus* 33:891–94.

Sear, F. 2006. *Roman Theatres: An Architectural Study*. Oxford University Press.

Sedley, D. 1999. "Lucretius' Use and Avoidance of Greek." *PBA* 93:227–46.

Segal, C. 1968. "Catullus 5 and 7: A Study in Complementaries." *AJPh* 89:284–301.

1970. "Catullan *otiosi*: The Lover and the Poet." *G&R* 17:25–31.

1989. "*Otium* and *Eros*: Catullus, Sappho, and Euripides' *Hippolytus*." *Latomus* 48:817–22.

Segal, E. 1974. "The Purpose of the *Trinummus*: For J. Arthur Hanson." *AJPh* 95:252–64.

1975. "Perché *Amphitruo*?" *Dioniso* 46:247–67.

1987. *Roman Laughter: The Comedy of Plautus*, 2nd ed. Oxford University Press.

2001. *The Death of Comedy*. Cambridge, MA: Harvard University Press.

Selden, D. 1992. "*Ceveat lector*: Catullus and the Rhetoric of Performance." In R. Hexter and D. Selden (eds.), *Innovations in Antiquity*. New York: Routledge, 461–512.

Seo, M. 2013. *Exemplary Traits: Reading Characterization in Roman Poetry*. Cambridge University Press.

Sharrock, A. 2008. "The Theatrical Life of Things: Plautus and the Physical." *Dictynna* 5.

2009. *Reading Roman Comedy: Poetics and Playfulness in Plautus and Terence.* Cambridge University Press.

2013. "Terence and Non-Comic Intertexts." In A. Augoustakis and A. Traill (eds.), *A Companion to Terence.* Malden, MA: Wiley-Blackwell, 52–68.

Silverstein, A. M., and A. A. Bialasiewicz. 1980. "A History of Theories of Acquired Immunity." *History of Immunology* 51:151–67.

Skinner, M. B. 1971. "Catullus 8: The Comic 'Amator' as 'Eiron.'" *CJ* 66:298–305.

1979. "Parasites and Strange Bedfellows: A Study in Catullus' Political Imagery." *Ramus* 8:137–52.

1981. *Catullus' Passer: The Arrangement of the Book of Polymetric Poems.* New York: Arno Press.

1987. "Disease Imagery in Catullus 76.17–26." *CPh* 82:230–33.

1989. "*Ut decuit cinaediorem*: Power, Gender, and Urbanity in Catullus 10." *Helios* 16:7–23.

1997. "*Ego Mulier*: The Construction of Male Sexuality in Catullus." In J. Hallett and M. B. Skinner (eds.), *Roman Sexualities.* Princeton University Press, 129–50.

2003. *Catullus in Verona: A Reading of the Elegiac Libellus, Poems 65–116.* Columbus: Ohio State University Press.

2007. "Introduction." In M. B. Skinner (ed.), *A Companion to Catullus.* Malden, MA: Wiley-Blackwell, 1–10.

Sklenář, R. 1999. "Nihilistic Cosmology and Catonian Ethics in Lucan's *Bellum civile*." *AJPh* 120:281–96.

Slater, N. 1990. "*Amphitruo, Bacchae*, and Metatheatre." *Lexis* 5–6:101–25.

1996. "Nero's Masks." *CW* 90:33–40.

2000. *Plautus in Performance: The Theatre of the Mind*, 2nd ed. Amsterdam: Harwood Academic.

Spencer, P. E. 2017. "'Mad' Rhoda in Acts 12:12–17: Disciple Exemplar." *The Catholic Biblical Quarterly* 79:282–98.

Starks, J. A. 2013. "*Opera in bello, in otio, in negotio*: Terence and Rome in the 160s BCE." In A. Augoustakis and A. Traill (eds.), *A Companion to Terence.* Malden, MA: Wiley-Blackwell, 132–55.

Stevens, B. E. 2013. *Silence in Catullus.* Madison: University of Wisconsin Press

Stokes, M. 1995. "Cicero on Epicurean Pleasures." In J. G. F. Powell (ed), *Cicero the Philosopher.* Oxford University Press, 145–70.

Striker, G. 1996. *Essays on Hellenistic Epistemology and Ethics.* Cambridge University Press.

Strong, A. K. 2016. *Prostitutes and Matrons in the Roman World.* Cambridge University Press.

Stroup, S. C. 2010. *Catullus, Cicero, and a Society of Patrons: The Generation of the Text.* Cambridge University Press.

Sussman, L. A. 1994. "Antony as a *miles gloriosus* in Cicero's Second Philippic." *Scholia* 3:53–83.

Syndikus, H. P. 1984. *Catull: Eine Interpretation, Erster Teil: Die kleinen Gedichte (1–60)*. Darmstadt: Wissenschaftliche Buchgesellschaft.

1986. "Catull und die Politik." *Gymnasium* 93:34–47.

Tatum, W. J. 1988. "Catullus' Criticism of Cicero in Poem 49." *TAPhA* 118:179–84.

Taylor, B. 2016. "Rationalism and the Theatre in Lucretius." *CQ* 66:140–54.

Taylor, L. R. 1952. "Lucretius and the Roman Theater." In M. E. White (ed.), *Studies in Honor of Gilbert Norwood*. University of Toronto Press, 147–55.

Taylor, R. 2008. *The Moral Mirror of Roman Art*. Cambridge University Press.

Temelini, M. A. 2006. "Pompey's Politics and the Presentation of His Theatre–Temple Complex, 61–52 BCE." *Studia Humaniora Tartuensia* 7:1–14.

Tesoriero, C. 2006. "Hidden Kisses in Catullus: Poems 5, 6, 7 and 8." *Antichthon* 40:10–18.

Thomas, R. F. 1984. "Menander and Catullus 8." *RhM* 127:308–16.

1986. "Virgil's *Georgics* and the Art of Reference." *HSPh* 90:171–98.

Thomson, D. F. S. 1967. "Catullus and Cicero: Poetry and the Criticism of Poetry." *CW* 60:255–30.

1998. *Catullus*, corrected ed. University of Toronto Press.

Uden, J. 2005. "*Scortum Diligis*: A Reading of Catullus 6." *CQ* 55:638–42.

2006. "Embracing the Young Man in Love: Catullus 75 and the Comic *Adulescens*." *Antichthon* 40:19–34.

2011. "Codeswitches in Caesar and Catullus." *Antichthon* 45:113–30.

Usener, H. 1901. "Italische Volksjustiz." *RhM* 61:1–28.

Van der Blom, H. 2010. *Cicero's Role Models: The Political Strategy of a Newcomer*. Oxford University Press.

Van Sickle, J. 1981. "Poetics of Opening and Closure in Meleager, Catullus, and Gallus." *CW* 75:65–75.

Vardi, A. D. 2000. "An Anthology of Early Latin Epigrams? A Ghost Reconsidered." *CQ* 50:147–58.

Vasaly, A. 1985. "The Masks of Rhetoric: Cicero's *Pro Roscio Amerino*." *Rhetorica* 3:1–20.

1993. *Representations: Images of the World in Ciceronian Oratory*. Berkeley: University of California Press.

Vessey, D. W. T. 1985. "Some Thoughts Inspired by Bergk's Emendation *gaudente* in Catullus, 31.13." *BICS* 32:101–8.

Wallace-Hadrill, A. 1989. "Patronage in Roman Society." In A. Wallace-Hadrill (ed.), *Patronage in Ancient Society*. London: Routledge, 63–87.

Walters, B. 2017. "The Circulation and Delivery of Cicero's *Post reditum ad populum*." *TAPhA* 147:79–99.

Walters, J. 1998. "Making a Spectacle: Deviant Men, Invective, and Pleasure." *Arethusa* 31:355–67.

Weber, C. 1996. "Roscius and the *Roscida Dea*." *CQ* 46:298–302.

Welch, T. 2005. *The Elegiac Cityscape: Propertius and the Meaning of Roman Monuments*. Columbus: Ohio State University Press.

Welsh, J. T. 2011. "Accius, Porcius Licinus, and the Beginning of Latin Literature." *JRS* 101:31–50.

Wheeler, A. L. 1910. "Erotic Teaching in Roman Elegy and the Greek Sources. Part I." *CPh* 5:440–50.

   1934. *Catullus and the Traditions of Ancient Poetry*. Berkeley: University of California Press.

White, P. 1993. *Promised Verse: Poets in the Society of Augustan Rome*. Cambridge, MA: Harvard University Press.

Wiles, D. 1991. *The Masks of Menander: Sign and Meaning in Greek and Roman Performance*. Cambridge University Press.

Williams, G. 1968. *Tradition and Originality in Roman Poetry*. Oxford University Press.

Wills, J. 1998. "Divided Allusion: Virgil and the *Coma Berenices*." *HSPh* 98:277–305.

Wiltshire, S. F. 1977. "Catullus Venustus." *CW* 70:219–26.

Winkler, M. M. 1983. *The Persona in Three Satires of Juvenal*. Hildesheim: Olms.

Wiseman, T. P. 1974. *Cinna the Poet, and Other Roman Essays*. Leicester University Press.

   1976. "Camerius." *BICS* 23:15–17.

   1979. "Strabo on the Campus Martius: 5.3.8, C235." *LCM* 4.7:129–34.

   1980a. "Professor Richardson and the Other Campus." *AJPh* 101:483–85.

   1980b. "Looking for Camerius: The Topography of Catullus 55." *PBSR* 48:6–16.

   1981. "Camerius Again." *LCM* 6.6:155.

   1985. *Catullus and His World: A Reappraisal*. Cambridge University Press.

   1994. *Historiography and Imagination: Eight Essays on Roman Culture*. University of Exeter Press.

Witzke, S. 2015. "Harlots, Tarts, and Hussies? A Problem of Terminology for Sex Labor in Roman Comedy." *Helios* 42:7–27.

Woodman, A. J. 1966. "Some Implications of *otium* in Catullus 51.13–16." *Latomus* 25:217–26.

Wooten, C. W. 1983. *Cicero's Philippics and Their Demosthenic Model: The Rhetoric of Crisis*. Chapel Hill: University of North Carolina Press.

Wray, D. 2001. *Catullus and the Poetics of Roman Manhood*. University of Chicago Press.

Wright, F. W. 1931. *Cicero and the Theatre*. Northampton, MA: Smith College.

Wyke, M. 1987. "Written Women: Propertius' *Scripta Puella*." *JRS* 77:47–61.

Yardley, J. C. 1972. "Comic Influences in Propertius." *Phoenix* 26:134–39.

   1987. "Propertius 4.5, Ovid *Amores* 1.6 and Roman Comedy." *PCPhS* 33:179–89.

Young, E. 2015. *Translation as Muse: Poetic Translation in Catullus's Rome*. University of Chicago Press.

Zagagi, N. 1980. *Tradition and Originality in Plautus: Studies of the Amatory Motifs in Plautine Comedy*. Göttingen: Vandenhoeck and Ruprecht.

Zeitlin, A. 2005. "Plutarch's *Moralia* 712C, Menander's Love Plots, and Terence's *Eunuchus*." In W. Batstone and G. Tissol (eds.), *Defining Genre and Gender in Latin Literature*. New York: Lang, 47–59.

Zetzel, J. E. G. 1972. "Cicero and the Scipionic Circle." *HSPh* 76:173–79.

Ziegler, K. 1936. "Der Tod des Lucretius." *Hermes* 71:421–40.

Zillinger, W. 1911. *Cicero und die altrömischen Dichter*. Würzburg: F. Staudenraus.

# Subject Index

Aedituus, Valerius, 71–72, 120
Aesopus, Clodius, 158, 161
Agamemnon, 57–60, 74
Archytas of Tarentum, 79–81
Aristotle, 59–60
    *phauloi*, 60
    *spoudaioi*, 59
*ataraxia*, 93, 98, 101, 104, 106

Caesar, C. Julius, 29, 57, 59
Cato, M. Porcius the Elder, 79–81, 89, 91
Catullus, C. Valerius
    Bithynia, 21, 25–35
    Catullan Revolution, 174–76
    domestic focus, 24–35
    everyday objects, 8–10, 12–13, 15–18, 20–25, 29, 113
    Greek identity, 21–23, 35–41, 72, 76
    objectification of people, 17, 26, 29, 134, 136–37, 142, 164, 169
    urbanity, 24–35, 151, 156–57, 160, 173
Catulus, Q. Lutatius, 71–73
Cicero, M. Tullius, 7, 45–50, 54, 57–58, 60–71, 73–93, 95, 97–98, 104, 107, 109, 113, 125, 127–28, 143–45, 147, 161
Cinna, C. Helvius, 28–30
comedy, Roman
    actors, 9, 12–13, 18, 20, 22, 45, 50–55, 61, 66, 68–69, 72, 75, 88, 95
    *choragus*, 10–13, 23
    costumes, 9, 21–24, 29, 53, 55, 96, 111, 159, 165
    Greekness, 21–23, 36–37, 72, 76, 81, 96, 146
    *machina*, 94–95
    masks, 2, 6, 46, 67, 69, 89, 95, 159, 175
    as mirror of life, 49–50, 54–55, 84–85, 91, 95, 104
    *pallium*, 20–23, 36, 184
    poetic program, 7–15
    props, 9–24, 26, 30, 43, 58, 134, 137
    as reformer of life, 83–85, 98

running slave schtick, 23
schticks/stock routines, 23, 129–30, 136, 143, 156–57, 160, 164
setting, 10, 23–26, 33, 36, 42, 96, 146, 156, 161
versus tragedy, 7, 60, 82, 174
wild goose chase schtick, 156–57, 160, 164
*contubernales*, 168–73
*curiositas*, 109–13

*deliciae*, eroticism of, 113, 126
divorce, 152, 156, 159

education, Roman, 81, 85, 91
    *fictio personae*, 68
    *sermocinatio*, 68
elegy, Roman, 3, 7, 43, 123, 141, 152, 176–82, 187
*epibaterion*, 31, 37
Epicureanism, 91–106
epigrams, 3, 37–42, 71–73, 120–25
Ethopoeia, 47, 68, 88
*exclusus amator*, 102–3, 177, 179
exemplarity, 10, 65–70, 73–74, 80–81, 84–85, 87, 89–91, 98, 101–4, 118, 151, 165–66

*fama*, 74, 95–100, 107
*fides*, 77, 176, 182
*flagitatio*, 54, 84, 161–63, 165

Hector, 82
Hellenistic aesthetics, 9, 37, 42, 71
Hercules, 18, 164–67
Heroic Badness, 128, 145–47, 149, 163–64, 166, 172–73, 186
Hippolyta, 164–66

*ineptia*, 16, 21, 76, 112, 117–18
intratextuality, 126–28, 139–41
*invidia*, 109–11

209

Juno, 39, 41
Jupiter, 37–42, 156, 159

*lepos/lepidus*, 8–10, 13–14, 23, 26, 173
Licinus, Porcius, 71–72
litter bearers, 26–27, 169
love
　as danger to the state, 63, 80–81
　divinely inspired, 77
　as illness, 4, 70–125
　monetary costs, 32–35, 95–100, 107–8, 176,
　　178, 183–88
　political vocabulary, 77, 108, 148, 176,
　　180–82, 184–86
　social costs, 72, 95–100, 107–14, 132–36
Lucretius Carus, T., 1–2, 4, 70, 73, 78–79, 88,
　91–107, 109, 112, 125
*ludi scaenici*, 45, 62–63, 104
*lusus/ludere*
　deception, 13, 32, 106
　erotic play, 96, 126

marriage, 24, 37–38, 40–42, 65, 70, 77, 148–49,
　152, 156, 159
material unconscious, 9, 17
Menander, 49, 76–78, 99, 116, 163
metapoetics, 8–9, 13, 15, 22, 95, 126, 132,
　184
metatheater, 10, 22–23, 25, 46, 50–56, 62, 90,
　95–96, 102–3, 156, 160–61
meter
　anapestic octonarii, 33
　comicus quadratus, 21
　of everyday speech, 49, 60
　iambic septenarii, 21
　limping iambic, 31, 33
*militia amoris*, 169
*miser*, as comic marker, 118–21
Mithridates VI Eupator, 29, 57, 59, 85
*mos maiorum*, 5, 7, 69–70, 81, 98, 150, 152
mythological comparisons, 38–42, 55–59, 82,
　164–65

Naevius, Cn., 82
Names, etymological wordplay, 32, 34, 37, 72,
　140–41, 164, 184
*negotium*, 5, 24, 33, 35, 42, 74, 151
Nero, 18, 55–57, 59–60, 62, 67
*nugae*, 6, 8–13, 15–18, 20, 23, 26, 29, 43, 54,
　144

*officium*, 95–100, 176, 181, 186
*optimates*, 73, 81
*ostentatio*, rhetorical, 87
*otium*, 33–35, 42, 74, 119

Parthenius of Nicaea, 29
persona
　etymology of, 6, 67
　performance of the self, 4, 6, 22, 24, 27, 46,
　　48, 53, 57, 62–69, 81, 116, 159, 175
　theory, 4, 6, 175
Pompeius Magnus, Cn., 57–60, 62, 74
　portico and theater of, 58–59, 160–61,
　　163–65
*postscaenia*, 102–6
pre-neoterics, 71–72, 176
Ptolemy Chennus "the Quail," 57

*ratio*, 89, 106, 125
Roscius, Sex. the Younger, 46–50, 61–63, 66
Roscius Gallus, Q., 45, 72, 75, 84, 158

*sal*, 8–11, 13–18, 21, 23, 30
Sappho, 36, 38, 71–72, 118–20
Saturnalian inversion, 150–54, 163–67, 172–73
Serapis, 27, 30
sex laborers, economic concerns of, 176
silence, 110–11, 113
　effeminacy of, 40, 72, 124, 163, 167
slaves
　freedom from *mores*, 51–53, 146, 150–51
　metaphorical, 145–47
　violence against, 21, 138
social competition, 5, 7–8, 13, 16–18, 24–30,
　42, 44, 62, 126–47, 150–54
*spolia opima*, 158
stock characters
　*adulescens amator*, 2–6, 11, 14, 34, 42–43, 50,
　　62–67, 72–125, 129, 131, 142, 153, 162,
　　170, 176, 178–88
　*adulescens rusticus*, 47–48, 61
　*lena*, 24, 177–88
　*leno*, 6, 11, 13, 18, 43, 50, 53–54, 61, 75,
　　129–30, 136, 162, 178
　*matrona*, 152, 158, 165
　*meretrix*, 6, 18, 26, 42–43, 50, 62–63, 99,
　　101, 113, 117, 123–25, 129, 142, 145,
　　149–54, 160–67, 170, 173, 176–88
　*miles gloriosus*, 6, 11, 27–30, 43, 61, 74, 124,
　　150, 158–60, 163–64, 169–73
　mixing of, 11, 13, 23, 27, 29, 42, 160, 163, 184
　*parasitus*, 6, 10–13, 15, 22–24, 27, 29, 43, 61,
　　75, 110, 129, 135, 158–59
　*senex amator*, 14, 29
　*senex durus*, 6, 14, 65–66, 107, 150, 159–63
　*senex lenis*, 65–66
　*servus bonus*, 153, 160
　*servus callidus*, 13, 18, 40, 43–44, 50–54, 62,
　　89, 99, 101, 116–18, 128–31, 134, 136,
　　139, 141, 143–47, 150–51, 153, 163, 167

*uxor*, 38–43, 151, 156, 159, 165
*virgo intacta*, 13, 42–44, 170
Sulla, L. Cornelius, 45

theatricality, 10–11, 46–50, 55–68, 74, 103,
    156, 163
theft, 15–22, 137, 165
transvaluation, 5, 8–24, 29, 107–13, 119,
    150–52, 180
triumph, Roman, 18, 45, 57–58, 158

Ulysses, 167

*venustas*, 14, 30, 32, 151

women
    "bad," 150, 186
    "good," 124, 148–49, 184
    social disadvantages of, 30, 149–54, 160, 165,
        167, 176
    violence against, 153, 161–62, 165

# Index Locorum

Aed. fr. 1: 71, 120
App.
 *BC* 2.67: 58
 *Mith.* 116: 59
Ar. *Eq.* 542: 45
Arist. *Po.* 1448a2–1459a12: 59–61

Caecil.
 *Hypobolimaeus*: 47
 inc. frr. 1–2 Ribbeck: 63
 inc. fr. 15 Ribbeck: 82
 *Synephebi*: 90
Call.
 *Epigr.* 25: 37, 40
 *Epigr.* 42: 72
Catull.
 1: 8, 10, 12, 15, 22
 2: 126
 3: 126
 5: 107–10, 113, 118, 185
 6: 23, 25, 111–13
 7: 109–10, 113, 118
 8: 2, 75–118
 9: 25
 10: 25–30, 33, 136, 150, 159, 169, 184
 11: 140
 12: 15–22, 28–30, 109
 13: 14, 25, 142
 14: 24
 15: 132–34
 16: 5, 8, 10, 14–15, 140
 17: 112
 21: 127, 134–36
 23: 140, 142
 24: 127, 143
 25: 20–23, 30
 28: 21, 29
 31: 29–36
 36: 170–73
 37: 24, 168–70
 39: 24

 42: 24, 154, 161, 178
 47: 29
 48: 137
 49: 127, 143–45, 163, 172
 50: 126
 51: 34–36, 118–21
 55: 154–57, 160–67, 178
 58b: 166–67
 64.314: 149
 68: 41
 70: 37–38, 40–42,
  122
 72: 122
 75: 122
 76: 70, 120–21
 81: 140
 85: 121–22
 99: 137–39
 100: 184
 103: 183
 106: 142
 109: 125
 110: 183–87
 111: 184
Catulus, Q. Lutatius
 fr. 1: 72
 fr. 2: 72
Cic.
 *ad Brut.* 1.2a.2.8: 32
 *Amic.*
  20: 79
  32: 79
  93–94: 79
  98: 79
 *Att.*
  7.3.5: 57
  7.3.10: 79
 *Brut.* 71–75: 175
 *Caec.* 27: 61, 75
 *Cael.*: 67, 89
  37: 57–66

*de Orat.*
  2.39.17: 32
  2.236: 84
*Fam.*
  1.9.19: 79
  7.1: 161
  7.1.2–3: 58
  11.21.1: 128
  15.6.1: 82
  15.12.7: 82
*Leg.* 2.36: 109
*N.D.*
  2.60: 79
  3.72: 79
  3.72–73: 90
*Off.*
  1.2.5–6: 97
  1.111: 68
  1.114: 68
  1.136: 68
  1.150: 79
*Orat.* 67: 60
*Phil.* 2.15: 61, 75, 79, 84
*Pis.*: 82
*Q. Rosc.* 20: 75
*Quinct.*: 82, 84
*Red. Pop.* 16: 128
*Rep.* 2.1.3: 87
*S. Rosc.*: 82
  42: 46
  43: 47
  46–47: 46–48
  74: 46
*Sen.*
  3: 80
  39: 79–81
*Tusc.*
  3.3: 85
  3.5: 70
  4.58–62: 88
  4.65–76: 81–91
  4.70: 91
  4.76: 79
CIL
  6.15346: 148
  6.19838: 149
  6.34045: 148

D.C.
  42.5.3–5: 57
  62.16.21: 55
  62.18.1: 55
  62.60.2: 56
  63.9.5: 18
  63.28.3–5: 56

Enn.
  *Sat.* 59–62: 13
Eur.
  *Hipp.* 380–85: 34
  *Tr.* 455: 57
Evanthius
  Excerpta de comoedia
    5.1: 49, 84
    5.5: 49

Gel.
  5.7: 67
  19.9: 71

Hor.
  *Ep.* 2.1.119–61: 175
  *S.*
    1.4.47–48: 60
    2.3.246–80: 99

Juv. 8.215–20: 56

Liv. 7.2: 175
Lucr.
  1.70–72: 105
  4.1–25: 107
  4.72–86: 2, 95
  4.292–301: 2, 95
  4.905–6: 95
  4.973–83: 1–2
  4.977–80: 104
  4.1037–1191: 91–107
  4.1048–49: 92
  4.1063–64: 103
  4.1063–72: 92–94
  4.1068–69: 70
  4.1069: 97
  4.1072: 97
  4.1113–20: 94–95
  4.1114: 97
  4.1117: 97
  4.1121–32: 95–97
  4.1121–91: 2, 4
  4.1124: 97
  4.1124–42: 112
  4.1132–34: 105
  4.1133–44: 98
  4.1135–40: 101
  4.1137–40: 103
  4.1141: 100
  4.1157–59: 104
  4.1160–69: 96
  4.1175: 103
  4.1177–89: 101–4
  4.973–83: 95

Lucr. (cont.)
   5.96: 94
   5.1113–14: 98
   5.1133–34: 97

Mart. 11.47.3: 160
Mel. *AP* 5.8: 38
Men.
   *Aspis* 147–48: 78
   *Dyskolos* 43–44: 77
   *Eunouchos* fr. 162 K–T: 78
   *Perikeiromene* 164–65: 78
   *Theophoroumene* fr. 227 K–T: 95

Naev. *Hector proficiscens* fr. 2 Ribbeck: 82

Ov.
   *Am.*
      1.4: 179
      1.6: 177, 179
      1.8: 177, 179
      1.10: 177–85
      1.13.23–26: 149
   *Ars*
      1.67: 160
      3.387: 160
   *Ep.* 4.36: 38
   *Met.* 7.801: 38

Pers. 5.161–74: 99
Pl.
   *Amph.*
      9–71: 159
      60–61: 60
      186–261: 158
      201–2: 103
      551–89: 159
      654–58: 159
      798–852: 159
      1009–14: 156
      1009–19: 157
      1032: 159
      1072: 159
   *As.*
      13: 13
      127–52: 115, 179
      128–29: 186
      167–75: 180–82
      167–88: 185–87
      187–93: 180–82
      276: 24
   *Bac.*
      54: 153
      87–88: 109
      362: 21

      500–25: 115
      786–93: 131
      1087–89: 129–30
      1118–70: 153
      1201–7: 153
   *Capt.* 778–79: 23
   *Cas.*: 152
      64–66: 75
      217–40: 14
      230–30a: 39
      317–24: 38
      323: 40
      328–39: 39
      406–8: 40
   *Cist.*
      406: 113
      487: 96
   *Curc.*
      280–98: 22
      462–64: 10
   *Epid.*
      1: 22
      192–95: 23
      453–54: 159
      719–20: 156
   *Men.*
      199–201: 165
      275: 24
      662: 165
      692: 165
      739: 96
   *Merc.* 805–8: 156
   *MG*: 169
      19–23: 28
      1099: 96
   *Mos.*
      655–58: 75, 119
   *Per.*
      1–6: 156, 164
      157–60: 13
      492–502: 130
      622–35: 13
      777–78: 130
   *Ps.*
      172–229: 178
      357–69: 162
      401–5: 50
      458: 54
      544a–45: 21
      562–73a: 51
      707: 54
      720: 54
      724–28: 53
      935–1018: 53
      1081–82: 54

1131–43: 95
1288: 54
1325: 24
*Rud.*
   223–28: 156
   931–1172: 18–19
*St.* 198–208: 110
*Trin.*
   12–13: 35
   642–51: 35
   655–58: 34
   820–24: 32
   838–39: 33
   844: 11
   854–60: 11
   930: 33
*Truc.*
   52: 96
   74–76: 35
   224–26: 24
   373: 108
   758–69: 115
Plin.
   *Ep.*
      1.16.6: 60
      5.3: 73
   *Pan.* 46.4: 55
Plu. *Cat. Ma.* 17.7: 70
Plb. 31.23: 35
Prop.
   1.3.41–46: 149
   4.8.75: 160
Ptolemy Hephaestion "the Quail" Phot. *Bib.*
      190.151a.16–18: 57

Quint.
   2.10.13: 61
   4.2.11: 87
   6.2.29–32: 87
   6.2.35: 88
   8.3.64: 87
   8.3.66: 87
   10.1.69: 49
   11.3.111–12: 157

Sapph. fr. 31: 36, 38, 71, 119
Sen. *Cl* 1.1.1: 87

Suet.
   *Jul.* 50.1: 59
   Nero
      21.3: 18
      38.2: 55
      39.3: 56
      46.3: 56
   *Poet.* 11: 78
Syrianus *Hermogenes* 2.23 Rabe: 49

Ter.
   *Ad.*
      120–21: 64
      713–18: 156
   *An.* 355–61: 156
   *Eu.*
      35–41: 5
      40: 121–22
      40–41: 88
      46–49: 90
      46–63: 100
      46–80: 115
      59: 100
      59–62: 86
      70: 123
      71: 118, 124
      72–73: 121
      74–78: 101
      83–84: 119
      95: 121
      98: 118
      175–77: 124
      216–25: 117
      223: 119
      383–84: 121
      549–56: 110
      558–62: 111
   *Ph.*: 61, 90
Tib. 1.03.83–88: 149
Trab. inc. fr. 1 Ribbeck: 82
Turp. *Leucadia* fr. 12 Ribbeck: 83

Var.
   fr. 39 Funaioli: 21
   fr. 306 Funaioli: 22
Vell. 2.1.1–2: 35
Vitr. 5.6.8: 24